Optimizing Learning Outcomes

Optimizing Learning Outcomes provides answers for the most pressing questions that mental health professionals, teachers, and administrators are facing in today's schools. Chapters provide a wide array of evidence-based resources—including links to video segments—that promote understanding, discussion, and successful modeling. Accessible how-to trainings provide readers with multiple sensory-based practices that improve academic success and promote behavioral regulation. Clinicians and educators will come away from this book with a variety of tools for facilitating brain-based, trauma-sensitive learning for all, realizing improved learning outcomes, improving teacher satisfaction, and reducing disciplinary actions and suspensions.

William Steele, PsyD, MSW, is the founder and was, for twenty-three years, the director of the National Institute for Trauma and Loss in Children (TLC), where he created trauma-specific, registered, evidence-based intervention programs and resources for schools and agencies. These programs are currently used in fifty-five countries. Now retired from TLC, he continues to write, consult, and train educators and practitioners across the United States.

Optimizing Learning Outcomes

Proven Brain-Centric,
Trauma-Sensitive Practices

Edited by
William Steele

Routledge
Taylor & Francis Group

NEW YORK AND LONDON

First published 2017
by Routledge
711 Third Avenue, New York, NY 10017

and by Routledge
2 Park Square, Milton Park, Abingdon, Oxon, OX14 4RN

Routledge is an imprint of the Taylor & Francis Group, an informa business

Library of Congress Cataloging in Publication Data
A catalog record for this book has been requested

ISBN: 978-1-138-67761-6 (hbk)
ISBN: 978-1-138-67762-3 (pbk)
ISBN: 978-1-315-56356-5 (ebk)

Typeset in Baskerville
by Keystroke, Neville Lodge, Tettenhall, Wolverhampton

To my family who keep me resilient and eager to continue to learn and teach Joyce, Monika, Darren, Tina, Gunnar and Ema

Contents

About the Editor

Ready to enter high school, Dr. Steele scored poorly on the schools entrance exam and was told he was not college prep material. This followed a difficult early start in life due to numerous family conditions that today would be defined as trauma inducing. Despite this poor start, Dr. Steele went on to earn master's degrees in Education and Social Work and later completed a doctorate degree in Psychology. Along the way he learned that there is no one teacher, no one professional, no one adult, environment or experience that fits the needs of every child. As a result he has always been passionate about collaborating with others in order to bring a collection of best practices to schools, communities, and families in need. Dr. Echterling, professor and doctoral coordinator of the graduate counseling programs at James Madison University, wrote the following about Dr. Steele's most recent publication, *Trauma in Schools and Communities: Recovery Lessons from Survivors and Responders*: "Bringing so many voices to this collaborative project exemplifies the spirit of best practices." *Optimizing Learning Outcomes: Proven Brain-Centric, Trauma-Sensitive Practices* exemplifies the same collaborative effort.

Dr. Steele began his work in the field of trauma by taking the lead in helping schools across the United States develop crisis teams in response to the epidemic of suicide among young people in the early1980s. These and other experiences led him to found the National Institute for Trauma and Loss in Children (TLC) in 1990. As its director for twenty-three years, he created a legacy of trauma-specific, evidence-based intervention programs and resources for schools and agencies now being used in fifty-five countries by many of the 6,000 professionals he trained while at TLC. These interventions are registered as evidence-based programs with the California Evidence Based Clearinghouse and the Substance Abuse Mental Health Services Agency (SAMHSA) Registry of Evidence Based Practices. Although now retired from TLC, Dr. Steele continues to train, consult and work diligently to bring best practices to those shaping the lives of children.

His work has been featured in such books as the *Handbook of Play Therapy, Children in the Urban Environment, Working with Grieving and Traumatized Children and Adolescents: Discovering What Matters Most Through Evidence-Based, Sensory Interventions,*

Understanding Mass Violence, Creative Interventions with Traumatized Children, Critical Incidents in Counseling Children and *Clinical Handbook of Art Therapy*, and in numerous journals. He has always considered it a gift and a privilege to have learned so much from the 80,000 professionals he has trained and consulted with over the years.

Contributors

Lindsey Biel, MA, OTR/L, is an occupational therapist in New York City specializing in pediatrics. She has worked with infants, toddlers, school-age children, adolescents, and adults with diagnoses including sensory processing disorder, autistic spectrum disorders, physical disabilities, learning disorders, and emotional/mood difficulties. She is a popular speaker across the country, running workshops and speaking at conferences to parents, teachers, therapists, and others about how to help children with special needs, especially those with sensory challenges. She is author of *Raising a Sensory Smart Child: The Definitive Handbook for Helping Your Child with Sensory Processing Issues* and *Sensory Processing Issues: Effective Clinical Work with kids and Teens.*

Chris Bye, MBA, MS, is the co-creator of MeMoves. As a featured speaker, he presents at numerous conferences/seminars on the topics of integrating movement and music into the classroom, reducing anxiety and depression at all ages, and developing tools to help those with special needs. Chris has taught numerous classes at UW Madison, UW River Falls and the University of St. Thomas.

Susan F. Cole, JD, MEd., is the Director of the Trauma and Learning Policy Initiative (TLPI), a joint program of Harvard Law School and the non-profit children's rights organization Massachusetts Advocates for Children (MAC). Prior to becoming a lawyer she taught in the Watertown MA and Woodstock CT public schools—experiences that continuously inform her current work. At Harvard she holds a joint appointment as Education Law Clinic Director and Lecturer on Law. Her work is based on research at the intersection of psychology, education, and law that links traumatic experiences to a host of learning, relational, and behavioral difficulties at school. She oversees TLPI's work in schools and its representation of families in the Education Law Clinic.

Richard Curci, Assistant Superintendent with Cohort 1 Elementary Schools in San Francisco Unified School District, was a former math teacher. Prior to taking on the responsibilities of Assistant Superintendent he was principal at Everett Middle School in San Francisco. During his tenure the school achieved a 75 percent reduction in school suspensions and a 40-point gain in Academic Performance Index when the pupils engaged in meditation twice daily.

Emily Diehl is Director of Professional Learning and Curriculum Design for Mindset Works, a social venture founded by Dr. Carol Dweck and Dr. Lisa Blackwell that works to help people grow and reach their full potential. She is a national speaker and trainer in cultivating growth-minded contexts in education at the classroom, school, and district levels and contributes to the design and development of Brainology for students and professional learning for educators through Mindset Works. She was formerly an instructional coach and a teacher, teaching at the secondary level in English-Language Arts and Adolescent Intervention.

Barbara Dorrington is a registered social worker and art therapist with a master's in Education Counseling. She has spent thirty years working for the London District Catholic School Board, the University of Western Ontario and Madame Vanier Children's Services. Between 2005 and 2007 she provided debriefing and art therapy for Hurricanes Rita and Katrina survivors in San Antonio shelters and St. Bernard Parrish, just outside New Orleans, and developed a photo project with children in the ninth ward of New Orleans to help raise money to continue with rebuilding efforts in Louisiana. She maintains a private practice specializing in trauma and loss, self-regulation, including REST, and school and social adjustment.

Anne Eisner, LCSW, LMHC, LMFT, is the Deputy Director of the Trauma and Learning Policy Initiative (TLPI). A licensed social worker, she leads the project's policy work. Anne participates in the work of the Safe and Supportive Schools Commission, which was established through the recently enacted Safe and Supportive Schools legislation in Massachusetts. Her twenty-six years of experience providing clinical services to and advocating for families and children impacted by domestic violence, child abuse, and neglect inform her current work with TLPI.

Michael Gregory, JD, is Clinical Professor of Law at Harvard Law School and Senior Attorney at TLPI. He also co-teaches Harvard's Education Law Clinic, where law students represent traumatized families and children in the special education system and participate in TLPI's larger systemic advocacy to create trauma-sensitive schools. He is a co-author of TLPI's landmark report and policy agenda *Helping Traumatized Children Learn*. In 2013, Governor Deval Patrick appointed Mike to serve on the Families and Children Requiring Assistance Advisory Board, a statewide panel that will advise the Commonwealth of Massachusetts on the implementation of the reformed CHINS law.

Ron Hertel began teaching in an inpatient psychiatric facility for adolescents, administered the Washington State Children's Group Care Program, and served the administrator of the state's Children's Mental Health Division/DSHS. Today, he is the Program Supervisor for Student Mental Health and

Wellbeing at the Office of the Superintendent of Public Instruction (OSPI), Washington's state education agency. In 2008, he led the development of the Compassionate School Initiative in Washington State, and he continues to train and assist schools across the country to become Compassionate Schools. He co-authored *The Heart of Learning and Teaching: Compassion, Resiliency, and Academic Success* and *Supporting and Educating Traumatized Students: A Guide for School-Based Professionals.*

Susan Hopkins, Ph.D., is the Executive Director of Dr. Stuart Shanker's organization, the MEHRIT Centre. As a one-time at-risk youth who quit high school twice, Susan went on to complete four degrees, including a master's in Educational Technology and a doctorate in Educational Leadership. Over the course of her career, she has been a teacher, school administrator, inclusive schooling coordinator, curriculum developer, educational researcher, and educational leader. She has worked in every area of education, from early years to post-secondary, from remote northern schools to the Department of Education, Italy, and the Northwest Territories.

Susan O. Kincaid, Ph.D., is Emeritus Associate Professor of Human Services at Western Washington University and co-author of *The Heart of Learning and Teaching: Compassion, Resiliency, and Academic Success.* She has taught courses in processes to initiate and sustain change in organizational, community, and global systems as well as social justice dynamics, diversity, and basic counseling skills. In 2011, Dr. Kincaid was the recipient of the Lenore McNeer Award for ongoing contribution to her field as an educator from the National Organization for Human Services.

Joel M. Ristuccia, Ed.M., is the Director of Training for TLPI and a co-author of both volumes of *Helping Traumatized Children Learn.* He is also a certified school psychologist with over twenty-five years' experience working in public schools. Joel provides consultations and trainings to schools to support the creation of trauma-sensitive learning environments. He is an Adjunct Professor at Lesley University, developing and teaching courses in a trauma-sensitive schools certificate program that is designed to support all students to be successful in the general education curriculum.

Kathie Ritchie, MA, MS.Ed., began teaching thirty-five years ago at the elementary and high school levels. She worked for the Collinsville School District in Illinois as a Special Education Coordinator at the high school level from 1985 to 2007, and since then has served as the Collinsville Elementary Special Education Coordinator. She is a certified trauma specialist through the National Institute for Trauma and Loss, and a department trainer.

Roberta Scherf is co-founder of MeMoves. When her second child was born on the autism spectrum, she learned all she could about embodied cognition, music, movement, mindfulness, and their impact on the nervous system, learning, and socialization. She has spent more than twenty years developing a program that helps people of all ages and abilities to calm their nervous systems, learn more easily, and increase their capacity for connection, friendship, and compassion.

Stuart Shanker, Ph.D., is a Distinguished Research Professor of Philosophy and Psychology at York University and the CEO of the MEHRIT Centre, Ltd. One of his many books, *Calm, Alert and Learning: Classroom Strategies for Self-Regulation* (2012), is a top-selling educational publication in Canada. His latest book, *Self-Reg: How to Help Your Child (and You) Break the Stress-Cycle and Successfully Engage with Life*, was published in June 2016. Over the past decade, he has served as an adviser on early child development to government organizations across Canada and the US, and in many other countries throughout the world.

David Ziegler, Ph.D., LMFT, LPC, a licensed psychologist, is Executive Director of Jasper Mountain, an agency in Oregon. His current treatment program is internationally recognized for its innovation and success with extremely difficult cases. Over the last thirty-three years he has lived with the children in his treatment program, giving him a first-hand glimpse of their inner world. Dr. Ziegler has numerous publications to his name and he has authored eight books, including: *Raising Children who Refuse to Be Raised* and *Traumatic Experience and the Brain*. He has provided training and consultation throughout the United States, and in Canada, Australia, Iceland, and New Zealand.

Acknowledgements

Over the past thirty years I have been privileged to work with, consult, and train over 80,000 educators. Their dedication to bringing best practices into the classroom is unquestionable. Their expertise and wisdom are at work throughout this resource. They have taught me so much and inspired this work and its focus on translating the neuroscience of learning into everyday classroom practices with all students, especially those struggling with anxiety, trauma, and sensory processing challenges.

I want to acknowledge additional appreciation to my colleague Barbara Dorrington, who read many drafts and provided so many helpful suggestions and wonderful stories of her experiences in the school setting that validated the importance of the strategies and messages this resource presents. The contributors to this work have also done much to advance the use of best practices in school settings. Their dedication has benefited all of us especially students. They deserve our thanks. Special thanks to Anna Moore, Senior Editor at Routledge, and her staff for their patience and expertise in helping to make this a timely, practical, and immediately usable resource.

The amazing resilience of the many survivors I have spent time with, following traumatic incidents in schools across the country, is a remarkable gift in itself and one that is at the core of believing in the capacity of all children to learn despite the challenges they may face. Thank you.

Introduction

William Steele

If we teach today's students as we taught yesterday's, we rob them of tomorrow.
(Attributed to John Dewey)

These are extraordinary times. Many past practices are no longer effective with today's students. That is the bad news. The good news is that despite the diversity of learning needs of students in classrooms today, what we have discovered and continue to discover about the neuroscience of learning and the regulation of challenging student behaviors has led to a number of very successful practices and strategies in our classrooms and schools. When the classroom environment, teachers' methods, their relationship and interactions with students, and the schools' response to dysregulated student behaviors match the neurological, deep brain learning needs of stressed, anxious, and traumatized students, everything and everyone change for the better.

This interactive resource presents brain-based, trauma-sensitive practices for creating learning environments where both teachers and students flourish. Although in-house training would afford readers more hands-on practices and demonstrations, the links to a variety of topic-specific articles and video segments provide the opportunity to read, hear, and see from a variety of resources as to how these practices are being used successfully. Their uses are achieving improved learning outcomes while significantly reducing challenging and disruptive behaviors.

The following questions reflect the challenges facing teachers and administrators today and address the brain-centered, trauma-sensitive approaches presented in this resource:

- **What conclusion did the Yerkes–Dodson Law of 1908 arrive at regarding cognitive and behavioral performance that neuroscience today repeatedly confirms?**
- **How does presenting students the opportunity to regulate their reactions to stressful situations change their behaviors and learning outcomes?**

- What simple activity can be done in every classroom several times a day to help students focus, improve academic performance, and minimize disruptive behaviors?
- What sixty-second activity is improving test scores?
- What role is sensory processing playing in the learning outcomes and behaviors of many students today?
- What would you do to realize the fastest student improvement statewide in a K-8 school that was plagued by violence, heavy presence of security guards, no backpacks allowed, hundreds of thousands spent on security, known as the "drop out factory," and ranked in the bottom five of all public schools in the state. There have been five principals in seven years. If you were the sixth, what would you do to change the situation?
- What one simple, trauma-sensitive, brain-based approach have some schools added to successfully reduce disciplinary action by as much as 90 percent while returning "disruptive" students quickly to their classrooms ready to learn rather than face "in-school" and "out-of-school" suspensions?
- What has one principal done to regulate his stress and change a school, known as the "fight school," to achieve a 75 percent reduction in suspensions, a 90 percent increase in attendance, and a rise from the bottom to the middle level of academic performance?
- What mindsets have proven most successful in helping children to learn and modify their behaviors?
- What verbal and nonverbal communication practices meet the universal learning needs of every child and promote regulation and resilience?
- What relational mindsets support a trauma-sensitive framework for optimizing the learning environment?
- What practices support teacher effectiveness, retention, sustained performance, and resilience?
- What change did the new principal make with teachers in one of the worst-performing schools in Kansas in 2007 to turn it into one of the best?
  What existing trauma-sensitive, brain-based *whole school* approaches are being used and achieving improvements in academic outcomes, in-school attendance, and behavioral regulation?

Unique Aspects

This resource has several unique aspects:

1. There are 100 links to YouTube segments that support, elaborate, and demonstrate the brain-based, trauma-sensitive learning and behavioral

regulation practices detailed in this resource. As educators in general you have limited time. Being able to virtually connect and quickly learn from your peers and leaders in the field (most segments are less than five minutes) makes this a practical and easily usable learning and teaching resource.

2. These virtual conversations also support the professional credibility of the entire work and simultaneously introduce you to a long list of additional resources and conversations specific to each topic area.

3. In addition the editor successfully presented the content of this resource to 1,200 teachers, counselors, social workers, and administrators in 2014/2015. Ninety-five percent of the participants were unaware of the many terms, practices, existing programs, and research that were presented. The relevancy, value, and practical application of the content in this resource are well supported.

4. Because there is no one practice or strategy that fits all students or schools, we have been fortunate to bring programs, strategies, and practices to you from a diverse group of educators. They present a variety of ways to accomplish the same goal-improve academic outcomes and student regulation of otherwise challenging behaviors.

Readers will learn:

- How our nervous systems and brains function under stress, and the impact these functions have on learning and behavior.
- Learning mindsets shown to improve student motivation to learn while realizing improved learning outcomes.
- Relational mindsets for teachers that are critical for remaining proactive rather than reactive to the challenging and sometimes disruptive behaviors of anxious and traumatized students.
- The well-researched role movement plays in enhancing learning outcomes.
- The well-researched role self-regulation plays in students' ability to learn and manage reactions to and behaviors triggered by stressful situations.
- The value of Restorative Resource Rooms.
- The challenges and solutions for students who are not autistic yet struggle with sensory processing issues, which negatively influence learning and behavior.
- The environmental conditions and resources conducive to learning and student regulation.
- How to make brief verbal and non-verbal Connections That Matter (CTMs) with students to support their efforts to learn, manage their behavior, and respond positively and successfully to you and your efforts to teach and assist them.
- Strategies and practices for creating a "whole school" infrastructure to optimize the learning experience for you as well as your students.

Students Today

Below is a very brief description of the growing number of students who are presenting learning and behavioral challenges for teachers in every classroom. Two out of every three children in the United States have difficulty with regulation of their reactions and behaviors (Transforming Education, 2015). Limited regulation decreases learning effectiveness and increases challenging behaviors in the classroom. The growing number of stressed, anxious, and traumatized students in our classrooms today as well as their unique learning needs and behaviors also present challenges that many teachers and administrators have not been trained to manage. Twenty-six percent of children in the United States will witness or experience a traumatic event before they turn four (Safe Schools Healthy Students, 2012). Different approaches are needed to optimize the learning experience for all students while helping them regulate their behaviors. Anxiety symptoms and disorders, including posttraumatic stress disorder (PTSD), are the number-one problem facing today's students (Goldman, 2009). In a Google search you will find 27 million references to anxiety's negative impact on learning and behavior.

The link between childhood trauma, learning, and behavioral challenges is also well established. Using the Adverse Childhood Experiences (ACEs, 1998) survey of elementary students in Spokane, Washington, the district found that those students with three or more adverse childhood experiences "had three times the rate of academic failure, five times the rate of attendance problems, six times the rate of school behavior problems" (Stevens, 2012). The ACEs survey asked participants if they had experienced any of the following: divorce, abandonment, death of a parent, homelessness, witnessing family violence, involvement with child protective services, substance-abusing parent, neglect, or mental illness. This was a landmark study involving 17,000 participants. It is being used today by a number of school districts to evaluate the number of students at risk as a result of their adverse experiences. There are also 20 million Google references to trauma's negative impact on learning and behavior. In essence, at least one-third of the students in every US classroom are struggling with regulation, stress, anxiety, and/or trauma symptoms.

The fact is any form of stress, worry, or fear is an impediment to learning and often triggers behaviors that become a barrier to learning and a challenge in the classroom. Basically, stress "hijacks" that part of the brain used for learning and regulation—the upper brain or the frontal cortex. When our mid-brain or limbic region is in an aroused state of stress, fear, chronic worry, or trauma, it is difficult to process information, and both concentration and focus are impaired (Levine and Kline, 2008; Perry and Szalavitz, 2006). Research also shows stress/anxiety/trauma induces and supports the release of glucocorticoids, such as cortisol, that can alter the left hippocampal area of the brain, increasing memory deficit (Perry and Szalavitz, 2006). Neurologist Dr. Bruce Perry (2004) indicated that traumatized children hear only about 50 percent of what is verbally communicated to them. Judy Willis (2013) also tells us that when in a state of stress, new learning is not retained. Further research reports that persistent stress, anxiety, and trauma cause students to develop a rigid cognitive style that conflicts with efforts to learn and leads to numerous learning and behavioral problems (Perry and Szalavitz, 2006; Ford, Chapman, Mack, and Pearson, 2006).

Traditional teaching methods simply do not help these students optimize their learning capacity while also regulating their behaviors. When we fail to meet the needs of the sheer number of students in every classroom who are struggling with regulation, stress, anxiety, and/or trauma, classroom outcomes suffer, teachers are less effective, and disciplinary actions increase. The good news is that brain-based, trauma-sensitive solutions are making a difference.

Why Brain-Based, Trauma-Sensitive?

All students, inclusive of stressed, anxious, and traumatized students, can benefit from the many brain-based, trauma-sensitive learning practices presented in this resource. For example, poor regulation impedes learning and is associated with behaviors that can be disruptive to others and certainly to the learning process. Traumatized students also struggle with self-regulation; however, the brain-based practices that help non-traumatized students with regulation also benefit traumatized students.

At the same time, all students can benefit from the core principles of what constitutes a trauma-informed/trauma-sensitive environment. For example, Lincoln High School in Walla Walla, Washington, had 798 out-of-school suspensions and 50 expulsions in the 2009–2010 school year. One year later, after initiating basic trauma-sensitive approaches, there were only 135 suspensions and 30 expulsions in the 2010–2011 school year. The principal, Jim Sporleder, said, "It sounds simple. Just by asking kids what happened to them (making a brief connection) they started talking. It made a believer out of me right away" (Stevens, 2012). He was describing the following mindset that emerged from the field of trauma: "Not what is wrong with you, but what *happened* to you?" This new way of thinking was the result of discovering how the brain and nervous system respond to chronic stress and that the challenging behaviors of traumatized children are primal, nervous system survival responses, not willful acts. Embracing just one of the neuro-based, trauma-sensitive mindsets can have significant outcomes for an entire school.

Silvia Cordero, principal of Eldorado Elementary School, stressed the importance of working within a trauma-informed framework when she stated, "It's important for trauma-informed practices to be paired with any program or framework, including Positive Behavioral Interventions and Support (PBIS) and Safe and Civil Schools, because [without the trauma lens] we miss components about what makes these approaches work or not work" (Stevens, 2012). Because of the large number of students that are dealing with regulation issues, worry, fear, chronic stress, and trauma, it simply makes sense that we adopt a brain-based, trauma-sensitive, "whole school" approach to learning.

Elizabeth Prewitt (2016), community manager and policy analyst for the ACEs Connection Network, recently wrote:

> In the text of the *Every Student Succeeds Act* (ESSA) signed on December 10, 2015, there is new life for providing support for students who are impacted by trauma. In the act, through funds made available, each state will be able to construct a series of strategies and activities to address the needs of the most challenged students.

Beyond the acknowledgement of the need for brain-based, trauma-sensitive schools, the resources needed to assist schools in this transformation are now being provided at the federal level. It is time for all to adopt the brain-based, trauma-sensitive learning mindsets, practices, and strategies that are improving learning outcomes and regulation of behaviors in schools that have already made the transition.

Chapter Progression

The first chapter provides an overview of the challenges facing anxious and traumatized students, their efforts to learn, our efforts to teach, the challenges they also face in their efforts to manage their behaviors, and how best we can assist them with the regulation of those behaviors. It includes numerous links to video segments so readers can hear directly from their peers as to what is helping them improve the learning outcomes and behaviors of their students.

Similar to the development of the brain, the other chapters follow a bottom-up approach. Because many of these students have dysregulated nervous systems and are frequently responding from their emotional brain or limbic region (lower regions), Chapter Two begins with a detailed discussion of self-regulation. Subsequent chapters address movement, which assists with regulation and learning, and Sensory Processing Disorder, often misdiagnosed and found in children and teens who are not autistic yet need sensory resources and activities in the classroom. These chapters focus on the many sensory practices that are critical for helping anxious, traumatized, and dysregulated students stabilize their more primal survival and emotional responses and reactions and behaviors to the stressors and sensory challenges they face daily. This attention assists with diminishing the more dominant emotional survival responses of students by restoring a more balanced use of the cognitive functions that are necessary for learning.

Following these four chapters, Chapter Five, "Brief Connections That Matter (CTMs): Student–Teacher Relationship," presents numerous strategies and practices to support trauma-sensitive, teacher–student relationships and those brief connections that matter most to students. Chapter Six, "Growth Mindsets for Learning: Effective Effort," is placed at this point since developing the mindsets that are necessary for learning and regulation of behavior is a cognitive process, and best developed and integrated by students when the lower regions of their brains are regulated. Because the most effective teachers are able to regulate their own reactions to the many stressors they experience daily, including the challenges that anxious, traumatized, and sensory challenged students present, Chapter Seven, "Teacher Resilience, Sustained Effectiveness, and Self-Care," is directed specifically toward teachers.

All of these chapters draw attention to the many components that describe a compassionate, brain-based, trauma-sensitive environment. Therefore, the final three chapters present several models for creating a "whole school" approach for developing an environment where today's students may flourish. These models are already used successfully in a number of schools across the country. A wide variety of resources, tools, practices, and strategies are presented in every chapter, and additional practices and strategies can also be found in the Appendix.

Not Asking You to Do More, Just Do Differently

This resource is not asking you to do more. It is asking you to take the time to learn what neuroscience has revealed about learning, how our brain and nervous system function under stress, and how the new mindsets and practices emerging from this new knowledge are transforming education, overall learning outcomes, and the reduction of disciplinary actions. This knowledge, and the many examples provided by teachers and administrators who have already introduced these brain-based, trauma-sensitive practices and approaches into their classrooms and schools, illustrates and supports that doing differently, not doing more, can have a significant impact on the performance and behavior of today's students. These practices are also bringing about improved teacher effectiveness, satisfaction, and retention. I hope you take the time to learn, see, and hear how your brain-centered, trauma-sensitive peers are optimizing learning and behavior outcomes with these students.

References

Adverse Childhood Experiences (ACEs) (1998). *Linking Childhood Trauma to Long-Term Health and Social Consequences*. Retrieved September 25, 2016 from www.acestudy.org.

Ford, J., Chapman, J., Mack, M., and Pearson, G. (2006). Pathways from traumatic child victimization to delinquency: Implications for juvenile permanency court proceedings and decisions. *Juvenile and Family Court Journal*, Winter, 13–26.

Goldman, W. (2009). *Childhood and Adolescent Anxiety Disorder*. Retrieved March 5, 2014 from www.keepkidshealthy.com/welcome/conditions/anxiety_disorders.html.

Levine, P. and Kline, M. (2008). *Trauma Proofing Your Kids*. Berkeley, CA: North Atlantic Books.

Perry, B.D. (2004). *Children & Loss*. Retrieved October 20, 2004 from http://teacher. scholastic.com/professional/bruceperry/childrenloss.htm.

Perry, B. and Szalavitz, M. (2006). *The Boy who Was Raised as a Dog and Other Stories from a Child Psychiatrist's Notebook.* New York: Basic Books.

Prewitt, E. (2016). *New Elementary and Secondary Education Law Includes Specific "Trauma-Informed Practices" Provisions.* Retrieved January 7, 2016 from www.acesconnection.com/blog/new-elementary-and-secondary-education-law-includes-specific-trauma-informed-provisions.

Safe Schools Healthy Students (2012). *National Center for Mental Health Promotion and Youth Violence Prevention, "Childhood Trauma and Its Effect on Healthy Development."* Retrieved June 8, 2013 from http://sshs.promoteprevent.org/sites/default/files/trauma_brief_in_final.pdf.

Stevens, J.E. (2012). *Author Archives.* ACEs Too High. Retrieved December 12, 2014 from http://acestoohigh.com/author/jestevens/page/25/.

Transforming Education (2015). *Let's Talk about Self-Management: Marshmallows, Stop Signs, Squeezy Balls, and Teaching.* Retrieved August 10, 2015 from www.youtube.com/watch?v=Oq9P0EdptZ8.

Willis, J. (2013) *A Neurologist Makes the Case for Teaching Teachers about the Brain.* Retrieved July 15, 2013 from www.edutopia.org/blog/neuroscience-higher-ed-judy-willis.

1 Twenty First Century Neuroscience, Learning, and Behavior

Not Doing More; Doing Differently

William Steele

There is nothing ordinary about learning and managing student behaviors in the twenty-first century. The students of today are not the students of yesterday. Consider that anxiety is the number-one diagnosis assigned to children today and that such anxiety does not respond well to verbal efforts to manage that anxiety and its associated behaviors. Also consider that one in four children will be exposed to a traumatic experience by age four. This represents approximately 5 million children every year who come into our classrooms with unique learning and behavioral needs. Also keep in mind that longitudinal research has repeatedly demonstrated that two out of every three children have poor regulation skills (Transforming Education, 2015).

Self-regulation is the ability to manage our emotional and behavioral reactions to what is experienced as stressful, fearful, or worrisome, and also to remain focused and patient when gratification is not immediate. In Chapter Two the authors explain regulation as the ability to "manage one's energy and attention." Poor regulation, as science now documents, significantly compromises learning and the management of challenging classroom behaviors. Neuroscience offers us irrefutable documentation that indeed stress, fear, worry, anxiety, trauma, and/or poor regulation compromise learning and trigger challenging student behaviors. **Past practices are simply not effective in helping these students realize their learning potential and manage their reactions and behaviors to stressful situations and conditions.**

The good news is that neuroscience has also led to new practices that educators are finding successful for optimizing learning outcomes and significantly reducing disciplinary responses and actions to challenging behaviors. This chapter provides an *interactive glimpse* into these successful practices and strategies. It reviews:

- The function of the brain and nervous system under stress, their negative impact on learning and behavior, and those brain-based, trauma-sensitive practices that are helping teachers more effectively help stressed, anxious, traumatized, and poor regulating students optimize their learning experience while managing their behavior.

- The research related to critical mindsets that motivate students to continue learning while improving outcomes, and those teacher mindsets that are critical for remaining proactive rather than reactive to the disruptive and often misunderstood behaviors of anxious and traumatized students.
- Various examples as to how "the experience" matters in changing cultures of violence into cultures of respect and optimal learning.
- The importance of integrating movement into the learning experience.
- The need to engage regulation practices throughout the day.
- The components of a brain-centered, trauma-sensitive environment.
- And the necessity of brief teacher–student connections to foster the kind of strength-based, resilient-focused relationship associated with optimal learning and behavioral outcomes.

Links to a number of video segments are also provided to address the questions and school scenarios presented in the Introduction. Subsequent chapters then expand on the practices and strategies related to these scenarios.

> **You are encouraged to visit the cited video segments to hear directly from your peers as to what is helping them, their students, and schools realize significant reductions in disciplinary actions and improved academic outcomes, despite the challenges of today's students.**

Worry, Fear, Anxiety, Trauma: One Commonality

When presenting training on creating brain-based, trauma-sensitive classrooms, I begin by reviewing the data related to the prevalence of anxious, traumatized, poor regulating students. I then ask participants to discuss the differences between worry, fear, anxiety, and trauma. The differences are not always known. They include:

- Worry is about a specific possibility that does not initially induce the intense physiological symptoms of fear or anxiety but can be stressful.
- Fear is a response to a specific threat with immediate neurobiological responses.
- Anxiety is an inexplicable range of reactions, including fear and worry, involving a preoccupation that interferes with ability to enjoy life and complete daily routines and expected tasks (learning).
- Trauma involves all the above.

The critical follow-up question is: "What do each of these have in common, in relation to learning and behavior?" The answer is: **"All are stressful and induce reactions that impede learning."** This process helps participants appreciate that the focus of the training is not solely about traumatized students but any student who is experiencing worry, new fears, or stress as a result of family or other challenging issues. At those times learning suffers unless those students are in a brain-based, trauma-sensitive environment. Given that it is not always possible to know the kind of stress a student might be experiencing, it becomes beneficial for all to engage in those practices that neuroscience now documents optimize the learning experience. Keep this in mind as you read through this resource.

The more intense and consistent our worry, fear, anxiety, or trauma symptoms, the more learning and behavior are compromised. The more inadequate our regulation skills, the more our cognitive and behavioral functions are also compromised. The lives of those around us also become complicated from the challenging behaviors associated with these reactions. In a moment we will take a more detailed look at how the brain functions under stress, and how that stress, whatever its form, impedes learning and triggers challenging behaviors. First, though, allow me, a college-educated professional, to present a personal example of how stress can alter our cognitive processes and lead to behavior that brings about negative consequences.

I was in my mid-thirties, single and living in a first-floor apartment with a door that led to an outdoor patio. It was only a few steps from the kitchen. One day the pot I was using somehow caught fire. The flames rose quite high and I had no fire extinguisher to hand. My first response was to the voice that said, "Remain calm." My next thought was: "I'm cool. I'll just take the pot outside, to the patio." I grabbed the pot and walked the five or six steps to the patio door, which was closed. I sat the pot on the linoleum floor to open the door. I then grabbed the pot and took it outside. When I came back in I saw the outline of the pot on the burnt linoleum. I thought I had been thinking clearly under the stress of dealing with that burning pot, so I could not believe what I had done. Although I lost my security deposit, I learned a valuable lesson.

Stress alters the way we think and process information and subsequently how we behave. This has critical implications for helping today's students optimize their learning experience, maximize their performance, and regulate their classroom behaviors.

Learning and Behavior Under Stress: Our Brain, Our Nervous System

The video *How Is Your Brain Wired?* (Olding, 2009) offers a seven-minute, fairly detailed description of how stress impacts the three regions of the brain. These are: the reptilian brain (sometimes referred to as our survival brain); the limbic brain (referred to as the mid-brain or emotional brain); and the cerebral cortex region (referred to as the upper brain or thinking brain). The video also discusses the right and left hemispheres of the brain and how these are connected by a bundle of nerves called the corpus collosum. It is this connection that allows for a balanced integration and processing of information to support optimal cognitive and emotional functioning, including self-regulation. It is worth watching before going into more detailed explanations related to learning and behavior under stress.

How Is Your Brain Wired?
www.youtube.com/watch?v=uOIWVo-4-lc

A Different Explanation

Another way to appreciate the function of the brain as it relates to learning and behavior is an adaptation of Daniel Siegel's *Hand Model of the Brain* (2012). I want you to make a fist, but put your thumb inside your hand. Now, as you look at your fist, also look at your forearm. Your forearm represents your reptilian brain, the first part of our brain to develop. The reptilian brain had three primary functions when it faced a potential or real threat—flight, flight, or freeze; the very same reactions we have when facing stress that is overwhelming or consistent. Now, open your hand and wiggle your thumb. Your thumb represents the next part of our brain to develop—the limbic region, the mid-brain, also known as the emotional brain. There is no language, reason, or logic in this part of the brain. We simply respond to what the brain senses needs to happen in order to survive.

Now, close your fist again. Your fingers represent the last part of the brain to develop—the cortex region—and your fingertips represent the frontal cortex. The cortex and the frontal cortex are those regions of the brain where language, reason, and logic reside and where the functions needed to learn as well as help regulate our primal survival responses take place. Now, open your fist and wiggle your thumb again. As you wiggle your thumb, picture all those students presenting with challenging behaviors and struggling with learning. Realize that many of them are functioning from *this* part of the brain, as opposed to the fingertip area (the cortex region). They are in a survival mode.

Basically, as you wiggle your thumb, you are depicting a dysregulated survival response to stress, where verbal information or talk is limited in its ability to calm down this part of the brain. This is critical because, when this limbic region of the brain remains active, it is very difficult to access the cognitive part of the brain, that thinking part that is needed to problem solve, process information, and regulate otherwise dysregulated, emotionally dominant reactions. When the body and brain are functioning in survival mode, children often display problematic behaviors, irritability, poor self-control, and hyperactivity symptoms. Learning and concentration are compromised (Maddox, 2006).

These processes are now documented by brain imaging technology that previously did not exist, but this is not new information. Interestingly, the Yerkes–Dodson Law of 1908 (Wikipedia, 2013) concluded that **the quality of our performance on any task, whether physical or mental, is related to our level of stress (emotional arousal). If we are feeling either very low or very high levels of emotion arousal, then our performance is likely to be impaired**. We have all experienced this at some point in our lives; now we have the learning science to better regulate our stress and help students regulate theirs.

Daniel Siegel's *Hand Model of the Brain*
www.youtube.com/watch?v=gm9CIJ74Oxw

Cognitive Limitations under Stress

Bio-neurological responses to stressful situations are difficult—often impossible—to control cognitively. Instead we need to take some action to regain control; we need to change the experience. Dr. Porges, who has done so much to increase our understanding of how the vagus nerve helps us with regulation, describes an experience he had that triggered a fear response he could not reason or take away. The video segment *The Polyvagal Theory: Looking at Trauma from a New Perspective* is well worth viewing.

Looking at Trauma from a New Perspective
www.youtube.com/watch?v=MKkDAOW2yd4

Hearing how difficult it can be to control our fear by our thoughts and how taking action matters more, it helps to appreciate how our nervous system functions when it senses something or someone who triggers a fear response.

The research is abundant. Stress triggers predominant processes in the limbic/subcortical and right hemisphere of brain (Perry, 2006; Schore, 2001), limiting access to the cortex (upper brain) and left hemisphere (Levine and Kline, 2007; Ford, Chapman, Mack, and Pearson 2006). This minimizes the student's ability to reason, think things through, make sense of what has happened, and use the cognitive processes needed to regulate their reactions and behaviors to what is being experienced as stressful or a danger to their physical and/or emotional wellbeing. When unable to regulate these stress responses and when exposure to stress is consistent and/or repetitive, students remain in an activated arousal/survivor response. Remember that approximately two-thirds of children today struggle with regulation, that anxiety is the number-one diagnosis assigned to students, and that one in four children will experience a trauma before age four. These students occupy every classroom today and establish the need for a "whole school" brain-based, trauma-sensitive approach to learning, teaching, and classroom management.

Our Nervous System: Its Impact on Learning and Behavior

It is impossible to talk about the functions of the brain without talking about the nervous system. The nervous system is highly sensitive to the possibility of threat and immediately prepares us for that possibility by triggering numerous chemicals and signals to our brain and body. *The Chemistry of Fear* video (Bytesize Science, 2013) describes how we react to sensory cues related to possible threat, our primal survival responses, and the critical roles of the sympathetic response (the gas pedal) and the parasympathetic response (the brake pedal), both of which relate to our efforts to regulate our responses. It was produced around Halloween, so after the opening we hear and see how the nervous system responds to fear.

The Chemistry of Fear
www.youtube.com/watch?v=e5jA2b9eEpE

Hyper–Hypo Arousal Behaviors

Not addressed in the above or other videos are the kinds of survival behaviors that emerge when students experience persistent anxiety or intense and/or chronic stress. These behaviors have frequently been mistaken for an array of disorders and responded to with disciplinary actions, including out-of-school suspensions. These actions are certainly not helpful to students, support a high dropout rate, and reflect a school environment that is neither brain-based nor trauma-sensitive. These behaviors are referred to as "hyper" and "hypo" arousal behaviors.

Arousal reactions and behaviors are on a continuum ranging from hyper arousal (a state of high nervous system arousal) to a low state of arousal, called hypo or passive arousal (Siegel, 2012). Anxious and traumatized students will move back and forth along the continuum, depending on what is happening in their environment, to them, and around them. As you review these behaviors and reactions, you will find that they describe criteria associated with a variety of diagnoses. Hyper-arousal reactions include anxiety, difficulties managing anger, irritability, verbal outbursts, aggressiveness, defiance, impatience, attention/focus difficulty, being easily startled, body agitation, and hypervigilance—a consistent state of fear or readiness for something bad to happen. Unfortunately, such behaviors can be misinterpreted as oppositional defiant disorder (ODD), or as attention deficit hyperactive disorder (ADHD), mood disorders, or many other diagnoses that are often erroneously assigned (Oehlberg, 2006; Dallman-Jones, 2006; van der Kolk, 2014). In the classroom setting they can be disruptive. Hypo—or passive—arousal involves avoidant behaviors, immobilization, lethargy, apathy, and helplessness. These students are "daydreamers" and also "shut down" or engage dissociative responses to cope with the stress they are experiencing (Levine and Kline, 2008). Although they may not upset the classroom climate, they are not actively engaged in learning as they struggle with their internal fears and need for safety and control.

Being brain-based and trauma-informed, we know the majority of challenging behaviors of students are not willful acts but dysregulated responses to the fears, worries, anxieties, and challenges they have or are experiencing. We now know that the informed response to these behaviors is not "What is wrong with you?" Rather, the informed response is "What is happening to you?" or "What has happened to you?" This brain-based, trauma-informed, trauma-sensitive response is just one of many that are now practiced in brain-based, trauma-sensitive environments to realize improved learning and student regulation. In case you did not read the example in the Introduction, it is repeated here to demonstrate that embracing just one of the brain-based, trauma-sensitive mindsets can have significant outcomes for an entire school. Lincoln High School, in Walla Walla, Washington, had 798 out-of-school suspensions in the 2009–2010 school year, and 50 expulsions. One year later, after initiating basic trauma-sensitive approaches, there were only 135 suspensions and 30 expulsions in the 2010–2011 school year. The principal, Jim Sporleder, said, "It sounds simple. Just by asking kids what happened to them (making a brief connection) they started talking. It made a believer out of me right away" (Stevens, 2014). The more informed we are regarding trauma, stress functions of the brain, and the nervous system, the more we realize that optimizing learning is not necessarily about doing more but about doing things differently, based on our understanding of the neuroscience of learning.

Not Doing More; Doing and Thinking Differently

Given what neuroscience is teaching us about learning and behavior, and considering the sheer number of students who have poor regulation skills, are traumatized, anxious, and exposed to a world filled with uncertainties and its associated stress, and that past practices have not been effective with these students, we realize that it is not about doing more; it is about doing differently. To that end, this resource is intended to present knowledge and resources that are transformative.

What, then, matters most in our efforts to optimize the learning experience for all students and help them learn and regulate their reactions and behaviors to all the stressors they face in the school and classroom environment?

> ## What Matters Most?
>
> - Regulation
> - Movement
> - Sensory Processing
> - Restorative Resource Rooms
> - The Environment/The Experience
> - Connections
> - Teacher Mindsets
> - Teacher Resilience and Self-Care
> - Growth Mindsets for Learning
> - Whole School Infrastructures

These topics are listed in the order in which they are addressed in subsequent chapters. In reality, they are all interconnected and represent ongoing processes in our efforts to create an optimal learning experience for students as well as staff. Each is briefly discussed below and then given detailed attention in their respective chapters.

Regulation Matters

Earlier we mentioned that two-thirds of students are poor self-regulators. This has major implications related to learning and behavior. The Marshmallow Test (Transforming Education, 2015) was initiated in the early 1960s and has been replicated with similar outcomes many times since. Children were given one marshmallow. They could either eat that marshmallow immediately or wait for up to twenty minutes and then get another marshmallow to enjoy. The children were then monitored for up to thirty years, with those who ate the first marshmallow compared to those who waited. Those who were able to wait for the two marshmallows rather than eat the first immediately scored better on their SATs, were more academically successful and socially competent, and were better able to plan and concentrate during stressful times.

There is more, so take the time to view the video.

> *Let's Talk about Self-Management: Marshmallows, Stop Signs, Squeezy Balls, and Teaching*
> www.youtube.com/watch?v=Oq9P0EdptZ8

Self-regulation matters. It involves communicating with and calming or stimulating critical regions of the brain and the nervous system in order to regulate reactions that otherwise interfere with learning functions and produce behaviors which are often disruptive. The majority of those who are poor self-regulators simply have never been taught the various ways they can manage their reactions and behaviors. Teaching students how to regulate and providing daily opportunities for them to do so within or outside the classroom help decrease disruptive behaviors and improve academic success. **For example, Dr. Melrose's evidence-based program Brain Charge has students using a series of sixty-second, cognitively focused activities that improve concentration, decrease test anxiety, and improve academic performance outcomes (Melrose, 2013).**

Meditation is another form of regulation that has enjoyed great success in schools. Four schools in the San Francisco School District that were experiencing high levels of violence, poor attendance, and low academic performance initiated two fifteen-minute periods per day for students to be guided in mindful meditation. Introducing calm and reflection into the school day had amazing results: there was a 75 percent reduction in suspensions and a 40-point improvement in API scoring in the first year. For more about this story, see the video below.

Meditation Curbs Violence at San Francisco Schools
www.nbcnews.com/watch/nightly-news/meditation-curbs-violence-at-san-francisco-schools-378464323951

Movement Matters

Movement benefits all students. "Elementary aged children can only absorb 15 to 20 minutes' worth of material at a time. Simple movements have the ability to improve cognition in just seconds" (Wikipedia, 2014). When engaged in brief movements throughout the day, students can focus more easily on tasks. Several studies have found that children with ADHD are better able to regulate their behavior and focus after exercise; and all children show scholastic improvement after brief periods of exercise (Fun and Function, 2014). "The more learners used learning activities with movement, the higher their academic achievements" (Shoval, 2011, p. 462). "While little evidence exists to show that extra time spent working on academics each day is beneficial to student achievement" (Movement and Learning, 2014), a host of evidence supports the positive impact of movement on learning.

Just two to three minutes of movement several times a day will make a significant difference in student performance and behavior. For example, MeMoves, which has a longer practice history than most school-based movement programs, uses three-minute movements to calm students and increase their focus and concentration. Most of all, MeMoves helps children of all ages to calm their minds as it removes the stressors that hinder development (MeMoves, 2014).

Melinda Radcliff, an early childhood specialist in Godfrey, Illinois, reported:

> I tracked off-task behaviors for two weeks prior to introducing MeMoves, then off-task behaviors after MeMoves was introduced to the class and done prior to academic instruction. My research showed a 71% decrease in off-task behaviors during academic instruction. The average time to perform the movements was 3 minutes.
>
> (MeMoves, 2014)

MeMoves in the Classroom
www.youtube.com/watch?v=55OGz8PVrRI

Sensory Processing Matters

Just as movement helps with self-regulation, it also helps students with sensory processing issues. Neuroscience has once again helped us appreciate the sensory needs of many students as a result of how their nervous systems receive information and then turn that information into behavioral and motor responses. Often the symptoms and behaviors associated with sensory difficulties are mistaken for defiance, aggressiveness, laziness, impulsiveness, hyperactivity, or social adjustment issues, to name but a few. Many students–an estimated one in six (SPD Foundation, 2015)—struggle with some form of sensory integration processing difficulty or with sensory processing disorder (SPD). Although SPD is associated with autism, many non-autistic children struggle with sensory integration issues, in addition to 60 percent of traumatized children (Steele and Malchiodi, 2012, p. 35). Because problems with sensory processing negatively impact learning and behavior, it is critical that schools provide a variety of sensory resources and opportunities to help students function in the learning environment, in addition to the occupational therapy some of these students need outside of the school environment.

For a visual explanation of SPD, view the first of the three brief video segments listed below (MichaelGrass House, 2009). For a brief glimpse into the world of an adolescent with SPD who is not autistic, view the second video segment, which was created by that adolescent (Grant, 2012). The third video segment (Unique Prints Therapy, 2011) takes you inside an occupational room where children are engaged in a variety of activities to help them with motor skills, leading to better focus, concentration, and other essential school-related learning functions.

What Is Sensory Processing Disorder?
www.youtube.com/watch?v=6O6Cm0WxEZA

Sensory Processing Disorder (Adolescent)
www.youtube.com/watch?v=M4afWC-_d4Y

Sensory Integration Therapy–Pediatric Occupational Therapy
www.youtube.com/watch?v=02JlnqUhXeU.

This last of these three videos shows us a therapeutically fitted room. School resource rooms are not generally therapeutically outfitted, but they provide the essentials for regulation. In fact, occupational therapy has developed a wide range of activities and resources directed at the variety of sensory issues students can experience. These resources and activities are now being made available in varying degrees in school resource rooms. Sensory integration activities for schools will be discussed in Chapter Four, with additional practices outlined in the Appendix.

Restorative Resource Rooms Matter

Understanding the brain-based, trauma-sensitive needs of students, a number of schools now allow students who are struggling with regulating their behavior in the classroom access to a separate, sensory-based room, where they engage in movement and regulation activities before returning to the classroom to learn. Previously, such students would frequently suffer some form of disciplinary action, including out-of-school suspension. These "restorative resource rooms" have many names. Several examples follow.

"Southwick Elementary New Sensory Room Increases Success in the Classroom" (EACS, 2013) is the headline of a news report that describes the success of a project that provides dysregulated students with opportunities to regulate their destructive and disruptive behaviors. East Allen County Schools, Indiana, reported that "This shift has resulted in a decrease in destructive and disruptive behaviors along with an increase in student focus and productivity in the classroom." Similarly, Cindy Terry, County Administrator, Gwinnett County Public Schools, Georgia, reported, "I'm a huge believer in creating school environments where our kids can be successful. We have Sensory Rooms throughout our district, and teachers see the change in behavior almost immediately. With a modest investment, we experience the benefits every day" (Fun and Function, 2014).

Principal Sylvia Cordero of San Francisco's Eldorado Elementary School reported, "If a student starts to lose it, the teacher can give a pass to go to the Wellness Center." Students sign in and can use a feelings chart to show the staff person what activity may be most helpful. The staff member starts a timer for five to ten minutes based upon previous use by that student. "It's not a punishment room. It's not a time-out room. It's not an in-school suspension room. **It's a room where you feel better going out than when you went in"** (Heimpel, 2014).

Although each resource room is outfitted differently, students can sit on a couch, beanbag, rocking chair, or even in a corner with a blanket to regulate. They can listen to the music that best fits their needs or shut out all noise while wearing headphones. They can squeeze rubber balls to relieve tension and anger, or talk to a staff member. They can run, jump, or engage in some other physical activity that helps them regulate.

The Environment and Experience Matter

Given the neuroplasticity of the brain and its ability to adjust, compensate, and redesign itself (Grafton, 2007) in response to changes in the environment, it makes sense that our efforts also focus on creating and sustaining brain-based, trauma-sensitive, learning environments. In essence, this entire resource is about rewiring our brain to match or fit the nervous systems and brains of today's students. It is not about doing more, but about doing differently. Neuroplasticity is a relatively new discovery that reveals how our brains are constantly being rewired by our environment and the experiences we have in the various environments we navigate daily. The video below provides another brief trip inside our brains to demonstrate this plasticity and the capacity to learn throughout life.

Neuroplasticity
www.youtube.com/watch?v=ELpfYCZa87g

Today the evidence is very strong that brain-based, "trauma-sensitive environments are a necessary precursor to any formal learning that might be offered to any child" (Bath, 2008, p. 17). However, even before neuroscience confirmed the influence the environment has on the development of all functions of our brains, inclusive of our nervous system responses, Malinowski (1960) and many others had substantiated, through practice outcomes, that when the environment fits the regulatory and sensory needs of children, they and the environment flourish (Bloom & Farragher, 2010; Brendtro, Mitchell, and McCall, 2009; Bronfenbrenner, 2005; Yehuda, 2002). Our brief discussions to this point have been addressing these needs. One environmental change, in the way students experience their environment, can dramatically change the way those students perform and behave. Ask yourself a question:

> **What would you do to realize the fastest student improvement statewide in a K-8 school that was plagued by violence, heavy presence of security guards, no backpacks allowed, hundreds**

of thousands spent on security, known as the "dropout factory," and ranked in the bottom five of all public schools in the state. There have been five principals in seven years. If you are the sixth, what will you do to change this situation?

Think about the one change you might make. I always present this scenario in training. In a room of 200 attendees, under 5 percent arrive at the correct answer. The reason for this is a mindset that is not yet attuned to children's sensory needs and their critical role in creating optimal learning and behavioral outcomes. Once you have your answer, take a look at the video that is listed at the end of this chapter, with the title *Orchard Gardens School* (we have not provided the link here, because the URL includes the answer).

Chapters Two and Three will provide additional practices and environmental resources that are conducive to learning and behavior regulation—fidgets, lighting, sound, seating, standup desks, transitions, predictability, safety and other essential elements, resources, and practices. For example, standup desks with swinging foot rails are helping some students improve their test scores by 20 percent (Up Desk, 2014).

The *Orchard Gardens School* video demonstrates the power of one experience in changing the environment from one plagued by violence to one that is thriving. It also addresses the importance of a "whole school" approach—one that provides an infrastructure to support that as well as the practices presented to this point and those that will be presented in subsequent chapters. The whole school approach refers to creating a brain-based and trauma-sensitive infrastructure to support the learning experience for all children.

Mindsets Matter

A mindset is a core belief that influences how we react to and interact with others at all levels. In 2015, I posted a blog titled *Milkshakes & Mindsets: Pathways to Academic Success-Regulating Behavior.* In it I discuss a study where two different groups were given the same milkshake. However, one group was told it had many unhealthy ingredients, while the other group was told that it had only healthy ingredients. The two groups had very different biological responses to drinking the milkshake. This study demonstrates that our mindsets matter. Related to optimizing the learning experience, the mindsets that teachers have about their students' capabilities and behaviors, and the mindsets students have about their own capacity to learn, directly influence outcomes. In Chapter Five we identify those teacher mindsets related to anxious and traumatized students that are needed to maximize students' learning outcomes as well as help them regulate their behaviors. Chapter Six identifies specific growth mindsets for effective learning, largely developed by Dr. Carol Dweck of Stanford University. Abundant research has demonstrated the growth in learning outcomes that can be realized when students change their fixed mindsets.

Connections That Matter (CTMs)

Implementing any one of the practices in this resource can produce positive outcomes. However, the most effective and sustained learning and behavioral student outcomes are direct results of the relationship between teacher and student. Practitioners have known for years that the one constant environmental characteristic that is associated with resilient children is their connection to caring, protective, and compassionate adults. This is why some children do better than others when faced with identical, terrifying, traumatic situations (Werner and Smith, 1992; Bowlby and Winton, 1998).

However, it is no secret that large student populations and the demands placed on educators make it difficult for teachers to spend a great deal of time with each student, especially in the classroom. School social workers across the United States have 300-plus students on their caseloads, and they are often responsible for covering several schools in a single district. Unfortunately, there is a persistent mindset that significant gains can be made only when a teacher or social worker can spend substantial time with a student week after week. As a result of this mindset, the value and powerful influence of *brief* connections for establishing positive student learning and behavioral outcomes have been minimized.

Many years ago, Cheever and Hardin (1999) found that those individuals who have effective connection to a significant other did better than those who did not when under stress. Brief connections build resilience and can bring about regulation when under stress. Brief connections with students make them feel significant and help them see us as significant. When this is experienced, outcomes improve. We refer to these brief connections as Connections That Matter (CTMs) to indicate the components that make some connections more effective than others.

CTMs

To be effective, CTMs must be made by teachers who respond with a trauma-sensitive mindset, and who consistently address the four universal needs of every child. Furthermore, when students are stressed, CTMs must be co-regulatory in nature, using non-verbal behavioral communications that address the student's dysregulated sensory responses.

What are the four universal needs of every child/student, and how can teachers meet them? While terminology may vary, a dozen major models of youth development are grounded in four evidence-based essentials:

- Belonging;
- Mastery;
- Independence; and
- Generosity.

These are universal brain-based *needs* and *strengths* (Brendtro and Mitchell, 2015; Van Bockern and McDonald, 2015). They can be reinforced verbally by constructing statements, similar to those listed below, which are specific to each need.

Addressing Students' Universal Needs

Alecia: It is always good to see you. (Belonging)
Jacob: I didn't realize how much you know about . . . (Mastery)
Carlita: I really appreciated the way you took the initiative to . . . (Independence)
Omar: That was really nice, the way you helped out Susan yesterday. (Generosity)

Non-verbal Connections

It is also important to keep in mind the earlier discussion of how our brains have difficulty processing verbal communication when under stress. Without the appropriate body language, the meaning and intent of our verbal communications can be lost. A UCLA study found that when we send a message, its meaning is derived from three sources: 20 percent from the spoken/written words; 25 percent from tone of voice and expressed attitude; and 55 percent from body language (Oakes, 2012). This is especially important in relation to co-regulation with stressed students, whose mid-brain or limbic region responds first to our sensory communications—our body language, facial expressions, tone of voice. If what we are communicating at a non-verbal level is attuned to their needs for sensory reassurance, connection, comfort, and safety, their initial aroused stress response begins to calm down, allowing for easier access to the upper brain—the cortex region—where verbal communication is processed and put in a meaningful context.

Co-regulation

A wonderful example of the power of co-regulation and non-verbal communication can be viewed in the *Still Face Experiment* video (UMass Boston, 2009). Watch how the infant responds to her mother's body language, facial expressions, and tone. Then watch how the same infant responds when her mother stops the non-verbal interactions. Finally, watch how quickly the infant positively interacts with her mother when she resumes her non-verbal interactions. The brief ways we connect with, interact with, and respond to students matter. They are necessary and definitely make a difference in the ways students reciprocate.

> *Still Face Experiment: Dr. Edward Tronick*
> www.youtube.com/watch?v=apzXGEbZht0

In a study, Emmy Werner (2012) found that every child who had survived adverse experiences had one person who believed in their potential. These brief connections, what we say, how we say it, how we react, and the time we take to connect, send very strong messages to students. Our body language, facial expressions, tone, and words all say, "You are important to me. I have taken the time to watch you, listen to you, encourage you, and spend time with you when you are struggling because you matter. I want you to do well."

This is crucial to understand. It is rarely discussed or written about. The same nervous system that prepares us to fight or flee from whatever or whomever is frightening also prepares us to fight our way *toward* the activity, the place, and—most importantly—the person that allow us to feel significant. This relationship leads to trust, and that trust supports achievement. A qualitative study (Shelden et al., 2010, p. 159) found that "not only was trust associated with greater gains in student achievement, but also with lasting gains in achievement." By engaging in brief connections that matter —CTMs—this kind of teacher–student relationship can be developed. Chapter Five presents the necessary teacher mindsets regarding sensory-challenged, anxious, and traumatized students as well as verbal and non-verbal sensory-based CTM strategies that are essential for helping students with self-regulation, behavior, and learning difficulties.

Teacher Resilience and Self-Care Matter

It is well established that the most resilient and effective teachers are themselves regulated and engage in practices that help them manage the stressors they face daily. Teachers who practice self-regulation/self-care are also far more consistently proactive than reactive to the challenges that students and our educational system present today. Sustaining a proactive response day after day necessitates consistent self-care. Consider this: "Public schools in the USA began the 2014–15 school year with an unprecedented demographic profile: For the first time ever, white students are the minority, according to the U.S. Department of Education" (Toppo and Overberg, 2014).

Teachers must learn how to apply differentiated, sheltered, and multicultural instruction within a "standards-based reform" framework. A parent trying to raise three children experiences a good deal of stress. Imagine a teacher trying to teach and relate to thirty diverse students in ways that will allow all of them to reach the same academic goals every day. This is also stressful and demands good self-care in order to remain physically energetic and positively proactive, rather than reactive to the diverse learning styles, needs, and behaviors students present today.

Needless to say, teachers face many additional stressors in the school environment. These are addressed in Chapter Seven. Numerous sensory-based strategies are provided for regulating the nervous system under these very challenging conditions. Particular mention should be made of those strategies that have demonstrated important roles in teacher satisfaction and retention, especially in a teacher's first few years of practice. Students are reflections of their teacher's ability to regulate their responses to the challenges that the students present. The rationale for discussing teacher self-care later in the text is that earlier chapters provide a strong argument as to the importance of self-care as it relates to teacher resilience, sustained effectiveness, and optimization of the learning experience for students.

Whole School Infrastructure Matters

A number of brain-based, trauma-sensitive-informed teachers are already using the practices that are described in this resource. These teachers are committed to bringing the best learning practices of the twenty-first century into their classrooms so that they and their students benefit. However, sustaining these practices requires an infrastructure whose policies, procedures, and resources "fit" within a brain-based, trauma-sensitive framework. Establishing a whole school approach provides the best opportunity to create an infrastructure where everyone can flourish.

Recognizing that no one program fits the needs and personalities of every school, the Trauma and Loss Policy Initiative group (TLPI, 2014), from Massachusetts, and the Compassionate Schools group (Compassionate Schools, 2014), from the State of Washington, were asked to share the policies and strategies they developed for creating a whole school infrastructure that supports teachers in their efforts to meet the learning and behavioral needs of today's students, including anxious and traumatized students. Numerous schools have found their strategies, policies, and practices very helpful in their efforts to create safe and supportive environments where learning can be optimized for all.

Prior to publication, we had a discussion about whether to place these chapters at the beginning or the end of this resource. Feeling that they might be more meaningful once readers had an understanding of the neuroscience of stress and trauma, as well as the science of learning and behavior as we know it today, we ultimately decided to place them at the end. In essence, the preceding chapters present researched, outcome-driven rationales for establishing a brain-based, trauma-sensitive, whole school approach.

Summary

This resource provides multiple choices, examples, and practices that relate to mindsets, movement in learning, self-regulation, sensory processing, experiences and environmental resources and practices, teacher self-care, teacher–student connections, and whole school trauma-sensitive and compassionate approaches.

Practice outcomes tell us that using the practices described in any one chapter will benefit both teachers and students, but all of the chapters are equally important. The practices discussed in one support and complement those in the others.

You will also find that one practice will accomplish several objectives. For example, introducing movement activities every thirty minutes in the classroom schedule helps students focus more effectively, concentrate, and perform throughout the day. It also helps with self-regulation. Mindsets help not only with motivation and learning outcomes but with forming positive teacher–student interactions and relationships. They also help teachers manage their own stress.

As indicated in the Introduction, the chapters follow a bottom-up approach that mirrors the way the human brain developed. The lower regions of the brain, where there is no reason or logic, and where many anxious, traumatized, and sensory-challenged students spend much of their time, must be regulated in order to utilize the cognitive processes that are needed for learning. Chapter Two begins with a comprehensive discussion of the role self-regulation plays in optimizing learning and behavior, and provides a number of practices to support efforts to help students learn to self-regulate their reactions to the stressors in their daily lives.

Answer to the question:

> What would you do to realize the fastest student improvement statewide in a K-8 school that was plagued by violence, heavy presence of security guards, no backpacks allowed, hundreds of thousands spent on security, known as the "dropout factory," and ranked in the bottom five of all public schools in the state. There have been five principals in seven years. If you are the sixth, what will you do to change this situation?

Orchard Gardens School
http://dailynightly.nbcnews.com/_news/2013/05/01/18005192-principal-fires-security-guards-to-hire-art-teachers-and-transforms-elementary-school?lite

---

Note

The discussion of specific programs does not constitute an endorsement of that program by any of the contributors. It does reflect critical elements from these programs that are brain-based, trauma-sensitive, have demonstrated their effectives, and are being used in schools today. These elements constitute a framework for evaluating other approaches that are referred to as brain-based and/or trauma-sensitive. Understanding that no one program or approach fits everyone's needs and environment, this resource introduces you to a number of programs, practices, and resources, with additional resources in the Appendix.

References

Bath, H. (2008). The three pillars of trauma-informed care. *Reclaiming Children and Youth*, 17(3), 5.

Bloom, S.L., and Farragher, B. (2010). *Destroying Sanctuary: The Crisis in Human Service Delivery Systems*. New York: Oxford University Press.

Bowlby, J., and Winton, J. (1998). *Attachment and Loss: Separation, Anger and Anxiety*. New York: Basic Books.

Brendtro, L., and Mitchell, M. (2015). *Deep Brain Learning: Evidence-Based Essentials in Education, Treatment, and Youth Development*. Albion, MI: Starr Commonwealth.

Brendtro, L., Mitchell, M., and McCall, H. (2009). *Deep Brain Learning: Pathways to Potential with Challenging Youth*. Albion, MI: Starr Commonwealth.

Bronfenbrenner, U. (Ed.). (2005). *Making Human Beings Human: Bioecological Perspectives on Human Development*. Thousand Oaks, CA: Sage.

Bytesize Science (2013) *The Chemistry of Fear*. Retrieved September 12, 2014 from www. youtube.com/watch?v=e5jA2b9eEpE.

Cheever, K.H., and Hardin, S.B. (1999). Effects of traumatic events, social support, and self-efficacy on adolescents' self-health assessments. *Western Journal of Nursing Research*, 21(5), 673.

Compassionate Schools (2014). *Compassionate Schools: The Heart of Learning and Teaching*. Retrieved April 15, 2014 from www.k12.wa.us/compassionateschools/.

Crum, A. (2014). *Change Your Mindset, Change the Game*. Retrieved Ausgust 12, 2015 from www.youtube.com/watch?v=ev65KnPHVUk.

Dallman-Jones, A. (2006). *Shadow Children: Understanding Education's # 1 Problem*. Lancaster, PA. RLD Publications.

EACS (2013). *Southwick Elementary New Sensory Room Increases Success in the Classroom*. Retrieved December 16, 2014 from www.eacs.k12.in.us/news/archived_news/2013-2014/october/southwick_elementary_new_sensory_room_increases_su/.

Ford, J., Chapman, J., Mack, M., and Pearson, G. (2006). Pathways from traumatic child victimization to delinquency: Implications for juvenile permanency court proceedings and decisions. *Juvenile and Family Court Journal*, Winter, 13–26.

Free Dictionary (2015). *Mindset*. Retrieved November 18, 2015 from www.thefree dictionary.com/mindset.

Fun and Function (2014). *Chillspa Sensory Room*. Retrieved December 17, 2014 from http://funandfunction.com/chillspa-sensory-room-silver-4640.html.

Ginsburg, K.R. (2006). *Building Resilience in Children and Teens, Giving Kids Roots and Wings*. Elk Grove Village, IL: American Academy of Pediatrics.

Grafton, S.T. (2007). Evidence for a distributed hierarchy of action representation in the brain. *Human Movement Science*, 26(4), 590–616.

Grant, K. (2012). *Sensory Processing Disorder*. Retrieved July 12, 2014 from www.youtube. com/watch?v=M4afWC-_d4Y.

Heimpel, D. (2014). *Aces too High: How Can Big Data Help Improve Child Maltreatment Response and Prevention?* Retrieved July 20, 2015 from https://acestoohigh.com/2014/10/.

Levine, P.A., and Kline, M. (2007). *Trauma through a Child's Eyes: Awakening the Ordinary Miracle of Healing*. Berkeley, CA: North Atlantic Books.

Levine, P.A., and Kline, M. (2008). *Trauma Proofing Your Kids*. Berkeley, CA: North Atlantic Books.

Luthar, S. (2006). Resilience in development: A synthesis of research across five decades. In D. Cicchetti and D. Cohen (Eds.), *Developmental Psychopathology*, Volume 3: *Risk, Disorder, and Adaptation* (2nd ed.), pp. 739–795. Hoboken, NJ: John Wiley & Sons.

Maddox, S. (2006). *Trauma in Children and Related Learning Problems*. Retrieved August 10, 2015 from www.psychiatry.emory.edu/PROGRAMS/GADrug/Feature%20Articles/Parenting/2006%20Trauma%20in%20Children%20and%20Related%20Learning%20Problems.pdf.

Malinowski, B. (1960). *A Scientific Theory of Culture and Other Essays*. New York: Oxford University Press.

Melrose, R. (2013). *K-12 Curriculum "Brain Charge" Is Now Evidence-Based*. Retrieved February 13, 2013 from www.drmelrose.com/2013/01/31/k-12-curriculum-brain-charge-is-now-evidence-based/.

MeMoves (2014). *Stories and Testimonials*. Retrieved January 15, 2014 from http://thinkingmoves.com/testimonials/.

MichaelGrass House (2009). *What Is Sensory Processing Disorder?* Retrieved September 25, 2016 from www.youtube.com/watch?v=6O6Cm0WxEZA.

Movement and Learning (2014). *What the Researchers Say*. Retrieved December 18, 2014 from http://movementandlearning.wordpress.com/about/.

Oakes, D. (2012). *What You Said Isn't What I Saw*. Retrieved July 29, 2015 from http://daveoakesseminars.com/what-you-said-isnt-what-i-saw/.

Oehlberg, B. (2006). *Reaching and Teaching Stressed and Anxious Learners*. Thousand Oaks, CA: Corwin Press.

Olding, S. (2009). *How Is Your Brain Wired?* Retrieved September 25, 2016 from www.youtube.com/watch?v=uOIWVo-4-lc.

Perry, B., and Szalavitz, M. (2006). *The Boy who Was Raised as a Dog and Other Stories from a Child Psychiatrist's Notebook*. New York: Basic Books

Regan, T. (2014). *Carol Dweck: A Sudy on Praise and Mindset*. Retrieved December 9, 2014 from www.youtube.com/watch?v=NWv1VdDeoRY.

Schore, A. (2001). The effects of a secure attachment relationship on right-brain development, affect regulation, and infant mental health. *Infant Mental Health Journal*, 22(1–2), 7–66.

Shelden, D., Angell, M., Stoner, J., and Roseland, B. (2010). School principals' influence on trust: Perspectives of mothers of children with disabilities. *Journal of Educational Research*, 103, 159–170.

Shoval, E. (2011). Using mindful movement in cooperative learning while learning about angles. *Instructional Science*, 39(4), 453–466.

Siegel, D. (2012). *Hand Model of the Brain*. Retrieved January 26, 2016 from www.youtube.com/watch?v=gm9CIJ74Oxw.

SPD Foundation (2015). *What Sensory Processing Disorder Looks Like*. Retrieved July 7, 2014 from www.spdfoundation.net/about-sensory-processing-disorder/symptoms/.

Steele W., and Malchiodi, M. (2012). *Trauma Informed Practices for Children and Adolescents*. New York: Routledge.

Stevens, E.S. (2014). *San Francisco's El Dorado Elementary Uses Trauma-Informed & Restorative Practices; Suspensions Drop 89%*. Retrieved February 14, 2014 from www.socialjusticesolutions.org/2014/01/29/san-franciscos-el-dorado-elementary-uses-trauma-informed-suspensions-drop-89/.

Thinking Moves (2010). *MeMoves in the Classroom.* Retrieved December 12, 2014 from www.youtube.com/watch?v=55OGz8PvrRI.

TLPI (2014). *Helping Traumatized Children Learn.* Retrieved April 12, 2014 from http://traumasensitiveschools.org.

Toppo, G., and Overberg, P. (2014). *Diversity in the Classroom.* Retrieved September 25, 2016 from www.usatoday.com/story/news/nation/2014/11/25/minnesota-school-race-diversity/18919391/.

Transforming Education (2015). *Let's Talk about Self-Management: Marshmallows, Stop Signs, Squeezy Balls, and Teaching.* Retrieved August 10, 2015 from www.youtube.com/watch?v=Oq9P0EdptZ8.

UMass Boston (2009). *Still Face Experiment: Dr. Edward Tronick.* Retrieved August 10, 2011 from www.youtube.com/watch?v=apzXGEbZht0.

Unique Prints Therapy (2011). *Sensory Integration Therapy–Pediatric Occupational Therapy.* Retrieved September 14, 2013 from www.youtube.com/watch?v=02JlnqUhXeU.

Up Desk (2014). *Standing Desks Help Students Perform 20% Better on Standardized Tests.* Retrieved August 12, 2014 from www.myupdesk.com/blog/standing-desks-help-students-perform-20-higher-on-standardized-tests.

Van Bockern, S., and McDonald, T. (2015). Creating circle of courage schools. *Reclaiming Children and Youth,* 20(4), 13–17.

van der Kolk, B. (2014). *The Body Keeps Score: Brain, Mind and Body in the Healing of Trauma.* New York: Viking.

Wall Street Journal (2008). We want comfort when stressed. September 30, p. C6.

Werner, E. (2012). Risk, resilience, and recovery. *Reclaiming Children and Youth,* 21(1), 18–23.

Werner, E.E., and Smith, R.S. (1992). *Overcoming the Odds: High-Risk Children from Birth to Adulthood.* Ithaca, NY: Cornell University Press.

Wikipedia (2013). *Yerkes–Dodson Law.* Retrieved January 22, 2013 from http://en.wikipedia.org/wiki/Yerkes%E2%80%93Dodson_law.

Wikipedia (2014). *Movement in Learning.* Retrieved December 9, 2014 from http://en.wikipedia.org/wiki/Movement_in_learning.

Yehuda, R. (2002). Post-traumatic stress disorder. *New England Journal of Medicine,* 346(2), 108–114.

Your Dictionary (2015). *Mindset.* Retrieved November 12, 2015 from www.yourdictionary.com/mind-set.

2 On Becoming a Self-Reg Haven

Stuart Shanker and Susan Hopkins

The Self-Reg Tsunami

It is hard to believe that we launched Self-Reg only three and a half years ago. Two extraordinary things have happened in this short time. The first is that Self-Reg has spread right across Canada, faster and further than anyone would ever have dreamt possible. This occurred entirely by word of mouth. If anything, our intention was the exact opposite: to keep it small and roll out Self-Reg gradually, beginning in preschool and early primary settings. But it was because that first group of teachers was so enthusiastic about the changes they were seeing, and shared this with their colleagues, that Self-Reg took on a life of its own. Before we knew it, we were working with middle and secondary schools, and now with colleges and universities.

Our thinking at the start may have been to keep in firm control of the reins, but we soon found ourselves holding on for dear life. And that really speaks to the second big aspect of what has happened. Without fully realizing it, we were involved in a different approach to professional development. Rather than the standard "expert-model," with a scripted manual and all sorts of "fidelity" checks, we were involved in a "community of learning," where everyone shared their expertise and experience, their successes and failures, all guided by a vision of how much Self-Reg benefits both students and teachers: students of all ages and teachers in every conceivable environment.

Right from the start, teachers realized that Self-Reg wasn't about acquiring a new set of tools or techniques for managing students' challenging behaviours. Self-Reg amounts to a paradigm revolution in how we see our students: the different stresses they are struggling with in one or—as is often the case—all five of the domains of Self-Reg. Self-Reg is about understanding the nature of *stress* and the myriad *hidden* as well as overt stressors that children and youth must contend with today. It is about recognizing the difference between misbehaviour and stress behaviour, and noticing subtle signs of stress behaviour that we never saw or understood before. It is about pausing to ask: "Why am I seeing this behaviour?" and "Why now?" before we react. It is about the little experiments that we conduct with an individual student or class, with school routines, with our school environment and after-school activities, all designed to enhance self-regulation. It is about truly connecting to the self-regulation needs and resources of a community, and the transformation from being an "educational institution" to becoming a "Self-Reg haven."

That word "haven" speaks to the importance of having our students feel safe and secure from the moment that they enter school; emotionally as well as physically. Only in this way can we turn off a kindled limbic alarm that blocks the very ability to learn. Indeed, only in this way can we increase the energy that sparks the very desire and not just the capacity to learn. And one of the most striking consequences of the shift from "survival brain" to "learning brain" that occurs when students are calmly focused and alert is, not surprisingly, that a teacher's own stress level is sharply diminished. This may be the ultimate reason why we have seen a "Self-Reg tsunami"; it is certainly one of our primary objectives.

The first link below provides additional information related to Self-Reg, the Mehrit Centre, and its resources. The second link is to a blog that discusses "The Paradigm-revolution: Self-Regulation for Schools and Communities." The third link is to a video presentation by the authors, and the final link is to additional information about self-regulation in a graphic format.

Self-Reg Information
www.self-reg.ca/shanker-self-reg/

The Paradigm-revolution: Self-Regulation for Schools and Communities
www.self-reg.ca/wp-content/uploads/2015/09/Viewpoints-Paradigm-Revolution-interactive.pdf

Self-Reg in the Community
www.youtube.com/watch?v=9Z_sWSwoa5M&feature=youtu.be

Understanding Stress Behaviour for Teachers: Self-Reg Infographic
www.self-reg.ca/wp-content/uploads/2015/09/Infographic-Feb-2016-Teacher.pdf

---

Self-Reg and the Shanker Method™

Self-Reg enables us to recognize not just when a student or a class or even a whole school is becoming dysregulated, but what to do about it: the process that will enable us to experience that calmly focused state where learning and growth can occur. There are five steps to Self-Reg, commonly referred to as "The Five Rs" of the Shanker Method™:

• Reframe the behaviour
• Recognize the stressors
• Reduce the stressors
• Reflect
• Respond

The first step involves distinguishing between misbehaviour and stress behaviour, recognizing that something that we automatically assume is due to a lack of self-control is, in fact, a sign of an excessive stress load (see *Self-Reg Infographic* above). Important examples of when we may need to reframe behaviour are things like: restlessness; a negative outlook; emotional volatility; sudden outbursts; heightened impulsivity; low frustration tolerance; aggression; oppositional behaviour; social withdrawal; and a lack of empathy.

One of the drawbacks of explaining this method in print is that it makes it seem like one does these steps in a linear order. It is not linear; there are multiple points of entry and we can be working on many steps at the same time, weaving back and forth. The goal is always the "self" in self-regulation—in other words, for the student to do this for himself/herself. The path to this goal is unique to the person involved.

The truth is that which of the Five Rs you start with depends on the individual student or class, and, what's more, may be something that you return to several times (Figure 2.1). This is especially true in regards to the "first" step outlined here: the "reframing" of behaviour. Our understanding of a student's actions is constantly evolving, especially in regards to the student's stresses. So often, what we thought was the major stressor turns out to be part of a more complicated "stress complex" or the result of some deeper stressor.

In some ways, the five steps of the Shanker Method™ seem quite simple and straightforward. However, in our experience, in practice, it is complex, messy, and often full of surprises. The application requires more than a selection of strategies to try; it requires knowledge of Self-Reg and the neurobiology beneath any behaviour, a commitment to detective work, great patience, and those necessary "soft eyes" for the student in front of us who is struggling.

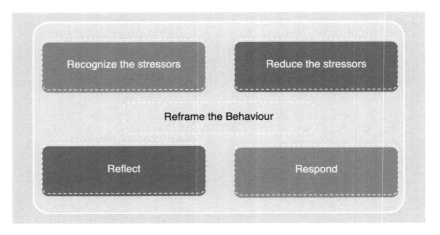

Figure 2.1

Self-Reg and Teaching

At the root of so many struggles teachers are facing in their classrooms today is a story of a stress system gone awry. With the understandings of behaviour that Self-Reg brings comes great hope. As we understand *why* a behaviour is happening, we can also begin to understand what to do about it. Gone are the days of ignoring the "blackbox" of the brain and just focusing on modifying or managing the behaviour. There is a whole population of young people for whom this approach did not work, and through Self-Reg we now understand why and what to do about it (Figure 2.2).

Many of our master teachers have been practicing a form of Self-Reg their entire careers. They are naturals, so learning about Self-Reg is part reinforcer of beliefs, part validator of past practice, and part extender of knowledge, as new science is illuminating new paths every day. In addition, we have to keep in mind that the incredible expansion of modern-day stressors in all five domains of our students' lives is also affecting the lives of our teachers. Excessive stress, especially when exacerbated by the hidden stressors we are unaware of that are at work on our "survival brains," increases tension and drains the energy reserves of many teachers, leaving less energy for the very demanding work of teaching itself.

Although it may feel like you do not have the time for Self-Reg, we strongly believe that, without it, some of your biggest behaviour challenges faced daily in the classroom will continue day in, day out. With the roots of the problem still locked away in the "blackbox," there is often not enough understanding of the *why* and *why now* of the behaviour to move beyond the surface level of what is going on.

What is SELF-REGULATION?
According to Dr. Stuart Shanker:

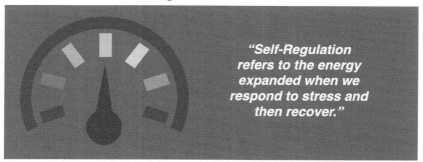

"Self-Regulation refers to the energy expanded when we respond to stress and then recover."

The MEHRIT Centre

Figure 2.2

So the next question is: where to begin? Relationships are always the starting point. Self-Reg reveals just how important relationships are, especially for the student who seems to be struggling the most.

Teaching, Relationships, and the Interbrain

Sometimes we hear teachers who are learning about Self-Reg refer to the "interbrain" as *the* relationship." It's definitely the science that explains the neurobiological roots, but it's perhaps more accurate to think of it as the shared space between people where the relationship lives. Just think of any individual whose presence you find soothing or with whom you share a sense of knowing that doesn't require words. Think of the "wordless" energy of a choir singing together, a well-drilled sports team, a grandfather holding the hand of his granddaughter as they walk through the park. Interbrain: it nourishes us throughout our lives, and it holds much magic for teachers looking to apply Self-Reg strategies in the classroom, especially with struggling students.

We know that young children learn to self-regulate by being regulated. Not to be confused with "being managed," this natural mechanism of learning self-regulation is facilitated by the interbrain, which acts like a wireless connection between the baby's and the caregiver's brains. Since newborns' brains are premature and executive functions within them have not yet formed, the baby requires a higher-order adult brain to serve as an "external brain" to regulate his/her physiological states. The higher-order brain reads the baby's cues—such as facial expressions, posture, movements, and sounds—and adjusts actions accordingly to up (stimulating) or down regulate (regulating) the baby as necessary. These dyadic experiences are vital to help the baby to develop the capacity for self-regulation, emotions, the HPA axis (our central stress response system), perceptual skills, cognitive skills, and communicative skills. This is relevant for early childhood educators and parents, of course, but it is equally important for all teachers of students who are developing self-regulation.

The research into the interbrain, this Bluetooth-like communication channel between a caregiver and an infant, is showing us the neurobiological "dawning" of relationships. This need for the interbrain continues throughout our lives; it just changes form. A Self-Reg teacher is naturally regulating to the students in his/her care, sometimes as the "external brain," sometimes in the co-regulation dance, and sometimes simply as that trusted adult who set the stage for the "self" in self-regulation to emerge and grow in a student or the classroom as a whole. The first link below reviews self-regualtion in the early years. The second is a brief video for early childhood educators.

Self-Regulation: The Early Years
www.self-reg.ca/wp-content/uploads/2015/09/What-you-need-to-know-Self-reg-early-years-print.pdf

Early Childhood Educators Video: Dr. Shanker
www.youtube.com/watch?v=F4qwr271voY&feature=youtu.be

Energy-Centered Teaching

In a series of blogs on the Self-Reg view of mindfulness (see the three links below), Dr. Shanker explores the relationship between the very popular trend towards mindfulness in education and Self-Reg, with a discussion of the similarities between the two, the many differences, and the implications for practice. Via a Self-Reg lens, we are looking first to understand "mind blindness" and then to remove the cognitive blinders that are, in a way, blocking our view and colouring our interpretations of what we are seeing. In teaching, this applies to learning about "stress behaviour" and how to read, and to the building of healthy relationships with students and their families.

Self-Reg View of Mindfulness
www.self-reg.ca/dr-stuart-shankers-the-self-reg-view-of-mindfulness/
www.self-reg.ca/dr-stuart-shankers-blog-the-self-reg-view-of-mindfulness/
www.self-reg.ca/dr-shankers-blog-self-reg-view-of-mindfulness-33/

The four facets of Energy-Centered Teaching (ECT)—protect, connect, collect, detect—can help with removing the cognitive blinders that get in the way of practicing Self-Reg in the everyday classroom (see Figure 2.3). As we focus on "seeing" each student's behaviour as a story of energy—presented, depleted, and diverted from the "calm and alert" learning brain that we need—we carry these four practices in our tool belt.

Protect

Self-Reg first! Always. To get the learning brain back online, first ask: what can I do to turn off this student's "I am not safe" internal alarm? Much like the "Housing First" movement cities are using to address homelessness, this step puts Self-Reg first. Before we dive into trying to understand behaviours that have complex roots, we soothe and we make it safe, physically, emotionally, culturally, socially—in every way. If the student's alarm is on, or if they are in a state of hypervigilance—regardless of how they got to that point—our first priority is always to make them feel "safe."

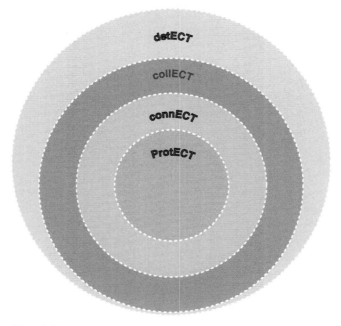

Figure 2.3

Connect

Build relationships with students and their families (see link below). Relationships are the core of the "haven" of Self-Reg. Ask how you can build and strengthen the relationship of trust with this student. This is not a new idea; healthy relationships are the core of good teaching. For Self-Reg teachers, these healthy relationships come naturally with most of the students. But there are often a few with whom it's not so easy to connect. Noticing the state of each relationship and then with the group as a whole is part of the process. Noticing what our experience of the challenging relationships is through a lens of hidden stressors can help open up awareness of what might be going on in the challenging situations. In other words, is there something about this particular student that is setting off your stress response system? Sometimes this is obvious—aggression or rudeness, for example—but there are often more layers. For example, many teachers find experiencing the distress of others very energy expensive (prosocial domain). This speaks to the deep caring nature of those within this profession. Yet, in situations where we see a student in distress but are unable to soothe them (a crying student, a withdrawn student), it can be very dysregulating to our stress response systems. Brain-to-brain communication is taking place continually. We must always keep in mind our own Self-Reg in any situation of challenge with a student.

In the video link below, the authors address their comments to families.

Parents

www.youtube.com/watch?v=n_YKVMueKTA&feature=youtu.be

Collect

Collect Self-Reg knowledge as you build your toolbox of strategies. Understanding the *why* is key to success in applying the *how*. Learn to "be the barometer" and ask: are there signs that this student is caught up in a stress cycle that he can't simply "will" his way out of? We cannot emphasize enough the importance of learning Self-Reg. Moving from the "head" knowledge to embodied understandings of Self-Reg is part of the process. A priority for any Self-Reg practitioner, including the authors of this chapter, is always to develop deeper understanding of the brain–body systems and their complexities across the five domains: biological, emotional, cognitive, social, and, prosocial.

Detect

Begin the process of applying the Shanker Method™ simply by asking: *why* and *why now?* Student behaviour always has a "why," and for those students who are struggling most we find the why is often not about a bad choice, a deliberate action, seeking attention, or any other of the myriad possible misbehaviours. These students' "tanks" are almost empty and they are operating on "survival brain" most of the time. They simply have no reserves to be the good student that everyone wants them to be. Detective work can change a student's trajectory. It is an incredibly rewarding experience for Self-Reg teachers as the *"aha"* moments come and you see a trajectory begin to shift.

Self-Reg: A Five-Domain Framework

There are five domains in the Self-Reg Framework: biological, emotional, cognitive, social, and prosocial. Each of these domains is unique to the individual student, and to ourselves as teachers and parents. Self-Reg is not a program—it is a framework through which teachers can better understand a student (colleague, parent, and even themselves). All five domains (Figure 2.4) are essential components that are necessary to understand holistically why a student may be acting the way they are and how we can help them to achieve their potential. The Framework provides an organizational structure for thinking about self-regulation with considerable flexibility and adaptability for application.

As we look a little closer at each of the five domains of the Self-Reg Framework (Shanker, 2012), it's crucial to keep in mind that the work of Self-Reg is always about all five domains together, as a whole. Strategies can be starting places but

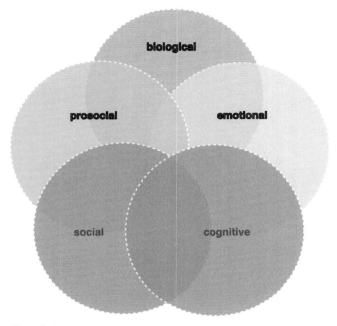

Figure 2.4

the shift comes as Self-Reg moves into the school culture as a foundation for student well-being and student learning.

Self-Reg is grounded in a vibrant new understanding of how genes operate in a web of co-actional interactions, ranging from the cellular material in which strings of DNA are enmeshed, to the social structure in which a child and her family are enmeshed. All of the levels in a child's "developmental manifold" interact with and influence all of the other levels. So, to understand something as complex as how a certain kind of "personality" becomes entrenched, we need to look at all of the levels of the manifold and the interactions between them.

The same point applies to Self-Reg. When we set out to understand the stresses that a student is under, we always need to look at all five domains (biological, emotional, cognitive, social, and prosocial). For here, too, we see the same sort of "co-actional interactions": a "multiplier effect" in which one kind of stress—say, the noisy assembly—makes a student more sensitive to other stressors. Put him in a crowded room and he becomes much more sensitive to noise and light. Back in the classroom, he cannot settle or focus on an assignment; the slightest frustration leads to an outburst; he starts to quarrel with the other students and refuses to comply with his teacher's wishes. His whole stress system is increasingly dysregulated, with each of the stressors intensifying his reactivity to all of the others.

A school is itself a dynamic system, with each class possessing its own unique set of stressors. Some of these stressors are highly functional. Indeed, learning itself is a stressor: one of the most beneficial kinds a child or youth can experience. But, just as a student can get caught in the grip of a dysregulated stress system, so can a school. Below we discuss the five domains and the practices that may be used to address each of them.

Biological Domain

When we are trying to understand a student's stresses, we typically begin with the biological domain, even in cases when we are dealing with a problem that stands out in one of the other domains. Quite often, a student who is struggling in one of the other domains has a low-level biological challenge that constitutes a constant drain on energy reserves and compromises recovery functions and attention.

The first step is to consider whether a student demonstrates some sort of sensory hypo- or hypersensitivity. A student who is very sensitive to, say, auditory or visual stimulation will have to expend considerable energy trying to stay regulated in a noisy or visually overstimulating environment. The same point applies to all of the student's senses, including those internal "body" senses that are so important for feeling comfortable and relaxed. We also need to factor in how well the student is replenishing their energy needs (e.g., sleep hygiene, nutrition, physical activity).

For many students, the problems they are having in the biological domain are due to:

- noises, crowds;
- too much visual stimulation; and/or
- not enough exercise.

Starter Strategies in the Biological Domain

Whole school/whole class level:

- Declutter, declutter, declutter.
- Conduct a "visual noise" scan of classroom. Look for bright colours, busy walls, busy carpets, more clutter that you missed.
- Consider other elements of distraction (remember this is just from the perspective of students and the bio domain), such as scents, sparkly and dangly jewelry, visually distracting clothes, where you stand (i.e., in front of a window).
- Consider every item on the wall: why is it there, who uses it, and how?
- Change harsh lighting to natural lighting options where possible. See microenvironments strategies (below) for more ideas.
- Create lighting "microenvironments" so students can pick and choose, moving from one to another as needs require.

- Replace laminated posters with co-created versions with students. For example, the alphabet designed with the class, with pictures chosen by the children that are associated with specific letters, or visual schedules with pictures of actual activities.
- Ensure all content intended for learners is at their eye level.
- Clear away the content in the upper part of the classroom wall.
- Do a spring clean and bring in tricks of the "home-makeover" world: use bins for storage, sheets to conceal the bins, etc. The local thrift shop is a great place to look for clutter clean-up resources.
- Remove hanging items from the ceiling.
- Do a noise audit. What are the "background" noises or brain alarm-triggering noises and can they be eliminated or at least minimized? Think of bells, humming electrical equipment, squeaky chairs, and students' voices. (We want them to engage, so this isn't about enforced silence. But "library voices" and "restaurant voices" are different from "playground voices.")
- Observe your own voice and how you use it.
- Have earbuds and noise-reducing headphones available.
- Consider non-alarm-triggering sound sources, like rainsticks.
- Bring nature into your space: plants, rocks, sticks, foliage—if it's from nature, you really can't go wrong.
- Use natural colours in your classroom. Bright primary colours everywhere are overstimulating to many students, so choose and use primary colours, especially yellow, very carefully—they go where you want the students' attention to go.
- Have a variety of seating options and allow students to choose what fits them best.
- Set up a hydration station and plan, and, if possible, a healthy snack program.
- Create sensory stations with regulating materials, including rocking chairs, beanbag chairs, bins of sensory materials, silent bikes, and couches (see Figure 2.5).

Individual student level:

- The individual level is always about practicing the five steps of the Shanker Method™: (1) Read and reframe; (2) Recognize the stressors; (3) Reduce the stress; (4) Reflect; and (5) Respond.
- Learning more about the student can help. There are many ways to conduct your biological domain stress detective work. Figure 2.6 presents reflection questions based on Dr. Shanker's work that will get you started.

Creating a Self-Reg "haven" is not about spending a lot of money. It's about developing awareness of the sensory experiences of your students (and yourself) and of your classroom as both a "canvas" for learning and a third teacher.

MICROENVIRONMENTS

A VARIETY OF PLACES FOR STUDENTS TO DO THEIR WORK THAT CAN MEET A VARIETY OF NEEDS

- To change body position: a counter-height table or bookcase, a couch, beanbag chair, and alternatives to sitting such as a standing area, or a bike with an easel, carpet/floor area with clipboards

- To down regulate or calm: tent – fabric over a desk, a comfortable chair/couch away from the desks, under a table along the side of the room or a closet with curtains and pillows, etc.

- To reduce visual/auditory stressors (desk or table in hallway, LA room, library, etc.)

- To up regulate (stationary bikes/foot pedals under desks, sit and wiggle)

- Has the use of the available micro-environments been explicitly taught to your students? Teach why you might use them and when they may be used during class time.

Figure 2.5

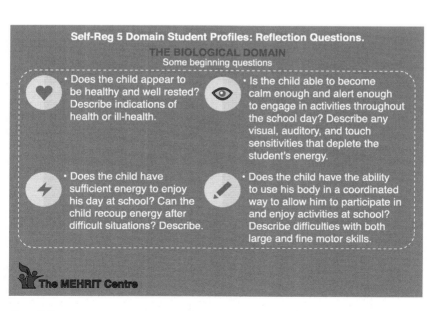

Figure 2.6

Source: Shanker, 2012.

Remember that classes may change quite significantly from one year to the next. Co-creating your learning space is a shared process and part of the Self-Reg detective work and relationship building; it should always feel like it belongs to the students too.

Emotional Domain

Emotion regulation is generally seen either through the lens of self-control—i.e., the emphasis is placed on teaching techniques to rein in explosive emotions—or as a meta-cognitive issue—teaching the meaning of different emotional terms (through picture boards, stories, role-playing, etc.). In Self-Reg the emphasis is placed on promoting the student's embodied understanding of the *physical–emotional nexus*: that is, the connection between their physical state and their emotional experience.

The first step is to help students recognize the connection between when they are in a low-energy/high-tension state and the negative emotions they experience in that state. Just as important, however, is for them to learn the connection between the positive emotions they experience when in a state of high energy/high tension. Finally, they need to learn what it feels like to be relaxed—i.e., the emotional as well as the physical feeling of being in a low-tension state. For many students, the problems they are having in the emotional domain are due to strong emotions, both positive (overexcitement) and negative (anger, fear).

Starter Strategies in the Emotional Domain

Whole school/whole class level:

- Recognize that developing Self-Reg in the emotional domain is not a standalone lesson of some kind. The practice of Self-Reg in the emotional domain is infused throughout the school day: in the everyday routines; through relationships; through problems that emerge, are worked through, and resolved; and, in the growth that happens over time.
- Build students' awareness of the biological–emotional nexus. Help the students become aware of the connection between their physical state and the emotions they experience: e.g., low energy/high tension and negative emotions; high energy/high tension and positive emotions. This is the key to the emotional domain.
- Remember that positive emotions are critical. We are not just trying to reduce negative emotions; the positive/negative equation is crucial to Self-Reg.
- Nurture a "positive bias."
- Scan your classroom for the "Self-Reg friendly" places where students can choose to go.
- Create a microenvironment plan for your classroom that moves beyond the general whole class "rethink" suggested in the biological domain strategies and considers individual needs.

- Introduce predictable routines that include care for transition time planning.
- Apply a "necessary for some, good for all" strategy to guide the planning of your space to support the Self-Reg needs of students who are processing strong emotions:

  o squirrel-away areas (caves, cubbies);
  o tents, tepees;
  o provide materials for camp building;
  o weighted items, like blankets, rice-filled socks;
  o have the whole class make personal pillows or weighted snakes;
  o knitting zone, puzzle area, personal "stuffies" zone for younger children.

- Consider the expectations around the use of microenvironments. Ask if the student has the option to self-select when to use a microenvironment and for how long.
- Allow Face Time with a caregiver as needed. Check in on your belief systems around this practice and a student's Self-Reg needs. These beliefs are as crucial to its success as the strategy itself.
- Encourage parents, grandparents, or siblings to make personal video clips, write letters, or produce pictures that students can "visit" for comfort when needed.
- Allow space for the emotions—whatever they may be. If our model was self-control, we would expect students to suppress strong emotions or move through them quickly. But it's Self-Reg, so we know that they can't simply suppress, even if they want to.
- Teach students that tears are "cortisol cleansers" and serve a purpose.
- Take it outside whenever you can.
- Use a preventative health model wherever possible with your support team (see www.youtube.com/watch?v=ZMcnIKHr2Ls&feature= youtu.be).
- Adopt a "Self-Reg First" philosophy. We all want to get on to the curriculum; prioritize turning on the "learning brain" and having a student who is calm, focused, and alert first.
- Move away from a focus on whole class calming strategies. Many of these exacerbate the dysregulation in students. Give each student what they need. Students who are always moving need to move. That's how they self-regulate.

Individual student level:

- The individual level is always about practicing the five steps of the Shanker Method™: (1) Read and reframe; (2) Recognize the stressors in all five domains; (3) Reduce the stress; (4) Reflect; and (5) Respond.

- "Explosive" emotions are rarely as explosive as they seem. Work with each student on "nexus," the understanding of the physical–emotional connection and the meaning of each emotion.
- Watch where students naturally go when given the opportunity to choose; look for the Self-Reg within that choice.
- Test out all sorts of strategies with individual students to identify those that work (each student is unique), such as 1–2–10 (1 awareness; 2 deep breaths; count to 10) or certain microenvironments (using the class spin bike). Ideally, each student wants to figure out a "bag" of strategies that helps them return to being calm, alert, and focused.
- Start a personal Self-Reg journal and document your own Self-Reg, energy and tension, and/or experiences of stressors in the five domains throughout the school day.
- Read Dr. Shanker's blogs: *The Self-Reg View of Kids Gone Wild* (www.self-reg.ca/wp-content/uploads/2015/09/viewon_kidsgonewild.pdf) and *The Self-Reg View of ADHD* (www.self-reg.ca/the-self-reg-view-of-adhd/).
- Learning more about the student can help. There are many ways to conduct your emotional domain stress detective work. Figure 2.7 presents reflection questions based on Dr. Shanker's work that will get you started.

For students with kindled alarms who are carrying the heavy burden of allostatic overload, the school bus driver, the custodian, the receptionist,

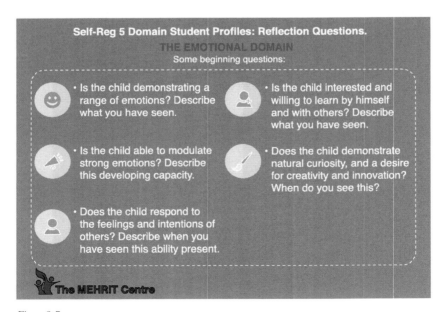

Figure 2.7

Source: Shanker, 2012.

the education assistant, the principal, and the teacher down the hall each registers as either "safe" or "threat" to the student's constantly monitoring limbic system. Make the environment "safe, safe, safe" by applying Self-Reg to the whole school: train the full team to understand, at minimum, the Energy-Centered Teaching model (protect, connect, collect, detect), the difference between stress behaviour and misbehaviour, and how to respond.

In the emotional domain it is crucial for teachers and students alike to learn how to "read" their physical state from their emotions. Self-Reg studies the significance of all emotions, rather than trying to suppress some and bolster others. Emotion is not some separate domain that we can "teach" through "domain-specific" exercises. For example, if we practice emotional vocabulary out of context we disconnect from the embodied experience of the emotion—crucial information for Self-Reg, especially for students with explosive behaviours.

Cognitive Domain

The cognitive domain is a classic example of when a student's problems may be mistakenly seen as due to a lack of effort when they are, in fact, due to a stress overload. The problems we are dealing with here are generally attentional: e.g., a limited ability to stay focused on a task; heightened distractibility; poor organizational problem-solving skills. Historically, such problems were treated with some form of punishment-and-reward, but in recent years we have seen the development of effective techniques to compensate for challenges in these areas (e.g., executive function coaching). Self-Reg enhances the effectiveness of these strategies by working on the sources of the student's cognitive problems.

This requires an understanding of the unique nature of *cognitive stressors*, the amount of energy expended in sustained concentration, and the effect of overall energy depletion on a student's capacity to pay attention. However, in many cases, the stress that arises when a student has trouble recognizing certain kinds of pattern is due to a processing deficit. The first step here is to identify such deficits and then scaffold learning experiences that will build up their ability to process this kind of information, thereby reducing the stress the student experiences when he does not readily see patterns in that area.

For many students, the problems they are having in the cognitive domain are due to difficulties with:

* processing certain kinds of information;
* having to sustain or switch attention;
* sequencing;
* remembering new learning;
* ignoring distractions;
* thinking in abstract terms; and/or
* seeing the relationship between cause and effect.

Starter Strategies in the Cognitive Domain

Whole school/whole class level:

- Create a Self-Reg haven in your classroom and school (see the biological and emotional domain starter strategies).
- Use predictable routines and schedules that are consistent, not ever-changing, yet also introduce novelty—the "new"—every day.
- Tell stories, listen to stories, look for the story within the learning.
- Do work that is meaningful to the students.
- Play, no matter the age, stage, or grade: play and learning are interconnected.
- Nurture interests. Whenever you can, bring the curriculum into the students' existing interests.
- Use flexible grouping: allow for different choices of grouping, including working individually. Make that choice a safe one.
- Move the classroom outdoors, into the community, and into authentic environments.
- Co-create visual schedules and routines with those schedules with the students.
- Wherever you can, allow for learning to flow for longer blocks of time and without interruptions that set off the limbic alarm.
- Remember that "boring" and "bored" are stress responses. Ask yourself frequently if the stressors might be coming from the cognitive domain.
- Use questioning to make the learning visible and "see" inside a student's or group of students' thinking.
- Use multi-modal approaches to bootstrap a "weaker" pattern recognition sense with a stronger one (e.g., number with tactile).
- Build movement and exercise breaks into your learning day, not just for the physical health benefits but also to support Self-Reg in the cognitive domain.
- Some additional advice to reduce stressors in the cognitive domain comes from our Director of Research, cognitive psychologist Dr. Brenda Smith-Chant:
    - o   Apply practice and repetition to aid cognition. Practice allows cognitive processes—reading, arithmetic, keyboarding, etc.—to become automatic (or fluent) and thus lowers stress. Once a process is fluent, it requires less effort and memory, and attention can be moved to more complicated aspects of the skill, such as comprehension.
    - o   Design learning for the multiple brain pathways which decode words, do math, etc. This is very important, because it means that even if a single pathway in the brain is barred due to injury or developmental disability, there is usually another pathway that can be used to get around that barrier.
    - o   Elaborate, expand, build on whatever it is you are learning or sharing with students. One of the best ways to enhance memory and recall is through elaboration. This may seem counter-intuitive, as elaboration

is about adding details, narrative information, and connections to related concepts to the information you want to remember. Oddly, though, adding more detail makes the information more memorable. So add stories and examples to illustrate whatever you want the students to learn.

o   Look for multiple sources of evidence of learning. In cognitive psychology, we understand that learning can be happening even when an individual cannot recall information on demand (e.g., answer the question on the test). Even when something cannot be recalled, learning is evident when a person can recognize the answer (e.g., in a multiple-choice format). Even if information cannot be recognized, it may be evident that some learning has occurred when it takes less time to reteach the information. A skilled instructor will appreciate these changes are all evidence of learning.

o   Learn about working memory and its connection to anxiety, stress, and thus Self-Reg. Working memory is known as the "bottleneck of the cognitive system"—we seem to be able to keep only very limited information within the active and working part of our memory at any given moment. Anxiety and stress have been shown to reduce the size of this bottleneck—the more stress or anxiety we suffer, the less information we can hold in the active part of our memory. We can see the impact on cognitive processes—there are fewer resources available for active thinking.

o   Recognize that part of what makes a cognitive task difficult is ignoring (or filtering) distracting information from our perceptual system but also from our memory. This can make even simple cognitive tasks more difficult and leads to errors.

Individual student level:

•   The individual level is always about practicing the five steps of the Shanker Method™: (1) Read and reframe; (2) Recognize the stressors in all five domains; (3) Reduce the stress; (4) Reflect; and (5) Respond.
•   Learn to recognize the shift from "learning brain" to "survival brain." Students shift to "survival brain" when they do not understand what they are experiencing, why people are acting as they are, or when there is just too much information for them to absorb.
•   Learning more about the student can help. There are many ways to conduct your cognitive domain stress detective work. Figure 2.8 presents reflection questions based on Dr. Shanker's work that will get you started.
•   Read Dr. Shanker's blog: *The Self-Reg View on Literacy* (www.self-reg.ca/wp-content/uploads/2015/09/viewon_literacy.pdf).

Make the environment "safe, safe, safe" by making Self-Reg whole school: train the full team to understand at least the Energy-Centered Teaching model

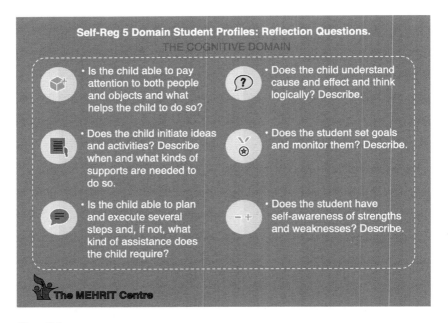

Figure 2.8

Source: Shanker, 2012.

(protect, connect, collect, detect), the difference between stress behaviour and misbehaviour, and how to respond. For students with kindled alarms who are carrying the heavy burden of allostatic overload, the school bus driver, the custodian, the receptionist, the education assistant, the principal, and the teacher down the hall each registers as either "safe" or "threat" to the student's constantly monitoring limbic system.

The Social Domain

The standard approach to working on problems in the social domain is some form of skills training, where one attempts to teach the student social conventions or concrete strategies for dealing with interpersonal conflict. As always, Self-Reg seeks to work on the underlying causes of the student's problems in this domain: in this case, the effect of an excessive stress load on the student's social behaviour; and, in particular, the effect of *social stress* on the student's ability to "mind-read" and "mind-display."

One of the effects of being in a state of allostatic overload is that the student's limbic alarm is kindled and he or she sees threats everywhere, even when none is present. A benign facial expression, an innocuous remark, a casual gesture, and so on are experienced as threatening, and the student responds in "fight-or-flight" mode. A further aspect of the stress that a student may feel in social situations is the amount of nonverbal information that is rapidly—and in many ways subliminally—processed. Unsure of what others are thinking or feeling on the basis of their body language ("mind-reading"), or unable to recognize the effects of their own behaviours on others ("mind-displaying"), the student is overwhelmed by the complex social situations that proliferate in school life.

Instead of trying to "explain" the rules of appropriate social behaviour, Self-Reg sets out to reduce the stress of social situations by reducing the student's overall stress load, building in the necessary restorative breaks, and exposing them to simpler social demands. This allows the student gradually to acquire the implicit mind-reading and mind-displaying knowledge that is needed to co-regulate effectively. Work on resilience has shown that a strong interbrain relationship is pivotal for self-regulation in this domain.

For many students, the problems they are having in the social domain are due to:

- mindreading deficits;
- trouble reading the effects of their own behaviours (mind-displaying);
- too much "social information" for them to process (e.g., class activities); and/or
- the challenge of cultural diversity: different kinds of affect cues, social expectations.

Starter Strategies in the Social Domain

Whole school/whole class level:

- Recognize that (as in the emotional domain) developing Self-Reg in the social domain is not a standalone lesson of some kind. The practice of Self-Reg in the social domain is infused throughout the school day: in the everyday routines; through relationships; in problems that emerge, are worked through, and resolved; and, in the growth that happens over time.
- Intentionally design activities and experiences that promote relation-ship building, starting simple (to keep it "safe") with, for example, a bridge-building or balloon tower challenge. Frame "success" as meeting the challenge, not as winning a race or a competition. Recognize (talk about, explore) "diversity as strength" in the team.
- Include a variety of age-appropriate activities that help students become aware of themselves and others.
- Practice turn-taking through shared times, such as during class, in small group discussions, or during class meetings.
- Introduce team-building games and collaborative exercises (start small).
- Invite older students to mentor younger children.
- Use age-appropriate self-reflective exercises (e.g., journaling).
- Invite adults into your classroom (principal, other teachers, assistants) during student working time (play centers, inquiry or collaborative project work, etc.), provide them with a few (open-ended) questions and have them

circulate, asking these questions. Teach the students in advance how to introduce themselves.

- Use circles for problem-solving class challenges that emerge or just as a general settling practice. One approach that supports turn-taking and builds social inclusion is pass the rock or "talking stick." Allow "passing" (not forcing a response) as an option (goes to safety) as the rock moves around the circle. Begin with "safe" questions that everyone can answer, such as: what is your favourite colour/animal? Or, for older students: what is your favourite band? Frame hearing the same answer more than once as a celebration of something in common.

- Play drama games, such as mirror opposites (in partners). Assign the leads ("'A's put up your hands, you lead first, then 'B's follow," etc.). Then, when you see they are ready, encourage the students to move the leadership of the mirror back and forth, without words.

- Play "vote with your feet" games, such as four corners, designated by the season when the students were born (winter, front left; summer, back right; etc.) or favourite out of four ice-cream flavours. Once they have voted with their feet, allow the groups to connect around whatever is common to the corner they have chosen.

- In the early years, include a dramatic play center or zone. Put out a variety of materials and then watch what the children create from them. (You may think it will be a doctor's office and they may turn it into a veterinarian's surgery.) Then add more materials to the zone as "invitations" to learning and see where they take it next. Never force play in this zone. If a child is still at the parallel play stage, they will make this clear with their choice of where to go during center time.

- Play games that encourage oral language development: charades, twenty questions, I-spy, Simon says. (These have many other Self-Reg benefits, too.)

- Create a "café" event for a parents' visit to the classroom. Design the classroom with the students to look like a café, design the menus, create the food and drinks, provide the service. Include entertainment (a play, or singing) or the sharing of student work ("All About Me" books) within the event.

- Create classroom products to which everyone contributes: class books with collections of poetry, stories, art, etc.; math word problems with all the students in the class included; "I wonder" questions; collections of lyrics to favourite songs; identifying various creatures—anything that can be celebrated collectively. Provide scaffolding for all those who need it.

- Model respectful engagement even in challenging situations where another is not showing respect and "think out loud" where possible/appropriate to describe your inner dialogue (during or afterwards).

- Apologize when you notice in retrospect that you should have responded differently to a relational or behavioural challenge that happened within the classroom. Students can learn so much from your open acknowledgement of what you might have done differently, especially if you explain what happened in terms of Self-Reg (e.g. "I was tired, feeling frustrated, and the noise level in the class had drained my energy when XYZ happened yesterday, so I didn't respond as well as I would have liked. I should have done this: . . .").

- Take field trips to a variety of settings with different social expectations. Explore and practice these before the trip and then discuss them afterwards. This can be applied to any field trip as well as in the school or with special guests to the classroom. Dialogue, repetition, and scaffolding the development of socially acceptable behaviours in any context are important. Note that this is not a behaviour management approach. Recognize the stressors for the child (new, unknown context; sense that others know the rules and they don't; hyperarousal from the "excitement").
- Normalize ruptures in relationships between students. Friends, even adult friends, have disagreements.

Individual student level:

- The individual level is always about practicing the five steps of the Shanker Method™: (1) Read and reframe; (2) Recognize the stressors in all five domains; (3) Reduce the stress; (4) Reflect; and (5) Respond.
- Common stressors in the social domain include difficulty picking up on social cues and understanding the effect of behaviour on others.
- Read Dr. Shanker's blog: *The Self-Reg View of Resilience* (https://self-reg. ca/2016/03/10/the-self-reg-view-of-resilience-2/).
- Learning more about the student can help. There are many ways to conduct your social domain stress detective work. Figure 2.9 presents reflection questions based on Dr. Shanker's work that will get you started.

The Prosocial Domain

Teachers consistently report that they find students most "challenging" or difficult when they are mean, selfish, or outright cruel. Often, our automatic response to such behaviours is to lash out at what we perceive as an irreparable "character defect." But here, too, Self-Reg teaches us to pause and reflect on the stresses that the student is experiencing. The goal is not to develop some sort of saintly tolerance in regards to deplorable behaviour, but rather to recognize and reduce the stresses that the student is experiencing, including the uniquely prosocial stress of empathy.

In the heat of the moment, we often fail to register how our own "limbic arousal" is a sign of what we might call the "costs of empathy." The fact is that we find someone else's distress intensely draining. It requires enormous amounts of energy to remain calm when someone else is distressed, let alone try to help regulate them. And one of the great paradoxes of the prosocial domain is that this point applies even to cases where we ourselves are the cause of the other person's distress!

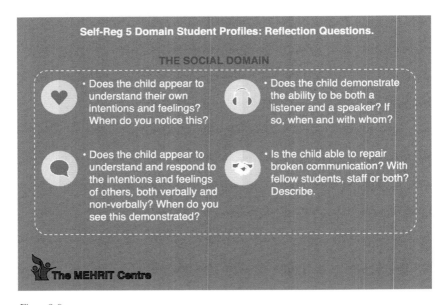

Figure 2.9

Source: Shanker, 2012.

Quite often what is happening with students who repeatedly engage in antisocial acts is that they are seeking to "discharge" their chronic limbic arousal on someone else. They may register the distress that another feels in their presence without fully appreciating why they are feeling it; or they may not know how to assuage the anxiety this provokes. Thus, the student may find himself/herself caught in a downward spiral of antisocial behaviour that intensifies the prosocial stress they are experiencing.

With Self-Reg in the prosocial domain (see the video below) we set out to help such students by first identifying and reducing the causes of their limbic arousal, and then developing adaptive strategies for remaining calm, even in the face of someone else's distress. Our first step is always to down regulate. Only when the student is calmly focused and alert can we broach the elements of "character education."

Prosocial Domain
www.youtube.com/watch?v=ghpb2kN0ow4&feature=youtu.be

For many students, the problems they are having in the prosocial domain are due to difficulties in coping with other people's stress.

Starter Strategies in the Prosocial Domain

Whole school/whole class level:

- Design your environment with student belonging in mind. Ask: what more can I do to have each and every student know or feel: "I am invited in"; "I am welcome here"; "I have a place"; "I fit"; "This is my space, too"; "I am not a tourist or temporary resident here"; "My family is welcomed"; "My culture and language belong and are always welcomed"; "I belong, you belong"; "We all belong"?
- Create a family feeling in your classroom. No family is perfect, but everyone belongs. Take a picture of the whole class and print a large version of it to put on the classroom door. If the students have cubbies or spaces for their possessions, mark these with names and pictures. Have student-created materials and designed spaces in the classroom to communicate: "This is *our* space."
- Healthy relationship are always the foundation for student well-being. Build, build, build relationships with children, families, and communities.
- Where the feeling of healthy relationship building is not yet reciprocated, be kind, patient, and available when the door opens for more.
- Introduce debates in the older grades. Start to release the responsibility slowly and gradually. The "me–we–you" model can help scaffold this. "Me"—teachers debate and/or watch debates on the web. "We"—teacher led with students. Then, when ready, "You"—student led. Celebrate diversity of perspectives and the debating skills of thinking critically and challenging others' ideas, but always respectfully. Honour the non-debaters; there are many roles to play in a debate. One student might write a news article about the debate, another moderate the debate, others play the roles of reporters, artists, or researchers.
- Initiate whole class role dramas exploring complex social issues that affect the local community, such as a planning proposal for a new shopping plaza or pipeline.
- Hold student parliaments—"we"-oriented activism.
- Start events like "Pay It Forward" and "Random Acts of Kindness."
- Participate in all the wonderful events that are already celebrated at the community or national level (e.g., Terry Fox Run, Cops for Cancer).
- Use age appropriate literature to explore identities: self and others. Explore hero figures in their complexity and humanness (imperfections included).
- Research a current news item from different perspectives, analyze the news coverage of it from different magazines, papers, broadcasters, and compare and contrast the differences.
- Care for animals or plants.
- Start a school community garden.
- Collect stories from the parents and families of your students to share, learn from, and build on.

- Become involved in community-driven initiatives (see www.youtube.com/watch?v=Ef-e2pL1Zs0&feature=youtu.be).
- Consider the culture(s) of your students. What do you know already? What are the "visible" and "invisible" aspects of their cultures? Do you hold any biases or assumptions? What might be some of the hidden stressors for a particular student? What are you deeply curious about learning? Who are the "keepers" of the cultural knowledge? Students? Parents? Elders?
- Learn about student or community culture alongside your students.
- Bring in elders and local experts for cultural experiences and teachings.
- Find curriculum links to use open-ended inquiry (or action research) to explore the diverse cultures in the classroom.
- Explore what caring looks like in different cultures and communities.
- Learn what "respect" looks like, and sounds like, in the cultures of the students.
- Set up a "Be the Teacher" unit in which students teach others in the class or school about their cultures. Allow choice for forms of presentation.
- Tap into technology: "visit" your students' communities and cultures virtually.
- Set up a "Learn about my Culture/Community" library check-out week, where students and classes can "check out" individuals to interview about their culture or community.
- Allow for the discomfort of students "not knowing" an answer (this includes their discomfort, but also yours in the prosocial domain). Give them the gift of figuring it out (without intervention) whenever this can fall in the zone of "safe"—in other words, when they have the internal and external resources and skills to cope with the discomfort and work through the problem. Scaffold the learning if necessary, but look for that "edge" first to see if it is needed. (Note: Sometimes, as teachers, we jump in too quickly to resolve, often because we try to reduce our own stress in the prosocial domain. It can be very dysregulating to watch another person struggle, so we need to acknowledge that struggle, risk-taking, and failure are all healthy, normal, and full of learning. Our role is to create the space for this in our classrooms and programs, to make such risks "safe," and then to observe through our Self-Reg lens (with the five steps of the Shanker Method™ always close at hand) the students' progress/experience and our own stress responses that may emerge.)

Individual student level:

- The individual level is always about practicing the five steps of the Shanker Method™: (1) Read and reframe; (2) Recognize the stressors in all five domains; (3) Reduce the stress; (4) Reflect; and (5) Respond.
- Read Dr. Shanker's blogs: *The Self-Reg View of Music* (https://self-reg.ca/2016/01/03/dr-shankers-blog-on-the-self-reg-view-of-music/) and

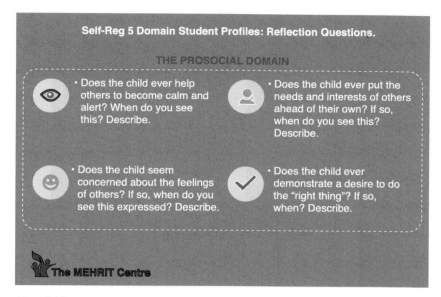

Figure 2.10

Source: Shanker, 2012.

> *Expanding Our Understanding of the Meaning of Safe* (www.self-reg.ca/wp-content/uploads/2015/09/Viewpoints-Meaning-of-Safe-print.pdf).

- Learning more about the student can help. There are many ways to conduct your prosocial domain stress detective work. Figure 2.10 presents reflection questions based on Dr. Shanker's work that will get you started.

Teachers who come to Self-Reg seeking affirmation of what they have always known find it in the form of the brain–body science that explains what they do naturally. They also find fellow "Self-Reggers"—a term that has grown through engagement with our grassroots movement. The community of learning discussed in the introduction to this chapter is part of this swell of Self-Reg that is spreading across continents, cultures, communities, and professions.

Conclusion

We have stressed throughout this chapter that the goal of Self-Reg is to create a haven in our schools: a place where everyone—students, teachers, parents—feels safe from the moment they enter. We do this not only because of the powerful impact this has on mental and physical well-being, but also because of the effect it has on educational outcomes. Indeed, the recent advances in neuroscience have taught us that these two sides of "student success" are inextricably linked.

If you create such an environment, even the most overstressed of students will quickly shift from "survival brain" to "learning brain."

It is remarkable how much being in "survival brain" mode constricts a student's ability to learn. The systems needed for inhibition are suppressed. So too is the ability to pay attention, ignore distractions, solve problems, and deal with frustration. Even the ability to hear the human voice and process what it is saying is significantly impaired. Moreover, the student's ability to co-regulate, repair interactional breakdowns, experience empathy, and feel "connected" to their peers, teacher, and/or school are all highly constrained. Create an environment where they feel safe, though, and all these abilities naturally come back online.

Every school can become such a haven, but the big question is: *how?* A good place to start is with the strategies that we have presented in this chapter. What we are doing here is paying close attention to environmental factors that add to students' stress load. This is why we abandon the use of alarms or shrill bells to signal class transitions, and why we reduce the low-frequency sounds coming from the HVAC or lighting ballasts. Students with chronic limbic arousal find such low-frequency sounds exceptionally draining, and therefore much more difficult to stay calmly focused and alert. We provide different kinds of seating and desk arrangements or calming prosthetics and apparatus.

As important as all this is, however, it isn't nearly enough to turn off a limbic alarm that has been kindled. Therefore, our use of Self-Reg strategies has to be grounded in a profound aspect shift. We have to see our students not through the lens of self-*control*, but through the lens of self-*regulation*. Using Self-Reg strategies without such a grounding can end up as just another form of behaviour management. It may be more effective than resorting to punishments and rewards, but it is still just behaviour management. To create an environment where a kindled limbic alarm can truly shut off, we need everyone in the school thinking as well as practicing Self-Reg.

This is so important because we send signals of safety or threat to our students in numerous unconscious ways: through the prosody of our speech; facial expressions; eye gaze; body language; gestures; even something as basic as proximity. The problem is, when we view a student's behaviour through the "cognitive blinder" of self-control, our irritation or frustration "leaks" into our affect cues. We start to speak in sharp, staccato tones; grimace instead of smile; drum our fingers; stand rigidly. Regardless of what we are saying, our "body language" keeps that student in a state of limbic arousal.

The more our thinking is guided by the science that underlies Self-Reg, the more empathy will take over and the more our unconscious affect cues will transmit messages of safety. This entices and enables a student to return to social engagement. Moreover, the better we understand Self-Reg in all five of its domains, the more we instinctively know what to do and when, regardless of the situation or the provocation. Our automatic reaction is pivotal: not just *when* to soothe rather than punish, but *how* to do this for different students and classes at different times.

The effect of this aspect shift on teacher stress is just as profound as its effect on student stress. This is hardly surprising, because the two cannot be separated. That is, we need students to feel safe for our own well-being as much as for theirs. By facilitating a student transition from "survival brain" to "learning brain," we don't just feel less strain, but actually experience a surge of restorative neurohormones.

The goal here, though, is not to go down the road of creating "helicopter institutions"; rather, it is quite the opposite. It is to help students—*all* students, not just those who are thought to be at risk—develop the skills that they need to understand and manage the stresses in their lives on their own. Students today, perhaps more than ever before, need to learn how to read the internal signs that tell them when they are overstressed and what they need to do in order to rest and restore. It is only by recognizing and responding to these internal signals in a positive manner that they will begin to learn, and we will be able to teach.

Reference

Shanker, S. (2012). *Calm, Alert and Learning*. Don Mills, ON: Pearson.

3 Multi-Sensory Practices for All

Changing Physiology, Behavior, and Performance

Roberta Scherf and Chris Bye

In every classroom there are students who are calm and focused, those who are just a step away from becoming dysregulated, those who are dysregulated, those who have very low energy and those of high energy, and those who are anxious, traumatized, or living with a variety of sensory challenges. The challenge for teachers is to help all these students regulate their nervous system/brain functions in ways that allow them to focus and engage those cognitive processes that are needed to learn. There is no doubt that movement can help all students with regulation. That is the good news. However, **when movement is integrated with rhythmic music and movement patterns, comforting voice frequencies, and visual patterns, and synchronized with expressive features of emotion and the movement of others, teachers and students realize many more benefits**. This integrated process supports a number of biophysiological and neurological functions, including:

- calming the hyper-aroused student, and energizing the hypo-aroused student;
- creating a sense of safety;
- improving social engagement, positive teacher–student interactions, and student–student interactions;
- supporting cross-modal attention in students, increasing their focus and performance; and
- reducing off-task behaviors.

The previous chapter presented a very comprehensive approach to understanding the need for self-regulation in the five domains. It presented a process for identifying students' regulation needs and suggested a variety of excellent practices to apply in each domain. The regulation needs of students will vary from needing little assistance to needing more than can be provided in a classroom setting alone. Furthermore, some children who are in need of self-regulation assistance and practices may also be experiencing sensory challenges.

Chapter Four focuses specifically on practices that assist students with significant sensory processing challenges, including sensory processing disorder (SPD). This wonderful selection of practices and resources addresses all the senses. They assist with issues around lighting, sound, smells, touch, vision, motion, and so much more. These students, when identified, are often screened by an occupational therapist for SPD and assigned a variety of sensory interventions. Similar to the Self-Reg approach, some of these practices can be carried out with the student in the classroom, while others are provided individually by an occupational therapist in the school setting or another clinical setting. **However, as stated earlier, *all* students—regardless of ability or sensory challenges—can benefit from very brief periods of movement. Movement enriches the hoped-for outcomes of all the approaches and practices that will be discussed throughout this resource.**

This is why we wanted to create a program around movement that would:

- meet the diverse regulatory needs of all students of all abilities in the classroom without singling out those individual, sensory-challenged students in need of occupational therapy;
- require no training by teachers;
- eliminate the need for special equipment or reconfiguration of the classroom;
- feed the universal need of all children—social engagement and the resilience that we know develops from experiencing positive connections with others (see Chapter Five);
- be easily used by parents at home as well as by occupational therapists, and even by pediatricians in clinical and medical settings as a supportive intervention;
- take no more than three minutes to complete in consideration of the unbelievable demands on teachers' time; and
- enhance children's self-regulation/behavioral organization, attention, expressive language, and learning.

My Story

I (Roberta) am frequently asked what has driven me to conduct such extensive research in multiple fields related to the body, the nervous system, and the brain, and the role they play in regulating everyday stress, acute stress, and other sensory challenges. This is my story:

When I was seven months pregnant with my first child our house in rural Wisconsin burned down in the middle of the night on one of the coldest nights of the year. The fire inspectors said it was a miracle that my husband and I made it out alive, but that miracle came with a heavy price in the form of PTSD. We had a perfect, healthy son, but we had lost part of our minds to bodies that were constantly on the edge of panic. I decided to investigate my own nervous system, which came in handy several years later when my daughter was born with autism. That was twenty years ago, when there was little understanding of the key role the nervous system and body play in our health, emotional wellbeing, social engagement, communication, cognitive processing, learning, and behavior. Thereafter, I pursued extensive research in the fields of embodied cognition, music therapy, behavioral and cognitive neuroscience, autism spectrum disorders, mindfulness, attention deficit disorders, and social and emotional learning. That research gave birth to MeMoves.

MeMoves is designed to be used by an unprepared, first-year, substitute teacher who is taxed beyond their limits by a room full of forty behaviorally challenged second graders, speaking a variety of languages, in a Title 1 school. Completed in 2010, it received the *Children's Technology Review* Editor's Choice Award, "given to only the highest-quality children's products in the interactive media category." In the same year, it was awarded the prestigious National Parenting Publication Gold Award. Today, the program is used in schools, homes, and clinics throughout the world. Many classrooms use it at the beginning of the school day, after lunch or during recess, or before testing or learning a new or difficult concept. Barbara Dorrington, a school social worker, who uses it in neurotypical classrooms, wrote:

The teacher knows I am coming. The kids immediately get up from their tables and shift to the carpet, carefully making sure they allow room for moving arms and legs. MeMoves is put on the overhead screen. They know what to expect because it is our routine before book reading. I can see comfort in their faces in predicting this safe and calming exercise. We close our eyes and breathe in slowly, imagining sniffing a flower, and then out again, slowly blowing out one birthday candle.

The calm, steady beat of the music from the MeMoves video starts, and I can see the collective shudder of shoulders, raised and then lowered, before hands come into position. It is like a dance. The beat remains steady and is very reassuring. We are all watching the screen and stare into the faces of the MeMoves instructors, happy faces of different ages with wide-open eyes and calming smiles. It feels like we are all cabled together as one group, but separate enough to allow for variations in the moves.

Within about four minutes, MeMoves comes to a close and one can almost hear the group's final breath, as hands slip to the sides and children sit down in comfort. With a quick rub of foreheads and cheeks, quiet fills the room. It is to no one's surprise that children ask for MeMoves again later in the day. This is often before the teacher even suggests it. It cannot get better than that!

A first-grade teacher in a neurotypical classroom in Maine stated in an email:

My class LOVES MeMoves! They ask for it if I forget. We've been using it when they first come in, and as they enter from recesses. Instead of running in, they come in quickly and get started on MeMoves. When it's done, I keep my tone quiet and ask them to have a seat on the mat so we can start our lesson. Transition time heaven! I've had several teachers stop by and even join in (it's hard not to). Our OT teachers come in and instead of pulling the kids right out, use that time as part of their OT with the children.

Parents find it particularly helpful as a way to calm children before transition times, most often before and after school, before homework and bedtime, and before stressful appointments. It is also used to avoid meltdowns. Therapists use it both individually and in groups. Occupational therapist Nancy Lawton-Shirley wrote:

Within minutes, it calms even non-verbal students in distress.

The first video below presents a parent, student, and teacher who describe their experience with the program. Melinda Radcliff, an early childhood specialist, documented a 71 percent decrease in off-task behavior in her mixed pre/K classroom after using the program for less than four minutes each day. The second video segment introduces Dr. Tim Culbert, a developmental/behavioral pediatrician specializing in integrative care, and former director of pediatric integrative care at Minneapolis Children's Hospital. He discusses why he encourages families to use MeMoves and the benefits he sees with his clients.

MeMoves at Alton School St Louis, MO
www.youtube.com/watch?v=eF12PMyLpEs

Dr. Tim Culbert
www.youtube.com/watch?v=TKVLMn9jEjQ

In this chapter, we examine the benefits of integrating movement with music, voice frequencies, and visual patterns synchronized with expressive features of emotion and the movement of others. Each of these areas has been subjected to extensive research that has confirmed the benefits reported by those who participate in the MeMoves program. We begin with movement.

Movement

Movement has numerous benefits. For instance, it:

*   improves learning and mental performance (Shoval, 2011, p. 462; Movement and Learning, 2014);
*   improves expressive language (Rocco, 2012; O'Callaghan, 2014);
*   assists with positive social interaction (Dammeyer and Koppe, 2013; Ramseyer, 2013);
*   raises the levels of norepinephrine, dopamine, and serotonin, the three major neurotransmitters that help with mood regulation, anxiety control, the ability to handle stress and aggression, and the ability to become more attentive and social (Esch et al., 2007);

- mobilizes gene expression and is a simple way to maintain brain function, both of which promote brain plasticity (Cotman and Berchtold, 2002); and
- strengthens the cardiovascular system, the endocrine system, the immune system, and the central nervous system. It increases levels of brain-derived neurotrophic factor (BDNF), which stimulates the growth of new cells and increases resistance to brain insult (Griffin et al., 2011).

The movements in this program are designed to initiate all of these benefits. They are so simple that participants of any age can view the movements on screen and intuitively know what to do. They take no more than three minutes to complete. However, movement alone is not as effective as when it is accompanied by music.

Music

The movements are synchronized to music to create smooth rhythmic moves that activate the parasympathetic nervous system (PNS) into a calm but attentive state. The music sets the program apart. Each piece is compelling and uniquely identified with the program. All of the music was carefully written and performed to provide a strong emotional connection, while rhythmically grounding each movement with each breath. Emphasizing the frequencies of the female voice, the music brings with it recognition of a safe, reassuring sound that often begins to activate a calm state on its own. Many people listen to the music before going to bed at night to quiet their minds, dispel anxious thoughts, and encourage sleep.

When our son, Sam, was a baby, my husband and I spent many nights singing to him, rocking him, and carrying him, while we gently and quietly swayed back and forth, eventually lulling him back to sleep. I remember having hallucinatory, sleep-deprived thoughts that if I could just reason with him, he would understand how important it was for us finally to get some sleep. But he never understood anything I tried to tell him, as much as he really seemed to like it when I sang and hummed, "La la la. little baby" and "All the pretty little horses."

Age is no barrier to restless nights, as MeMoves' music is heard in the dark in nurseries and cognitive care centers in cities all over the world. The power of music warrants more attention.

The Power of Music

Much like social contact, music is hardwired into our bodies and brains. In fact, researchers at MIT have discovered cortical specialization for music: neural pathways in the auditory cortex that are specifically designed to react exclusively to music (Norman-Haignere, Kanwisher, and McDermott, 2015). Some researchers (Norton et al., 2009; Patel and Iversen, 2014) theorize that the neural structures that respond to music evolved earlier than the neural structures that respond to language, suggesting that speech evolved from music, not vice versa. Historically, music was an integral aspect of survival and socialization. Making music with other people in a tribe was an important part of what kept the group together (Koelsch, 2013). There is an interesting dynamic parallel between the temporal nature of auditory information and movement performance. Simply put, there is a strong connection between rhythmicity and brain function. New research continues to highlight the significant impact music has on emotional and physical well-being. For example, sound waves orchestrate patterns in the brain that facilitate learning (Kaye, 2013).

We knew that music would be a critical part of MeMoves for several reasons:

- It is strongly associated with the brain's reward system. The brain releases dopamine fifteen seconds *before* the moment of "peak pleasure," when we listen to a piece of music we know and enjoy and anticipate what is coming next as the music helps to calm and engage us (Salimpoor et al., 2011);
- It provides emotional perspective, letting us know what we should think about what we see (Cohen, 2000). The composer Hans Zimmer said that people always do the wrong thing in a scary movie: they cover their eyes when they should be covering their ears.
- It rewards us as it helps us to move and learn (Levitan, 2007). Music anthropologists list "eliciting physical response" as one of the ten basic functions of music in human culture.

Music has been used for thousands of years—informally and as part of specific healing rituals in many cultures—to elicit motor response and enhance motor behavior. Neuroscientists studying the impact of music on motor processes have concluded that auditory rhythmic stimuli can enhance or promote motor responses and elicit movement, and there is clinical evidence that other components of music also have an arousing effect on the motor system (Grahn and Brett, 2007).

Music with a beat seems to help people with motor disorders such as Parkinson's disease walk better than they do in the absence of music; patients actually synchronize their movements to the beat (Nombela et al., 2013). Some studies show that when people move together to a beat, they are more likely to cooperate with one another in nonmusical tasks (Rabinowitch and Knafo, 2015).

Learning is based on pattern acquisition, which is difficult without basic rhythmic skills. Rhythm underlies patterns of breathing and movement and helps to organize incoming sensory information into coherent new patterns of learning. *Steady beat* is an important precursor to language acquisition, and it helps us to detect patterns in incoming sensory information (Weikart, 1989). It is the most fundamental concept in music. It is the ongoing, steady, repetitive pulse that occurs in songs, chants, rhymes, and music. It is the part that makes you want to tap your toes, clap your hands, or jump up and dance as if no one is watching. It underlies our ability to pick up patterns of language as an infant, express the pattern as verbal language, and, finally, read that pattern.

Rhythmic movement competence can be learned, and it is strongly correlated with significant improvements in academic achievement and related abilities at both the elementary and high school levels (Taub, McGrew, and Keith, 2007). One study demonstrated a strong link between academic achievement and steady beat competence, particularly in math and reading achievement scores. The study of 237 second-grade children used piano keyboard training and newly designed math software to demonstrate improvements in math skills. The group who took keyboard scored 27 percent higher on proportional math and fraction tests than the children who used only the math software. Steady beat matters and it is part of the program (Kuhlman and Schweinhart, 1999).

Music therapy is powerful in part because of its unique capacity to reorganize cerebral function when this has been damaged (Sacks, 2007; Tramo, 2001). Sound and music can affect dysfunction in the brain and the nervous system, and they have been used successfully in treatment programs to reduce stress or lower blood pressure, alleviate pain, overcome various learning disabilities, improve movement and balance, and promote endurance and strength (Garza-Villarreal et al., 2014; Karageorghis and Priest, 2012).

My colleague and I were speaking at a behavioral health conference in North Carolina a few years ago. It was a wonderful program, designed to provide resources and respite care for entire families at a weekend retreat. Right after our talk, a very animated man pulled us aside. His words tumbled out rapidly as he told us what had just happened. His twelve-year-old son has severe autism and was in a constant state of arousal, sleeping barely a few hours each night. Always wound up and in motion, he was often destructive, using his fists more than his words. The man explained that someone had delivered a note during our talk, asking him to check on his son in the nearby activity room. He told us that he went with a heavy heart, fully expecting to pay for the hole that his son had likely punched in the wall, all the while trying to figure out how he was going to break the not-so-unexpected news to his wife and daughter, as this had happened several times before. He paused to take a breath and began to cry as he told us that as he entered the room filled with middle school children moving quietly to MeMoves, all of the adults put their fingers to their lips for him to be quiet. Then they pointed to his son, sound asleep on the floor in the middle of the room, as the music played softly in the background.

Since music is such an important part of MeMoves, we spent a lot of time investigating its use, strengths, and possible outcomes, exploring the work of various researchers. We came up with a very specific "ingredient" list that included types of instruments, genres, beats per minute, and frequencies, among other things. We were lucky to find some very talented musicians, scheduled the sessions, and went to work. The end result was beautiful music, but there was something about it that just wasn't right for the program.

If you recall, MeMoves came about because my daughter, Rowan, has autism. I had started to work on this project several years before. My husband, John, knew how important it was and how much work we had done. Serendipitously, he is also a producer and recording engineer, and the one who finally gave the program its distinctive voice. I talked with him, explaining the problem we were having with the music, and said, essentially, "You've recorded music all over the world for years, you even hear it in your sleep, so how hard could it be, really, to write just one song? And by the way, we don't have any money left."

We didn't talk very much about the details involved in the structure of composing a piece; we talked about what the music would do. We talked less about how to get there and more about where we wanted to end up, which always brought us back to where we began, with Rowan. And that was what made the difference. John wrote a piece of music out of love, for his daughter. I talked with him again and said, "By the way, we need ten more pieces of music. Also, could you play all of the instruments? And record everything? And perhaps you could do all of the video work as well? Because how different could audio and video possibly be?" And he did.

Shortly after the program was released, we began to receive phone calls and emails from people telling us how much they loved it, and all the different ways it was helping them. One of the most surprising uses was by people of all ages who had struggled with insomnia and sleepless nights. We were able to give John the most heartfelt, unusual compliment when we told him that his music put people to sleep.

Steady beat music with movement certainly helps with regulation. When this is synchronized with the movement of others, we meet the one universal need all of us share, especially children—the need to connect with others, the need for social engagement. This is also critical for helping students regulate their behavior.

Behavioral Challenges

Schools are overwhelmed by behavioral challenges that get in the way of learning (Brauner and Stephens, 2006). Many districts allocate significant resources for classroom management and teacher training. Large districts often employ "behavioral team specialists," whose role is to work with students identified by recurring and "unmanageable" behavioral challenges. Despite all the time and resources, it is an almost impossible task generating mixed results, in part because many protocols intellectualize what is essentially a physiological process (Barbetta, Norona, and Bicard, 2005).

Imagine the decision-making process of a first grader with autism spectrum disorder on the way to a "melt down." "I'm having a bad day and I feel overwhelmed. I'm also unable to communicate my emotional needs to my teacher, so I'm going to lose my temper even though I realize my emotional outburst will have consequences for those around me. But my emotional challenges are more important, so I think I will just go for it." This is a ridiculous example, but it highlights the fact that behavior is not determined intellectually. Yet, some behavioral interventions focus on consequences and outcomes. This works if the child's nervous state is regulated, but physiology takes over and consequences can become irrelevant once things get difficult and frustration sets in.

Bottom Up Not Top Down

Behavioral interventions that require processing by the pre-frontal cortex are known as "top down" approaches. MeMoves employs a "bottom up" approach, which activates the more primitive lower brain. With no instructions, words, or expectations, the program actively changes the user's physiology and behavior, regardless of age or ability.

Our body heavily influences our thoughts and behavior. The surprising research that demonstrates that our affinity or aversion toward another person may be determined by something as simple as whether we are holding a hot or cold beverage underscores just how little control we have over our own behavior (Williams and Bargh, 2008).

We need to think about the body and brain differently to see that emotions are rooted in biology. Previous chapters have discussed in detail the three primary regions of the brain and highlighted that it is difficult to forge successful relationships with other people or learn new things when the nervous system is in a high state of arousal and the lower parts of the brain are in charge. Many children and adults go through part of each day in a state of "fight or flight," frozen with anxiety, existing with less than their whole brain, unable fully to embrace what it means to be human.

Many self-regulation programs ask people to pay attention to, and modify, their behavior. Unfortunately, this kind of "top down" approach is ineffective when a person is already in "fight or flight," and conscious, rational thought and language are unavailable to them. We cannot just tell people to calm down and behave when they cannot hear us. We might as well try to explain how much we need sleep to a crying baby. MeMoves uses a visceral "bottom up" approach to calm the lower brain and activate the parasympathetic nervous system (PNS). There is no speech or language in the program, no directions or instructions. Instead, it uses the body to calm the system and shut down the "fight or flight" response. It activates the PNS, changing the body's physiology, and helps to sync our nervous system and brain by rocking or moving, and soothes it with soft, reassuring, rhythmic tones and music. Once calm, the whole brain can organize, regulate, empathize, and learn.

From *Me* to *We*: Social Engagement, Biology, and the Vagus Nerve

Social connection is an essential part of what it means to be human; to survive and to thrive. Our safety was rooted in tribes and extended families as people cared for each other and kept each other safe. That need for connection is still hardwired into our bodies and cells. Our very survival might depend on the connections that we are able to forge with complete strangers

(Lieberman, 2014). Deep social connections can alter the way that DNA is expressed within our cells, affecting our health and well-being. Such connections increase our resilience, health, productivity, happiness, and even our longevity. The most important aspect of mental health is being able to feel safe with other people and have healthy relationships. Safe connections are therefore an essential part of a meaningful life (Fredrickson, 2013).

Synchronized Movement

Positive, safe social connections develop through shared synchronicity that comes from facial expressions, eye contact, attunement, activating mirror neurons, and moving rhythmically with others. When synchrony is surreptitiously produced in experimental situations it breeds feelings of "liking" another person and oneself, cooperation, and compassion, as well as success in collaborative action. Studies show that more synchronized movement is associated with better relationship quality and better interactional outcomes. The quality of a relationship is thus embodied by the synchronized movement patterns that emerge between partners (Ramseyer, 2013). Furthermore, synchronized gestures also reflect and trigger the release of oxytocin, a hormone that is essential for bonding and secure, safe attachments (Uvnas-Moberg, 2003).

The Polyvagal Theory

Dr . Stephen Porges is a behavioral neuroscientist whose development of poly-vagal theory (Porges, 2011) is changing the way we look at social and emotional behavior, particularly trauma and anxiety. ("Polyvagal" refers to multiple branches of the vagus nerve, which connects the brain, lungs, heart, stomach, and gut.) Dr. Porges's theory emphasizes the biology of safety and danger, as it examines the interaction between the body's internal states and the faces and voices of the people around us. Once we understand that, we can work to change our nervous system's response so that we can change our behavior.

The theory emphasizes that our nervous system has more than one defense strategy, and that our defensive response is completely involuntary, beyond our control. Our nervous system constantly evaluates risk in the environment, making judgments and setting priorities for adaptive behaviors that are beyond our conscious control, keeping us safe in the face of danger. One of the most interesting aspects of polyvagal theory is the way it moves beyond "fight or flight" to examine the important role that social relationships play in understanding safety, danger, and trauma. It is a primary mechanism for neurological recovery and behavior modification.

Positive Social Engagement

If our nervous system perceives that our situation is safe, then the polyvagal system will trigger the most sophisticated adaptive response to stress, using the social engagement system. This connects the "social" muscles of the face (eyes, mouth, middle ear, larynx, sinus) with the heart. This level activates the ventral vagal complex (VVC), which is regulated by a myelinated branch of the vagus nerve. This is the most evolved strategy for keeping us safe.

If we have a problem at this level of stress, we will call out to others for help, support, or comfort. This form of communication is the one we use to beg for forgiveness, negotiate a solution, and straighten out misunderstandings. It is activated by eye contact, vocal prosody, and gestures. It fully energizes our own facial expressions and eye contact, speech and vocal prosody, as we gesture communicatively, using our whole body (face, voice, and gestures) to convey information. We are also able to listen well to others, in part through the contraction of the inner ear that allows us to distinguish human voices from other sounds in the environment more easily. If you have successfully talked your way out of a speeding ticket, this is why.

Earlier, we stated that we wanted to develop a program that would socially engage participants. Our first effort failed.

When we began to develop MeMoves we were fortunate to be able to use professional ballet dancers. It was breathtaking to see so many beautiful people move so perfectly. They were fluid and graceful as they traveled through space. And they moved exactly on the beat. There was little "time shifting" in the editing process. We were very excited, so we started to test MeMoves. Unfortunately, the people using the program weren't as excited as we were. They were intimidated and immobilized by the dancers' perfection. They felt awkward, flawed, and uncomfortable, and too embarrassed to move. We had inadvertently provided them with the exact opposite of a shared experience.

So we began again. This time we contacted people whom we knew: young, old, black, white, Asian, Hispanic. We asked them to come in and we showed them a few movements. Some of them had great difficulty; almost no one moved with the beat. But they were real people. The only thing we did was to tell them something about the people who would be using the program—that they might be having a bad day. We asked them to picture those people, to look at them and send them their love.

It was a different story when we tested MeMoves again. An elderly woman started to rock back and forth in time to the music as she watched the people on the screen. She began to cry and hug herself when she saw a young boy point to her and smile. A middle school boy with severe autism and limited speech imitated an adolescent boy on the screen. He watched as the boy completed his final movement and spontaneously smiled with a big "thumbs up." The autistic boy stopped suddenly, stood up tall, laughed, and said, "I think he likes me!"

You might enjoy the song about the polyvagal nerve that features in the video below.

Learn Polyvagal Theory with the Polly Vagal Blues
www.youtube.com/watch?v=hCCNv3P7jUs

We strengthen the various branches of our vagus nerve and their responses to stress and threat by connecting with others, who send signals of safety through their expressive facial features, eye contact, and voices. The people in this program with whom participants synchronize their movements accomplish just that. A special education teacher in rural Minnesota sent us the following note, one of many we receive regularly from those who use the program:

We use MeMoves several times a day with all of the kids in our program, and they love it. Some of the changes have been incredible and I wanted to let you know about one student in particular. She has severe autism and posttraumatic stress, a lot of anxiety. She's been in the district since kindergarten and has memorized her route to class after the bus drops her at school. She always looks at the ground and never makes eye contact with anyone. Three days a week she has such bad headaches that she has to go home. I started using the program in October. One morning just before winter break she didn't show up in class. I knew she had taken the bus to school and went to look for her. I couldn't believe it when I saw her. It was taking longer than usual for her to get to class because when she got off the bus that morning she stopped to smile and say, "Good morning!" to everyone she saw. And she has stopped having headaches. Thank you!

When we go from *me* to *we* our entire physiology changes. When done as a group, the entire environment changes.

The video below is from Riverview Elementary School in St. Paul, MN, where a number of students had suffered adverse childhood experiences associated with trauma. It shows the benefits of MeMoves for a broad population of learners in a challenging environment. Note that the principal mentions her students achieving high ACE scores.

Calming Students and Changing the Culture at Riverview Elementary
www.youtube.com/watch?v=b6wDQmHlXxU

Important Considerations

Do Not Use MeMoves Incorrectly by Having the Students Follow (Imitate) a Leader in the Classroom Instead of Those on Screen

One aspect of MeMoves that sets it apart from other programs is the consistency, reliability, and safety of the people on screen. They provide the same nonjudgmental, compassionate expressions every time, and appear in exactly the same way at exactly the same moment every time the video is played. Moreover, the variety of people in each sequence keeps the viewers engaged. This delivers enormous emotional benefits, which disappear when a parent or teacher leads the session in the classroom.

Do It Together When You Can

The program is designed as a shared activity that can help the whole family or classroom to become calmer and connect with one another. Research shows that there are significant benefits leading to affiliation and collaboration when a group of people is engaged together in simultaneous shared physical movement. The emphasis is not on identical simultaneous movement, but rather on the shared experience of being engaged in a singular activity at the same time. This does not mean that everyone needs to do the movement. **We realize that choice is an essential part of feeling safe**. Initially, some children may be more comfortable facing away from the screen. Our definition of participation is: **Everyone is participating as long as no one is engaged in a different activity than the rest of the group**. If the program is being used at home, the whole family should participate, without looking at, assessing, encouraging, or correcting the performance of any other family member. The three minutes to complete each segment will make a difference.

This Is Not a Competitive Activity or a Teaching Activity

The goal is not to learn to do any of the movements "correctly," or to improve (although this is generally a natural outcome). When the focus is placed on achievement, it becomes a competitive activity, which invalidates its strength as a calming, self-regulation tool. Each person is unique and will respond to the movements in their own way. It's fine for a person to stand motionless or sit, rocking back and forth in time to the music. Everyone finds their own level of engagement, which may change over time. Remember, people can respond only to the degree that their personal physiology allows.

Use It as a Transitional or Priming Activity

The program works well as a transitional tool or priming activity. Many families use it in the morning, before school, after returning home from school, before homework or a stressful activity, and/or before bedtime. Many schools use it at the beginning of the day, after lunch or recess, and/or before quiet learning activities. This will prepare students (and their nervous systems) to anticipate and welcome the calming sequences in the program. Some teachers incorporate the program into a social and emotional learning curriculum as a daily compassionate practice.

Summary

When writing this chapter, we wanted to stress the program's viability for school-age children of all levels of ability. We were concerned that if we highlighted its value for autistic children and teens, readers might discount it usefulness for other students. That said, it is already benefiting the autistic population and those who work with them in school and clinical settings. Allow us to provide two examples. The first is of a third grade autistic student; the second is of an autistic adolescent.

An occupational therapist from Iowa recently sent us one of her favorite stories:

I have been working with a third grader with autism who has a very hard time regulating his behavior and is unable to stay in one place for more than a few minutes. I began to use MeMoves in the fall and things changed so much that his teacher decided to let him be part of the holiday concert. He was very proud and so excited. I was also very proud of what he had achieved, but I was concerned that the excitement would be too much for him. I was horrified when I saw that his teacher had put him in the very center of the risers, right at the front of the auditorium. I was standing off to the side of the stage, holding my breath, trying to figure out how to pull him off stage and salvage the situation when I saw him start to shift his weight very quickly from side to side as he grew more and more anxious. All of a sudden, he closed his eyes, took a deep breath, raised his arms high above his head, and began to do the movements from MeMoves as he kept on singing. I could see his parents and grandparents in the audience take a big breath and start to cry at the same time I did. He sang the last two songs with his eyes closed while doing MeMoves. He was so proud that he was able to calm himself and finish the concert.

We also received an email from an occupational therapist who works with a mild to moderate cognitive disability vocational class of twelve–fifteen-year-olds.

For one student in particular, this program worked beyond the classroom. He is a young teenager of thirteen and he has autism. He demonstrates a lot of self-stimulation through arm and hand jerking, facial grimaces and body movements, but when anxiety is really high he tends to play with his teeth, eventually pulling healthy adult teeth from his mouth. This young man took to this program immediately, stating that it really helped calm him. On one occasion when he was home for the weekend, he received a "no" from his mother for a request he wanted to do. Typically, this would have sent him into a mini meltdown. Instead, he went into the living room and began to do the arm movements of the MeMoves program while listening to the music in his head that he remembered from school. He came back to school on Monday, telling us what he did, and he was so proud of himself for not melting down and being able to work through the challenge. Thank you!

It has been our experience—and that of many others—that movement alone is helpful to the learning process and, to some extent, self-regulation. We hope we have also demonstrated that when movement is **integrated with rhythmic music and movement patterns, comforting voice frequencies, and visual patterns, and is synchronized with expressive features of emotion and the movement of others, many more benefits can be realized by students as well as their teachers, parents, and/or therapists**.

References

Barbetta, P.M., Norona, K.L., and Bicard, D.F. (2005). Classroom behavior management: A dozen common mistakes and what to do instead. *Preventing School Failure: Alternative Education for Children and Youth*, 49(3), 11–19.

Brauner, C.B., and Stephens, B.C. (2006). Estimating the prevalence of early childhood serious emotional/behavioral disorder: Challenges and recommendations. *Public Health Reports*, 121, 303–310.

Cohen, A.J. (2000). *Film Music: Perspectives from Cognitive Psychology*. Middlebury, VT: Wesleyan University Press.

Cotman, C.W., and Berchtold, N.C. (2002). Exercise: A behavioral intervention to enhance brain health and plasticity. *Trends in Neurosciences*, 25, 295–301.

Dammeyer, J., and Koppe, S. (2013). *The Relationship between Body Movements and Qualities of Social Interaction between a Boy with Severe Developmental Disabilities and His Caregiver*. Retrieved January 12, 2016 from www.ncbi.nlm.nih.gov/pubmed/23834212.

Esch, T., Duckstein, J., Welke, J., and Braun V. (2007). Mind/body techniques for physiological and psychological stress reduction: Stress management via Tai Chi training: A pilot study. *Medical Science Monitor*, 13(11), CR488–CR497.

Fredrickson, B. (2013). *Finding Happiness and Health in Moments of Connection*. New York: Hudson Street Press.

Garza-Villarreal, E.A., Wilson, A.D., Vase, L., Brattico, E., Barrios, F.A., Jensen, T.S., Romero-Romo, J.I., and Vuust, P. (2014). Music reduces pain and increases functional mobility in fibromyalgia. *Frontiers in Psychology*, February 11. Retrieved June 4, 2015 from http://journal.frontiersin.org/article/10.3389/fpsyg.2014.00090/full.

Grahn, J.A., and Brett, M. (2007). Rhythm and beat perception in motor areas of the brain. *Journal of Cognitive Neuroscience*, 19(5), 893–906.

Griffin, É.W., Mullally, S., Foley, C., Warmington, S.A., O'Mara, S.M., and Kelly, A.M. (2011). *Aerobic Exercise Improves Hippocampal Function and Increases BDNF in the Serum of Young Adult Males*. Retrieved January 16, 2016 from www.ncbi.nlm.nih.gov/pubmed/21722657.

Karageorghis, C.I., and Priest, D.L. (2012). Music in the exercise domain: A review and synthesis. *International Review of Sports and Exercise Psychology*, December 7, 64–84.

Kaye, G. (2013). *How Does Music Affect the Learning Experience?* Retrieved January 11, 2016 from www.eolearning.com/2013/08/how-does-music-affect-the-learning-experience/.

Keogh, J., and Sugden, D. (1985). *Movement Skill Development*. New York: Macmillan.

Koelsch, S. (2013). *Processing of Hierarchical Syntactic Structure in Music*. Retrieved January 15, 2016 from www.pnas.org/content/110/38/15443.short.

Kuhlman, K., and Schweinhart, L.J. (1999). *Timing in Child Development*. High/Scope Educational Research Foundation. Retrieved September 26, 2016 from www.highscope.org/Content.asp?ContentId=234.

Levitan, D.J. (2007). *This is Your Brain on Music: The Science of a Human Obsession*. Boston, MA: Dutton Adult.

Lieberman, M.D. (2014). *Social: Why Our Brains Are Wired to Connect*. New York: Broadway Books.

Movement and Learning (2014). *What the Researchers Say*. Retrieved December 18, 2014 from http://movementandlearning.wordpress.com/about/.

Nombela, C., Hughes, L.E., Owen, A.M., and Grahn, J.A. (2013). *Into the Groove: Can Rhythm Influence Parkinson's Disease?* Retrieved January 15, 2016 from www.ncbi.nlm.nih.gov/pubmed/24012774.

Norman-Haignere, S., Kanwisher, N., and McDermott, J. (2015). Distinct cortical pathways for music and speech revealed by hypothesis-free voxel decomposition. *Neuron*, 88(6), 1281–1296.

Norton, A., Zipse, L., Marchina, S., and Schlaug, G. (2009). Melodic intonation therapy: Shared insights on how it is done and why it might help. *Neurosciences and Music III: Disorders and Plasticity*, 1169, 431–436.

O'Callaghan, J. (2014). *How a Child's Language Development Can Be Helped by Hand Movements*. Retrieved January 11, 2016 from www.dailymail.co.uk/sciencetech/article-2729665/ How-childs-language-development-helped-hand-movements-Gesticulating-makes-words-easier-understand.html.

Patel, A.D., and Iversen, J.R. (2014). The evolutionary neuroscience of musical beat perception: The action simulation for auditory prediction (ASAP) hypothesis. *Frontiers in Systems Neuroscience*, 8 (57). Retrieved October 5, 2016 from www.ncbi.nlm.nih.gov/ pmc/articles/PMC4026735/.

Porges, S.W. (2011). *The Polyvagal Theory: Neurophysiological Foundations of Emotions Attachment Communication Self-Regulation*. New York: W.W. Norton & Company.

Rabinowitch, T., and Knafo, A., (2015). Synchronous rhythmic interaction enhances children's perceived similarity and closeness towards each other. *PloS One*, April 8. Retrieved September 26, 2016 from http://journals.plos.org/plosone/article?id= 10.1371/journal.pone.0120878.

Ramseyer, F. (2013). *Synchronized Movement in Social Interaction*. Retrieved January 12, 2016 from http://dl.acm.org/citation.cfm?id=2557597.

Rocco, T. (2012). *Why a Long Island Speech Therapist Incorporates Movement and Sensory Activities into Speech Therapy Sessions*. Retrieved January 11, 2016 from http:// speechinmotion.com/blog/2012/10/22/long-island-speech-therapist-incorporates-movement-and-sensory-activities-into-speech-therapy-sessions.

Sacks, O. (2007). *Musicophilia: Tales of Music and the Brain*. New York: Knopf.

Salimpoor, V.N., Benovoy, M., Larcher, K., Dagher. A., and Zatorre, R.J. (2011). Anatomically distinct dopamine release during anticipation and experience of peak emotion to music. *Nature Neuroscience*, 14, 257–262.

Schrammel, F., Pannasch, S., Graupner, S.-T., Mojzisch, A., and Velichkovsky, B.M. (2009). Virtual friend or threat? The effects of facial expression and gaze interaction on psychophysiological responses and emotional experience. *Psychophysiology*, 46(5), 922–931.

Shoval, E. (2011). Using mindful movement in cooperative learning while learning about angles. *Instructional Science*, 39(4), 453–466.

Taub, G., McGrew, K., and Keith, T. (2007). Improvements in interval time tracking and effects on reading achievement. *Psychology in the School*, 44(8), 849–863.

Tramo, M.J. (2001). Biology and music: Music of the hemispheres. *Science*, 291(5501), 54–56.

Uvnas-Moberg, K. (2003). *The Oxytocin Factor: Tapping the Hormone of Calm, Love, and Healing*. New York: Perseus.

Weikart, P.S (1989). *Teaching Movement and Dance: A Sequential Approach to Rhythmic Movement*. Ypsilanti, MI: High Scope Press.

Williams, L.E., and Bargh, J.A. (2008). Experiencing physical warmth promotes interpersonal warmth. *Science*, 322(5901), 606–607.

4 Students with Sensory Processing Challenges

Classroom Strategies

Lindsey Biel

In Chapter One you had the opportunity to view three brief video segments describing sensory processing disorder (SPD). In this chapter additional detail is presented for each of the senses in school settings that can create learning challenges. This is important because we need to become more aware of the behaviors that are often mistaken for a variety of mental health disorders that, in fact, may be sensory processing issues students of all ages can experience. These behaviors are described throughout this chapter. With this in mind, it is even more critical that when these behaviors are observed, screenings are provided to identify indicators that sensory processing may be at the core of these behaviors. These screenings take only a few minutes to complete and are available on the internet for teachers and parents to use at no cost. Multiple references are presented in this chapter and in the Appendix. They can save children a lifetime of inappropriate and even harmful responses and interventions. In today's world it is recommended that all children presenting with learning and behavioral challenges be screened for possible sensory processing issues.

It is also important to keep in mind that **sensory processing challenges are not limited to autistic or traumatized children**. There are growing numbers of children without autism or trauma histories that experience sensory challenges. An estimated 5–13 percent of children in the general population are affected by sensory processing challenges in daily life (Ahn, Miller, Milberger, and McIntosh, 2004). In addition, a longitudinal study by members of the Sensory Processing Disorder Scientific Work Group, composed of developmental psychologists, clinical psychologists, occupational therapists, pediatric neurologists, and others, found that 16.5 percent of school-age children experience clinically significant sensory overresponsiveness to tactile and auditory stimuli affecting everyday social-emotional function (Ben-Sasson, Carter, and Briggs-Gowan, 2009).

Children first learn about the world through their senses, experiencing many sounds, sights, touches, movements, tastes, and smells. They see stationary and moving objects and people, smell their parents, food, and interesting objects, learn to move against gravity, and so on. Sensory processing is the neurological process of transforming those bits of sensory information into meaningful messages, which provide children with an accurate, reliable understanding of the world and how they fit in. For most kids, sensory processing skills develop automatically.

Occupational therapists are invaluable in helping teachers, parents, and students identify those resources and practices that will help them with sensory challenges. Unfortunately, not all schools have access to occupational therapists. Therefore, many of the practices that are presented in this chapter are designed to be helpful for teachers and those who support them, and they should feel comfortable trying them. As in any healing process, keep in mind that what works for one may not work for another. It is a matter of trying different approaches until you find the one or two that help the most.

It's a Different World

Children with sensory challenges experience the world differently from others. Sensory input can come in too intensely or too weakly. Sensory issues can range from the quirky preferences and intolerances most of us have to intense, out-of-proportion reactions to experiences that can be physically and emotionally painful. Being startled and frightened by an ambulance's blaring siren is not unusual for a toddler, but suffering a meltdown every time he hears a toilet flush or someone singing is a red flag. Sensory problems can cause distressing behaviors and developmental delays. If the sight and sound of boisterous classmates running around the playground alarms some children, it is no wonder they will only play in the sandbox in the corner rather than try to climb the chain ladder. And if students are distressed by every sight and sound in the classroom, they won't be available for learning.

Many of the activities presented in this chapter are structured to help students struggling with sensory issues both inside and outside the classroom in ways that support more effective learning outcomes. They are designed to help *all* students with sensory challenges, including those who are autistic or experiencing sensory integration issues as a result of adverse childhood experiences. Those with more significant sensory issues will benefit most from a combination of sensory activities and resources in the classroom and additional assistance outside the classroom that can include in-school assistance from an occupational therapist, sensory resource rooms (as discussed in Chapter One), and/or assistance in a clinical setting.

This chapter will assist with the identification of behaviors that may be the result of sensory processing challenges and provide access to sensory screening tools when such behaviors are observed. It also offers extensive descriptions of in-classroom and out-of-classroom practices to help students manage their sensory issues more effectively while improving their necessary learning functions. For example, some students may be particularly sensitive to loud or unexpected sounds, such as sirens, harsh voices, or whistles blown in the playground. They may have increased difficulty tuning in to what is being said, especially if they are hypervigilant or there is competing noise, such as others speaking or moving around the classroom or hallway. Once we are aware of theses challenges, the resources and interventions that are presented in this chapter can help students better manage their reactions and behaviors.

Common Signs of Sensory Problems

We begin with the common signs of sensory integration challenges, followed by a detailed description of the multiple senses children experience in school settings and how problems with these are manifested in challenging behavior. Following this is a list of the various interventions for each sensory challenge. These can be used in the classroom and/or school resource rooms, or with individual students while in school or in a clinical setting.

What, then, are some of the common behaviors that may indicate that students are struggling with sensory issues?

- over- or undersensitive to touch, movement, sounds, sights, tastes, or smells;
- dislikes getting "messy" with glue, paint, sand, lotion, and so on;
- bothered by clothing fabrics and tags, sock seams, etc.;
- always seems to be "on the go" or unusually sedentary;
- squints, blinks, or rubs eyes frequently;
- avoids grooming activities, such as toothbrushing and haircuts;
- refuses foods that most children enjoy;
- gets dizzy easily or never;
- seems clumsy or careless; and
- is uncomfortable in group settings, such as parties.

These problems can trigger a variety of behaviors, which are described in each of the subsections below.

The Senses at School

Touch

The tactile system is the first sensory system to develop and **our most primal means of comfort and self-knowledge**. It is the largest sensory organ in the body, with several kinds of tactile receptors in the multiple layers of the skin, including what lines the mouth, throat, digestive system, ears, and genitals. It is through touching that a baby learns where her skin-covered body ends and the outside world begins. She learns she is safe and loved through cuddles, kisses, and touches as well as by being surrounded by soft toys and materials. As the child experiences less pleasant tactile input, such as scratchy fabrics and sharp surfaces, she refines her perception of what feels good and what to avoid.

Light touch activates superficial tactile receptors and triggers protective responses. **Some students may be upset by an unexpected touch on their back while lining up to go to recess, by wearing a smock in art**

class, by getting paint on their skin, by the feeling of Play-Doh or sticky substances, by applying sunblock or deodorant, and so on. Firm touch that activates deeper tactile receptors is more reassuring, so a student may seek it out, rolling on the floor during circle time, or pushing his body into walls, furniture, and other students. Vibration from a toy or an air conditioner may be either alarming or soothing. Pain and temperature are also tactile experiences. Some children refuse to eat any food that isn't exactly the right temperature. Some are sensitive to a bump while others are unaware of a badly scraped, bloodied knee.

Touch can be especially problematic for the student with a history of trauma, particularly the survivor of physical abuse. Great care must be taken to make touch experiences at school voluntary and beneficial. Self-injurious tactile behaviors, such as cutting, hand-biting, and head-banging may also be serious tactile manifestations.

Auditory

Processing sound begins with hearing muted noise in the womb and is refined as we mature and learn to listen for important sounds. Listening involves both passively hearing and actively processing and making sense of the sounds that are heard. Sound has many dimensions: volume, frequency/pitch, duration (how long it lasts), and localization (where it is coming from). A student with sound sensory difficulties may have trouble putting these qualities together, making sound confusing for them. **A student with hypersensitive hearing hears too well, detecting sounds others don't hear. With so much auditory input flooding into the student's ears, it's hard for them to filter out irrelevant sounds and attend to what is important.** While most of us feel uncomfortable when sound exceeds a certain volume, an oversensitive student may become miserable at a much quieter level. Some are sensitive to higher sound frequencies (such as a ringing telephone) or to lower frequencies (such as a truck rumbling past). This is just another reason why our classrooms need to be equipped with resources to help *all* students with their sensory differences.

Students who have experienced trauma may be particularly sensitive to loud or unexpected sounds, including sirens, harsh voices, whistles blown in the playground or in gym class, bells for changing classes, musical instruments, and fire alarms. They may have increased difficulty tuning in to what is being said, especially if they are hypervigilant or if there is competing noise, such as others speaking or moving around the classroom or hallway.

Vision

The visual sense involves much more than whether our eyes see well or poorly. Of course, the eyes play a major role; but it is what the brain does with visual input that really counts. While the eyes require proper visual acuity (or correction via lenses), they also need to work together, like a pair of binoculars, with each barrel of visual information merging into a single image, follow moving objects, and keep the visual field stable during movement. **Poor visual acuity and impaired ocular-motor and other visual processing skills are common, and can make tasks such as playing ball, reading, and writing difficult. A student may be hypersensitive to color, patterns, lights, movement, and/or contrast. Some students are visually distractible.** Those who have experienced trauma may be triggered by visuals that are reminiscent of the traumatic experience, along with sensory annoyances such as glare, fluorescent and strobe lights, jarring patterns, and other visual inputs.

Taste and Smell

We taste only a few things: sweet, salty, bitter, sour, and umami (savory). Everything else is smell. For some students, school truly stinks—from cafeteria food to garbage cans to sweaty socks in gym class to the teacher's coffee breath. **Students with sensory issues are notoriously picky eaters. Food issues can be about taste, but most commonly they also revolve around tactile issues of texture and temperature, neuromuscular issues, such as low muscle tone or an exaggerated gag reflex that makes swallowing tricky, and certainly about smell, which is an essential part of whether we enjoy what we are eating.**

Of course, the nose smells much more than food. Smell is a primitive sense that alerts us to danger; we can smell smoke before we see it, for example. **Odor receptors send information directly to the brain's limbic system, the seat of emotion, long-term memory, pleasure, and motivation. This direct linkage explains why smell can remain a serious trigger for people who have experienced traumatic events.**

Proprioception

If you close your eyes and move your hand behind your head, your brain will know exactly where your hand is at all times due to proprioception, which uses information from sensory receptors in joints, muscles, ligaments, and connective tissue to locate where body parts are without seeing them. This internal body awareness provides a reassuring mental map of your position in space at all times, enabling you to lengthen and contract your muscles to find your way to the bathroom in the dark, braid hair without a mirror, type on a keyboard without looking at the keys, and so forth. **A student with poor proprioceptive skills may be clumsy, move slowly, and have trouble with fine motor tasks, such as handwriting, tying shoelaces, and combing hair. Some students crave proprioceptive input: they crash into walls, throw toys, and roughhouse to receive stronger sensory messages. Other students avoid it, preferring to sprawl over a desk or on the couch or floor like a wet noodle.**

A student with poor proprioceptive skills may feel lost in space much of the time. A child who has experienced trauma may use proprioceptive input as a means of self-comfort since it helps her to ground herself in space.

Vestibular/Movement

Whenever you change your head position—nod "yes" or shake "no," spin around, ski down a hill, ride in a car or airplane—vestibular receptors in your inner ear receive important information about the movement and gravitational changes. This enables you to maintain your balance, move efficiently, and feel safe and secure both physically and emotionally. By telling us which way is up at all times, the vestibular sense helps keep our world and our bodies in equilibrium. It works seamlessly with the proprioceptive and visual systems like a GPS system, telling us exactly where we are and how we are moving, twenty-four hours a day. Proprioceptors and vestibular receptors work together to make it possible for a child to adjust her movements in order to step from the sidewalk onto grass, walk in snow, jump off a diving board, come to the surface of the water, and swim to the edge of the pool.

Students with vestibular issues may have an exaggerated response to anti-gravity movements, becoming dizzy or nauseous when playing team sports, using playground swings and slides, or riding the school bus. Even subtle changes in head position, such as bending over to retrieve a dropped pencil, may be disorienting. Some students who have experienced trauma may use movement as a coping mechanism, finding emotional and physical escape through running, spinning, climbing, and other intense vestibular experiences.

Interoception

The interoceptive sense detects essential regulation responses for body functions, including heart rate, respiration, blood pressure, hunger, thirst, temperature, and bowel and bladder sensations. These body-based feelings, largely experienced at the border of consciousness, complete the picture of how we experience our bodies and define our place in the world. **They also play an essential role in our state of arousal, feelings, emotions, and self-awareness.** Interoceptive messages can have a strong impact when they reach our consciousness. For example, the student who becomes aware of a rapid heartbeat and increased blood pressure will need to judge whether it is proportional to the experience of jogging.

Most of the time, we are not aware of how quickly our heart is beating or how fast we are breathing unless something happens to increase these rates. For the student with increased sensitivity to these things, having basic involuntary functions such as heartbeat and respiration within their conscious awareness can generate

anxiety. Impaired processing of hunger and satiety can result in feeding problems and eating disorders. Students who cannot tell when they have to use the bathroom may have frequent accidents even after they have developed sphincter control because they simply cannot feel the need to go. Interoceptive sensory processing may be quite disrupted for the trauma survivor.

Global Sensitivity

Students who are hypersensitive tend to be globally sensitive—that is, chemically and nutritionally sensitive, experiencing strong reactions to harsh chemicals in cleaning products, such as ammonia, artificial colors and flavors, pesticides, and sugar. **They also tend to be deeply empathic, quickly detecting the moods and feelings of others.** Students who have experienced trauma may be hypervigiliant, scrutinizing facial expressions and nonverbal and verbal communication, always on the lookout for possible threat and ready to defend themselves. Some may become blunted and obtuse emotionally and socially in an effort to avoid the possibility of further negative interactions.

> For a more detailed discussion of sensory processing challenges and their impact on functions at home, school, and in the community, plus practical strategies and real-life solutions, see Biel (2014) and Biel and Peske (2009).

Helping the Traumatized Child with Sensory Issues

Those who work with and care about child, teen, and adult survivors should always keep in mind that traumatic experiences are encoded in feelings and sensations absent of language (van der Kolk, Burbridge, and Suzuki, 1997). Further, **it is essential to understand and respect that trauma survivors typically respond instinctually to sight, sound, smell, and other sensory reminders with responses that are poorly regulated or not at all regulated by conscious awareness** (van der Kolk et al., 1997). Thus, while it may require extra time, effort, and creativity to meet the traumatized student's needs, **it behooves educators, therapists, and administrators to make trauma-informed "sensory smart" decisions to meet students' sensory processing and emotional needs along with their academic requirements**. As was discussed in previous chapters, meeting these sensory needs greatly assists students with the use of the cognitive functions they need in order to learn.

The Sensory Challenge–a Good Fit

Schools and teachers may not realize the adverse affects of coercing a student to engage in something they are highly resistant to, or disciplining a student who refuses to comply. There are always alternatives available. For example, a non-competitive, individual sport that encourages "personal best" results, such as track or swimming, may be preferable. Even some of the most common and seemingly harmless activities, such as finger painting or modeling with clay, may be an emotional and sensory trigger. Providing a paintbrush or alternative arts and crafts media, such as markers and colored pencils, enables creative expression and access to the educational curriculum at the same time. **As a rule of thumb, it is best to provide a range of acceptable choices and empower the student to make a selection.**

Any caring teacher, related service provider (school-based occupational, physical, speech, or vision therapist) should recognize that care must be taken to avoid emotionally retraumatizing the student. **What is less transparent is that the same holds true for the trauma survivor's nervous system, which detects and responds to sensations throughout the day, frequently with disproportionate responses.** For the traumatized student who experiences heightened sensitivity and sensory vigilance, going to school can be heaven or quite the opposite. **So much depends on "goodness of fit" between a student's sensory experiences, temperament, and learning style and the school's educational approach, physical environment, and personal chemistry with teachers and school staff.**

Most schools emphasize auditory and visual learning and reward students who learn best through these sensory modalities. A student who thrives on reading, listening to a teacher speaking at the front of the classroom, and working independently on projects will excel in a quiet, structured setting in which students sit at assigned desks and have clearly defined behavioral and academic expectations. Students who thrive when physically active and engaged in hands-on learning will have difficulty sitting still and staying tuned in with their eyes and ears. These students would likely fare better in a classroom that encourages active student participation and opportunities for physical exploration. Even when students are fortunate enough to attend a school that is aligned with their needs, the school can inadvertently magnify sensory difficulties that existed before the trauma or emerged as a consequence of the traumatic event.

Everyday Experiences

Dealing with everyday life experiences that seem unremarkable to us can easily overwhelm people with sensory challenges. They may be able to deal with processing demands for a short period or even longer if the demands are less intense. However, if too much demand piles up for too long, the student is at increased risk of overload, especially when there are specific triggers related to the trauma. **It may help to think of sensory overload as putting too much food on a flimsy paper plate. The plate may hold up as you load on a hot dog, potato chips, and some coleslaw, but add potato salad and it falls apart. We need to put less food on**

the plate, create a stronger plate, or, ideally, do both. Similarly, when it comes to sensory processing demands, we can use "sensory smart" strategies to reduce toxic elements in the environment or activity to keep students more comfortable and capable. We can reduce sensory load, build their ability to tolerate sensory challenges through therapeutic interventions that develop sensory and coping skills, or, ideally, do both.

While everyone is different, highly sensitive students are most likely to find the following common school experiences uncomfortable or even painful:

- classrooms and hallways with harsh glaring lighting;
- crowded hallways, noisy classrooms, cafeterias, school buses, and assemblies;
- sudden loud noises, such as fire alarms, gym or recess whistles, and PA announcements;
- gym class and recess incorporating clothing changes, physical contact, and competition;
- transitioning between classes and completing tests and assignments in a short period; and
- lack of privacy in the bathroom, where students often congregate.

This is not to say that students should avoid every activity they dislike. The goal is for them to engage in every activity that is done by other classmates. There is a great sense of accomplishment and, ultimately, healing when they try something hard, unpleasant, or distressing and emerge victorious. This is easier said than done for the traumatized student who has experienced strong feelings of panic, fear, and/or helplessness. School staff must understand this. It is not a matter of bucking up and muscling through tough times and tasks. **Quite often, extremely challenging activities and tasks are best relegated to trauma-informed therapists working alongside compassionate school staff who can gently and knowledgeably assist students and help them move forward.**

Considerations for Assisting All Sensory Challenged Students

Working with OTs

The gold standard for assessment and treatment of sensory processing issues has always been occupational therapy (OT) with a therapist who has extensive training and experience in sensory integration theory and practice. Some OTs work alongside psychiatrists, psychologists, social workers, and other clinicians in mental health facilities, while many others work in schools, hospitals, and other practice settings.

In a school setting, especially when working with a student with a trauma history, collaboration between OTs and mental health clinicians is paramount. **The OT builds sensory processing, neuromuscular, fine and gross**

motor, psychosocial, and other skills, while the mental health clinician cultivates the client's self-awareness, coping skills, and ability to self-advocate in positive, prosocial ways. A small pilot study found that psychotherapy combined with sensory integrative therapy was far more effective than psychotherapy alone in treating traumatic stress (Kaiser, Gillette, and Spinazzola, 2010). In addition to implementing one-on-one therapeutic interventions to strengthen the student's proverbial paper plate, the OT should help to identify any necessary environment and task modifications that are required to empower a sensitive student to learn optimally—in effect, putting the "just right" food on the student's plate.

While OT with a sensory integrative component (OT–SI) is most appropriate when addressing sensory issues, the available school-based therapist may not have this training or be adept at connecting the dots between sensory issues and the student's ability to access the educational curriculum, which is the defined role of the school-based OT. Instead, the OT at school may focus on fine motor or gross motor skills development, handwriting skills, and visual perception. It is extremely important that any OT working with a traumatized student— whether it is someone working within the school or an outside OT clinician— has in-depth training and experience in SI as well as familiarity with conditions such as PTSD, attachment disorders, anxiety, fearfulness, and other sequelae of trauma. Finally, the OT *must* work with the student, school psychologist, teacher, family, and any outside therapists to address sensory issues, behavior, and school performance.

> The *Sensory Screening for School* and the *Sensory Screening for Home* tools, both available for download at https://sensoryprocessingchallenges.com, can help all team members tune in to what is happening for the student from a sensory standpoint.

Three Levels of Sensory-Based Care

Safe Havens

A safe retreat is the first line of defense (and help) for students who are overwhelmed, upset, stressed out, irritable, sad, or grouchy. Safe havens can take many forms: **a dedicated sensory room, a nook within the classroom, or a designated school staff member's office**. Whatever it is called, and whether it is a separate room or just a corner, a safe haven should never be used as a punishment or time-out space. If the student is overaroused or just having a bad day, this carefully designed haven can provide a soothing environment and materials that can help shift how the student feels and help them attain a state of calm, composure, and focus.

Sensory rooms (or other havens) are typically used for ten to fifteen minutes (with a timer) and may include: dim, non-fluorescent lighting, often with colored lights, lava lamps, or fiber optics; gentle music or sound-cancelling headphones with or without preferred music; tactile materials, such as stuffed toys or fidgets, including Koosh balls and hand exercise balls; a weighted blanket or weighted lap pad; a vibrating cushion; comfortable seating, such as a beanbag chair, rocking chair, Cozy Canoe or PeaPod (an inflatable, flocked cotton canoe, available from www.funandfunction.com or www.specialneedstoys.com); a picture book; high-quality essential oil (preferences typically include vanilla, sweet orange, and lavender); and other items.

For more on sensory rooms and calming tools, see: *Sensory Processing Challenges*
www.specialneedstoys.com and www.funandfunction.com.

One-to-One Intervention at School

OT interventions at school can take several forms, depending on resources and service mandate. OT may be mandated for consultation only, possibly recommending equipment, such as molded pencil grips and slant boards or organizing a group speech therapy session with students sitting on therapy balls rather than chairs to boost alertness. Other models include "push in," working with one or more students inside the classroom, possibly presenting a movement module or handwriting program to all the students or working with a single student to increase participation in classroom activities and routines. Finally, the OT may "pull out" the student to work in a separate room and build their skills.

In any scenario, the OT should help the student identify the sensory tools (many of which are discussed later in this chapter) that help him or her feel better, calmer, and more in control. The OT should work with the student, teacher, and other school-based support team members to develop a "sensory diet"—a schedule of regulating, sensory-based activities the student practices at set times during the school day which enable them to feel and function at their best. The link below provides access to a questionnaire that will aid in identifying sensory stressors and sensory organizers.

Sensory Challenge Questionnaire
https://sensoryprocessingchallenges.com/

Sensory Gyms

Located in an outside therapy center and in some schools, "sensory gyms" are therapy settings where a client works one-to-one with an OT using sensory equipment such as platform or Lycra swings, trampolines, scooter boards, ladders, climbing walls, and more. A sensory gym may be ideal for a student who is so physically active that he bounces off the walls and requires very intense movement and deep pressure, as well as for the student who is unwilling or unable to try a sensory experience in a high-stimulation setting such as a playground or gym class. An added benefit is that the student attends sensory gym outside of school hours, so he does not miss classwork or social opportunities. Ideally, the student who attends a sensory gym also receives services at school and at home to promote carryover of skills and to handle any necessary environmental and task modifications in their natural, "real-life" environments.

Informal Arrangements

Frequently, sensory strategies can be implemented without fuss with an understanding teacher who recognizes, for example, that taking short breaks throughout the day helps the student stay on task. In an informal arrangement, the school is not obligated to purchase equipment or implement a strategy. In order for a piece of equipment or any modification of the school environment or activities to be mandatory, it needs to be spelled out in a legal document, such as a 504 plan or an individualized education plan (IEP).

Making the School Day Easier

Note: The Appendix provides many more strategies and practices for each of the sensory issues reviewed below. Some of these strategies will benefit all students, such as the music examples discussed earlier, while others will primarily benefit sensory-challenged students, who may need them included in their IEP or 504 plans.

On any given day there are numerous opportunities to help sensory-challenged students manage and adapt to the many environmental elements and activities that would otherwise trigger more acute reactions to the sensory overload, confusion, and even pain that these environmental elements and learning-related activities can precipitate. These environmental elements and learning activities include starting the day off right, unstructured time, floor time, easy movements, lighting, visual overload, vision and reading issues, noise, writing time, meals and snacks, taking tests, fire drills, gym and recess, transitions, art classes, assemblies, and the end of the day. The restrictions of space make it impossible to discuss all of the activities and practices that may help sensory-challenged students, so a few key strategies are presented for each topic area. (The Appendix provides a more complete range of practices for use in the classroom, in resource rooms, and during one-to-one interventions.)

It is best to begin by helping students get off to a good start each day.

Start the Day off Right

- While riding the school bus, taking the subway, or entering the crowded school lobby at drop-off time, a sound-sensitive student can wear sound-reducing earmuffs, such as those by Peltor or other brands (http://earplugstore.com).
- The student may be calmed by holding a hand fidget tool, such as a squeeze ball, hand exerciser, or worry stone.
- Wearing a weighted vest or compression garment may be comforting and organizing at these times (resources available from www.weightedwearables.com, http://otvest.com, http://sensorycritters.com, and http://spioworks.com).

Unstructured Time

Children and even teens generally have a poor sense of time.

- A timer lets the student know how much time is left to play or tolerate being in a boring situation. Understanding how every minute counts can help students, too.
- Students who have trouble initiating tasks may procrastinate by sharpening their pencils, going to the bathroom, getting a tissue, getting a drink of water, and only then sitting down and getting down to work. They may then complain that they do not have enough time to complete the assignment. An appropriate timer will provide a visual indication of time that disappears as it elapses, which can be quite helpful for taking tests, writing essays, giving oral presentations, choice time, and more.
- While a clock is an obvious tool, the "Time Timer" (available from www.timetimer.com) may be an excellent choice for students who cannot tell the time or require a quick visual. It comes in several versions: a wristwatch for older students; a three-inch timer for personal use; a twelve-inch timer most people can see from across the room; iPad, iPhone, and Android apps; and desktop computer software. Set for up to one hour (or customized for longer periods on the apps and software), the Time Timer's signature red disk disappears as time elapses. Most versions also have an optional auditory alarm.

Floor Time

Floor time can be very difficult for sensory-challenged students because of poor muscle tone, poor body awareness, tactile issues of sitting on a hard floor, and difficulty processing auditory and visual input. To help these students:

- Schedule circle time or meeting time immediately after gross motor activity, such as recess or gym.

- Alternatively, teachers can incorporate physical activities beforehand to provide vestibular and proprioceptive input. For example, teachers can begin with two minutes of "shaking the sillies out." Some teachers worry this will rev up students when they need to be calm and quiet. In practice, it does the opposite, because jazzing up the muscles by stretching, bouncing, jumping, hopping, running, and other forms of movement input helps to reset bodies and brains, enabling students to sit and tune in with their ears and eyes.
- You will find movement activities that can be incorporated easily into the classroom throughout this resource and especially in the Appendix.

Desk Time

- If the student's feet cannot reach the floor, add a footrest. This can be an inexpensive footstool with a rubberized base (from Ikea or other retailers), a yoga block, a sturdy box with nonskid matting attached, or even a double-bagged container of dry beans.
- The Movin' Step (available from http://gymnic.com) is an inflatable footrest designed for students who push against the front legs of their desks. Instead, they push down into the cushion.
- Bouncy Bands (available from http://bouncybands.com) can be added to chairs or desks with support pipes that keep a sturdy elastic strap in place for a child to kick or push against.
- A strip of Theraband or Lycra across the front chair legs can also be used, though they tend to slip down.

Some students do best standing up, which lets them obtain vestibular input and burn off surplus energy and calories. Some schools now offer standing desks, such as the AlphaBetter Stand-Up Desk (available from http://worthingdirect.com), which let students either stand or sit and swing their legs silently on a foot bar. A few others now offer desks with pedal exercisers or elliptical trainers on the floor below (available from http://deskcycle.com and http://thefitdesk.com).

Easy Movement Ideas for the Classroom

Frequent movement breaks boost learning and mood by stimulating sensory receptors, increasing oxygen intake, and releasing excess energy in a beneficial way. Having an opportunity to move is especially important in helping students get ready for classwork.

- With smart boards in so many classrooms, it is easier than ever to do group movement activities. A favorite is GoNoodle (see www.GoNoodle.com), which offers a range of group activities, such as the arousing "Pop See Ko," which can be used to get the ya-yas out, and "Slo-Mo," which can help students slow down and reorganize.

- Brain Gym exercises are designed to get the two hemispheres of the brain communicating with each other, help get wiggles out, reduce stress, and stimulate brain function. Teachers can learn more about these activities in *Brain Gym: Teacher's Edition* (Dennison and Dennison, 1989) or find a course on http://braingym.org. See the Appendix for other recommended Brain Gym activities.
- A teacher might also play Martin Boroson's *One-Moment Meditation* video (www.youtube.com/watch?v=F6eFFCi12v8; also available as a smartphone app) to get the kids ready to start a lesson.

Lighting

Sensory-challenged students may have significant sensitivity to lighting. People who are sensitive to light and sound can see and hear fluorescent lights flicker as the voltage switches on and off. This is more common for older fixtures that cycle on and off sixty times per second; however, even newer fluorescents can be incredibly annoying. Fluorescent lighting has been associated with drowsiness, poor concentration, stress, eye strain, headaches, and migraines (Basso, 2001). Indeed, any downcast lighting can be problematic. Add a ceiling fan and you will get a strobe effect that is uncomfortable for some people and a serious risk factor for those who are prone to photoreactive seizures.

- Replace overhead fluorescent lights with fixtures that contain full-spectrum bulbs that cast even, pleasant, illumination.
- Fluorescent ballasts can be replaced with less noxious LED tubes from Home Depot and other hardware stores.
- If fluorescent fixtures cannot be replaced, add light diffusers that attach magnetically, such as Cozy Shades (available from http://abilitations.com). Or simply turn them off and use floor lamps.

Visual Overloading

Classroom clutter can be very overstimulating.

- Avoid unnecessary decorations on walls.
- Use a small area of the room as a reading or relaxation nook with reduced visuals and reduced lighting.
- Help students stay organized with chair pockets, such as the Aussie Pouch (available from www.aussiepouch.com), which fits over the back of the chair and can be used to organize notebooks, pencils, and other school supplies.
- Allow students to take tests and write in-class essays in a separate location (This must be included in the IEP or 504 plan.)

Vision and Reading Issues

A significant number of students with attention and sensory problems have undiagnosed visual acuity and/or visual processing problems. Signs to look for include squinting, rubbing eyes, blinking, covering one eye, tilting the head when looking at a book or object, and frequent complaints of headache, tiredness, or boredom when reading.

- While students are expected to be able to scan the written page easily from left to right, word by word, and then shift down to the left side of the next line, others need support to do this. For these readers, it should be okay to use a finger, a piece of plain paper, or a ruler placed over upcoming lines of print to allow them to scan across a line of print more efficiently by eliminating the visual distraction of the subsequent lines.
- Teach a student to use highlighter markers or strips (available from http://enasco.com) to focus on the most salient points in written materials. This enhances visual attention and makes reviewing for tests easier.

Dealing with Noise

Due to large class sizes and avoidance of sound-absorbing fabrics such as carpeting due to sanitary concerns, many classrooms can be far too loud for everyone.

- Allow students to wear ear protection, such as Peltor noise-cancelling headphones, at key times, such as during study hall, reading, assemblies, and so on.
- Use music judiciously in the classroom since it may help some students stay calm and focus, but irritate and defocus others. Consider letting students listen to their own music during reading and independent work. What makes one person relax may not help the student who needs quiet in order to focus. While music preference is subjective, it has been found that certain pieces have a positive influence on brainwave patterns in people with attention challenges. You might try:
  - Pachelbel's Canon in D
  - Bach's Brandenburg Concertos
  - Mozart's Symphony No.40 in G Minor
  - Chopin's piano études
  - Philip Glass's piano works
  - Brian Eno's ambient music
  - Nature-based music, such as *Gentle Sounds*, and *KidzJamz* CDs (available from from www.vitalsounds.com).

Writing Time

A continuous interaction between cognitive and emotional skills, fine motor, perceptual, language, and sensory components makes this a very complex task.

There are dozens of writing strategies, hand exercises, suggestions for handwriting and keyboarding apps to improve handwriting and written communication at https://sensoryprocessingchallenges.com.

- Some students find it difficult to write comfortably on a flat tabletop because they may have to crane their neck to see what they are doing or bend their wrist inward to write. Using a slantboard brings the materials closer to the face so the student does not have to bend over. Having students stand up and work on a smart board, dry erase board, wall easel, or paper taped to the wall is an engaging whole-body activity that can help the students see better, strengthen their bodies, and engage more effectively.
- Students with poor graphomotor skills should learn to keyboard early. Students with sensory issues may do best with a typing tutorial program that does not have distracting music or colorful graphics and games. One such program is UltraKey (available at www.bytesoflearning.com). Of course, if graphics and games will help to motivate the student, many alternative programs are worth investigating.

Taking Tests

Sensory issues can interfere with a student's ability to take tests to the best of their ability because of distractions from the sounds and smells of classmates, the glare of overhead lighting, and so on. Test accommodations are easily implemented but may need to be formally added to the student's IEP or 504 plan. Common test accommodations include:

- Taking the test in a separate location, such as a quiet, pleasantly lit room. This allows sensitive students to demonstrate what they know without forcing them to deal with sensory distractions.
- Extended time for students who take longer to process information or write slowly.
- Answers recorded in a variety of ways, such as typing into a laptop or dictating to someone.
- Allowing students to chew gum, drink water, or take a brief movement breaks during the test.

Fire Drills

Typical fire alarms ring at ear-splitting volume, which can traumatize a sensitive student. They may take hours, days, or even weeks to recuperate from a fire drill and become anxious in anticipation of the next one. Alarm systems with strobes can pack a double whammy for visually sensitive kids and those who are prone to migraines and seizures.

- Students should have the right to wear noise-reducing earplugs, headphones, or earmuffs in the event of a fire drill. They will still be able to hear the siren and instructions.

Gym and Recess

Gym and recess should be times when students can play, burn off excess energy, get physically fit, and feel great. Unfortunately, this is not the case for some students. General education gym classes tend to be held in large, brightly lit rooms that lack sound-absorbing materials, such as dedicated gymnasiums or school cafeterias.

- It helps to add sound-absorbing mats to the room and to eliminate shrill whistles if possible. Some students become disorganized at recess or in gym because of their intense craving for input. It will help them to make a plan before starting the gym session and to practice safe, appropriate behaviors (see the Appendix).

Transitions between Activities and Classes

Some students have trouble with transitions between classes or activities.

- Provide verbal notice about upcoming transitions. Use a visual timer if it helps.
- Try playing soft music to help kids recognize that something is about to change and they need to be ready to refocus their attention. Whether a young child is busy building a castle with blocks or reading a book, hearing this music—first at a very soft volume and then a bit louder—is an excellent cue. Some teachers gently play a tambourine or a triangle.
- Allow older students to leave the room first in order to get to their next class before the hallway is jam-packed with students. Or allow students to be a few seconds late without penalty. Keep in mind, however, that being first in the classroom is less noticeable and taunt-worthy than always being late.

Art Class

Art projects can present distinct and significant sensory challenges. Art media, such as paint, markers, glue, and clay, typically have strong odors that are intolerable for some students. Tactile exploration may be delightful for sensory seekers but completely unbearable for others. The goal here is participation, and sensory issues should not prevent this.

- If a student refuses to get messy, offer gloves and a long-handled paintbrush, or glue sticks instead of liquid glue. Sometimes having a damp cloth close by for wiping hands can make all the difference. Once students find pleasure in what they are doing, they are usually more willing to deal with the sensory issues.
- Special attention should be paid to ensuring good ventilation during art projects—open a window or use a fan, if necessary. The teacher should never invalidate a student by saying, "It doesn't smell." *It does to them.*

Everything smells like something. Even if the label states the item is certified nontoxic, it may still be toxic to a specific student's sensitive nervous system.

Assemblies

- Any large gathering is ripe for discomfort for an auditory-sensitive student. Students should be entitled to wear ear protection to any school assembly and should be allowed to sit at the end of the row, near an exit, so they can take a break if needed without disturbing their classmates. They should also be allowed to bring seat cushions and hand fidgets if these help.

End of the School Day

School dismissal may be a stressful transition. For students who have trouble getting organized, whether due to sensory distractions, concerns about homework, or other reasons, an aide or teacher can help make sure everything they need is packed in their book bags, and double-check that they have written everything legibly in an assignment notebook. If transporting books home is difficult, a second set should be available for them to keep at home.

Weigh after-school activities carefully. Many students with sensory issues and a history of trauma will be thrilled to let off some steam in an after-school tae kwon do or dance class, and they will still have plenty of energy for doing their homework afterward. Others may love the quiet discipline of an after-school chess club or drawing lessons.

Getting Teachers and Others on Board

Many parents assume that educators know about sensory processing and trauma issues and how to work around them in school. Or they may keep silent in the hope that this year's new teacher will not run into the same problems as last year's, or that an older child has finally overcome his issues because he had such a fabulous, happy summer break. All too often, when parents learn that this is not the case, they resent having to teach the teachers. But we are all learning. Many schools today are not brain-based or trauma-sensitive. On the other hand, many are, and their successes are paving the way for others. Teachers who care want to hear as much as they can about their students, especially from parents.

So parents should be encouraged to speak with teachers and let them know what works best for their children. Remind them that most general education teachers, teaching assistants, and paraprofessionals have received little, if any, training, in atypical development. Special education teachers have received more training, especially in teaching children with disabilities, but again a significant proportion of them have received little or no information about sensory issues or trauma. This does not mean that unrealistic demands should be made, or that a laundry list of things the teacher must do for the student should be drafted. Every child is different, and it behooves parents to help teachers learn how to work best with their children. After all, it is nearly always the parents who are the ultimate experts.

References

Ahn, R. R., Miller, L. J., Milberger, S., and McIntosh, D. N. (2004). Prevalence of parents' perceptions of sensory processing disorders among kindergarten children. *American Journal of Occupational Therapy*, 58, 287–293.

Allen, A.P., and Smith, A.P. (2011). A review of the evidence that chewing gum affects stress, alertness and cognition. *Journal of Behavioral and Neuroscience Research*, 9(1), 7–23.

Basso, M. R. (2001). Neurobiological relationships between ambient lighting and the startle response to acoustic stress in humans. *International Journal of Neuroscience*, 110, 147–157.

Ben-Sasson, A., Carter, A. S., and Briggs-Gowan, M. J. (2009). Sensory over-responsivity in elementary school: Prevalence and social-emotional correlates. *Journal of Abnormal Child Psychology*, 37, 705–716.

Bernardi, P., Porta, C., and Sleight, P. (2006). Cardiovascular, cerebrovascular and respiratory changes induced by different types of music in musicians and non-musicians: The importance of silence. *Heart*, 92, 445–452.

Biel, L. (2014). *Sensory Processing Challenges: Effective Clinical Work with Kids and Teens*. New York: W. W. Norton.

Biel, L., and Peske, N. (2009). *Raising a Sensory Smart Child: The Definitive Handbook for Helping Your Child with Sensory Processing Issues* (rev. ed.). New York: Penguin.

Copple, C., and Bredekamp, S. (2009). *Developmentally Appropriate Practice in Early Childhood Programs, Serving Children from Birth through 8* (rev. ed.). Washington, DC: National Association for the Education of Young Children.

Dennison, P., and Dennison, G. (1989). *Brain Gym: Teacher's Edition*. Ventura, CA: Education Kinesthetics.

Gertel Kraybill, O. (2015). *Trauma & Sensory Integration: The Egg & the Chicken*. Psych Central. Retrieved February 3, 2016, from http://pro.psychcentral.com/trauma-sensory-integration-the-egg-the-chicken/008673.html.

Hamstra-Bletz, L., and Blote, A. W. (1990). Development of handwriting in primary school: A longitudinal study. *Perceptual and Motor Skills*, 70, 759–770.

Ishihara, K., Dake, K., Kashihara, T., and Ishihara, S. (2010). An attempt to improve the sitting posture of children in classroom. *Proceedings of International Multiconference of Engineers and Computer Scientists, Hong Kong*. Retrieved September 26, 2016 from www.iaeng.org/publication/IMECS2010/IMECS2010_pp1922-1925.pdf.

Kaiser, E. M., Gillette, C. S., and Spinazzola, J. (2010). A controlled pilot-outcome study of sensory integration (SI) in the treatment of complex adaptation to traumatic stress. *Journal of Aggression, Maltreatment and Trauma*, 19, 699–720.

Leekam, S. R., Nieto, C., Libby, S. J., Wing, L., and Gould, J. (2007). Describing the sensory abnormalities of children and adults with autism. *Journal of Autism and Developmental Disorders*, 37, 894–910.

Pfeiffer, B., Henry, A., Miller, S., and Witherell, S. (2008). The effectiveness of Disc "O" Sit cushions on attention to task in second-grade students with attention difficulties. *American Journal of Occupational Therapy*, 62, 274–281.

Pontifex, M. B., Saliba, B. J., Raine, L. B., Picchietti, D. L., and Hillman, C. H. (2012). Exercise improves behavioral, neurocognitive, and scholastic performance in children with ADHD. *Journal of Pediatrics*, 162, 543–551.

van der Kolk, B. A., Burbridge, J. A., and Suzuki, J. (1997). The psychobiology of traumatic memories: Clinical implications of neuroimaging studies. *Annals of the New York Academy of Sciences*, 821, 99–113.

5 Brief Connections That Matter (CTMs)

Student–Teacher Relationship

William Steele

Before beginning this chapter, there are two tasks to complete. These are related to the use of sensory-based interventions and teacher mindsets.

Task One

Watch the *Boston 247* video listed below. Keep in mind the previous discussions regarding how our brains function under stress and the issues with regulation of our nervous systems under stress. The school had a rule of no hats, yet a few teens had brought their hats to school and had them sitting on a lunchroom table when a teacher came by and took just one student's hat. The student's reactions escalated until the principal stepped in. Unfortunately, the subsequent efforts by the principal and the teacher failed to help the teen regulate his reactions.

As you watch, ask yourself what one sensory intervention the principal and/or teacher could have used to prevent the student from eventually putting his fist through a glass panel.

Boston 247
www.youtube.com/watch?v=X9_WwuGF4dM

Task Two

How we react and respond to challenging behaviors is determined by our mindsets regarding such behaviors. In a trauma-sensitive environment (actually, in any environment), rather than asking a dysregulated child, "What *is wrong* with you?" we would ask, "What *has happened* to you?" This response underscores that we believe their behaviors are not conscious or willful but driven by fear.

Below are sixteen incomplete sentences that you are asked to complete. Your answers will provide a way for you to evaluate your current mindsets and how they are influencing your own emotional, cognitive, and behavioral responses to the challenging behaviors of students. As you will learn in the next chapter, our beliefs or mindsets regulate our behaviors as well as our biology. Completing these sentences will take several minutes, but as you compare your answers with those provided later in the chapter, you should find it a very worthwhile exercise. The mindsets presented in this chapter help teachers remain far more proactive than reactive to difficult situations and greatly assist them with their own need for self-regulation in a stressful environment that presents challenges every day.

1. Not "He's pushing my buttons" but . . .
2. Not "She's manipulating me" but . . .
3. Not "He is so oppositional" but . . .
4. Not "She thinks she'll get her way throwing a fit" but . . .
5. Not "He's always afraid" but . . .
6. Not "What's wrong with him?" but . . .
7. Not "He's a bad kid" but . . .
8. Not "Look at his behavior" but . . .
9. Not "He can't be trusted" but . . .
10. Not "Punishment will get his attention" but . . .
11. Not "We have the authority" but . . .
12. Not "He's disrupting the class" but . . .
13. Not what my students are doing wrong but . . .
14. Every student has the capacity to . . .
15. The student is not the problem; the . . .
16. Problems are opportunities to . . .

The answers to these two tasks are presented later, in the discussion related to teacher mindsets regarding student behaviors and those brief connections that matter, especially when students are dysregulated.

A lot has already been said about relationships being at the core of successfully teaching and helping students flourish. Subsequent chapters will add to the discussion because relationships are at the core of change, learning, behavior, growth, and resilience. In this chapter, the focus is on making brief connections with students and how these brief connections can have long-term impacts and help regulate behavior and improve academic performance. It also focuses on those brief non-verbal and verbal connections that matter when helping students with regulation as well as establishing relationships that are conducive to learning. However we communicate it, the repetitive message must be **"You matter."** In the video below Angela Maiers tells us why children need to hear this message early and frequently.

You Matter Initiative
www.youtube.com/watch?v=BS7kleRUkk4

One Moment: One Brief Connection

Chapter One mentioned the persistent mindset that only long-term relationships produce long-term gains, and, as a result, the importance of brief connections tends to be minimized. **The fact is it only takes one brief connection to create a long-term gain.** Any brief connection that is attuned to our need and attends to that need immediately has a significant and long-term impact on our behavior and learning performance.

I remember nothing about kindergarten. However, I do remember the most important part of my first morning in first grade. Family life was emotionally very difficult and as a result I was an anxious, fearful, and extremely shy child. It is an understatement to say that I was feeling anxious about the first day of school.

My mother walked me to school. It was a Catholic school, and I would attend it for the next eight years (a story in itself). New kids and parents were all gathered in one place. I'm sure my eyes never left my mother. As she started to leave I followed a distance behind. No one stopped her or me. I guess they were all too busy to notice us. We walked for what seemed like a very long distance. It wasn't until she stopped to cross the street that she saw me lingering behind. She did not hesitate to grab my hand and walk me right back to school, only this time she took me to the principal, who escorted us directly to the first grade teacher, Sister Joanna Mary. She immediately put me in charge of cleaning the chalkboard and erasers. I have absolutely no memory of what she said to me, but I do remember her showing me how to clean the board and erasers, which were not yet dirty but would be shortly. From that day on, I was eager to go to school and caused no one a problem.

When I tell this story, I can still visualize the white chalk clouds I made as I banged the erasers together. I can smell it in my nose and almost feel it on my hands. That one moment in time taught me many lessons. Most of all, I remember always being happy when I was with Sister Joanna Mary. It was an immediate, brief connection that also involved me doing something, a sensory action. It taught me how such brief connections can have a lifelong effect on students in the school setting. The blogs listed below, written by teachers, describe how they are connecting to their students and the benefits they are experiencing.

---

3 Ways to Make Meaningful Connections with Your Students
www.edutopia.org/blog/make-meaningful-connections-with-students-nick-provenzano

10 Ways to Make Real Connections with Students
www.catholicteacher.com/blog/archives/89-10-Ways-to-Make-Real-Connections-with-Students.html

---

Be Curious

Cleaning erasers worked for me, but it might not have helped another student who was experiencing similar anxiety. If asked at the time, I certainly would not have been able to tell Sister Joanna Mary I needed to clean erasers to feel okay in her class. I was far too anxious to talk or even think. This is why every teacher ought to have a curious conversation with students, when they are regulated, about those things that upset them and what helps them feel better. This will not only generate interest and provide an opportunity to build a positive connection; it can also alert teachers to actions they may take with students when they are dysregulated.

Expressing curiosity about a student's experiences takes only a minute or two, at most. Here is a sample script:

> You know we all get upset. Sometimes it's because of what others say or do to us. Sometimes it's when we can't get something to work or when something doesn't go right. The other day I . . . [self-disclose a troubling experience]. I was so upset. I'm curious what upsets you most. Okay. So, when you are upset, what do you do? Does that help or make it worse? What makes you feel better? Sometimes I take a walk. Sometimes I go to a quiet place. Sometimes I run. Sometimes I call a friend. What works for you? I wonder if you've tried . . . [offer sensory suggestions—taking a deep breath, going to a different part of the house, doing something different, playing a favorite game, talking about it, etc.]. Maybe next time you are upset you can try something different. Of all the ideas we came up with, which one or two do think might help? You know, we could even practice them to find which one feels best for you.

This connection takes less than two minutes, yet it yields wonderful information that can be used later to help the student and immediately tells them, "You are important to me." It also creates a sense of trust, which has a direct correlation with achievement. For example, Shelden and colleagues (2010, p. 159) found that "not only was trust associated with greater gains in student achievement, but also with lasting gains in achievement." In their study, those helpers who took the time to be curious, ask open-ended questions, and listen engendered more trust. This holds true for teachers, too.

The word "curious" is used deliberately, as curiosity is the cornerstone of empathy. Empathetic people have an insatiable curiosity about how others are experiencing their world. Curiosity is essential for determining what matters most to the student's efforts to regulate their reactions, and it is a wonderful way to create a positive connection. Hughes (2009, p. 169) wrote,

> When curiosity is directed toward the child's experience rather than toward the factual events in his life and when it is conveyed with both affective (non-verbal) and reflective features, the child is likely to go with us very deeply into his or her life story and experience a co-regulating of emotions related to what is being explored and the meaning given those events.

Curiosity clearly tells the child, "You matter." This is crucial, yet it is rarely discussed or written about.

The same nervous system that prepares us to fight or flee from whatever or whomever is frightening also prepares us to fight our way toward the activity, the place, or the person that is safe, attuned to (curious about us), and attentive to our needs.

Often the term "relationship" is thought of as something that takes time to develop. Actually, a relationship is simply a connection that is made between two people. That relationship is defined by the nature of the connection. Essentially, it is positive or negative, helpful or hurtful, useful or useless. When teachers make even brief connections that are attuned to and attend immediately to their students' needs, those students experience these as positive relationships. When these brief, positive connections are repeated, even over short periods of time, the students begin to flourish.

Brief Connections: Long-Term Results

It does not take long to form a relationship that has long-term benefits, and even brief connections can have long-term gains. For example, in one project that consisted of a six-session intervention with parents of children with varying degrees of anxiety, that anxiety was significantly reduced and the reduction was then sustained over a three-year period (Cathcart, 2012). The parents in this project were introduced to the developmental aspects of anxiety, assisted with cognitively reframing their thoughts (changing their mindsets) to their children's symptoms and behaviors, and given various ways to interact (connect) with their children.

Dewar (2016) describes a study by Ahnert and colleagues (2013) which showed that students who had a positive relationship (connection) with their teacher solved problems faster than those without such a connection when they were shown a picture of their teacher's face. Moreover, they were shown the picture for no more than a second prior to tackling the problems. If the student had a positive connection/relationship with their teacher, they did well; if not, they did less well. When the brief connections made with students are positive in nature—convey care, concern, curiosity, choice, excitement, joy, and inform—students do better.

Connecting to Regulate Behavior and Cooperation

Research also confirms the importance of teacher–student connections related to regulating behavior: "Kids who experience high quality student–teacher relationships (connections) in the early years have fewer behavior problems. They show more engagement in the classroom and better performance" (Dewar, 2016). Such connections have a positive influence on performance. For example, one study on performance with teenagers showed improved academic growth in mathematics from eighth to twelfth grades when students had a perceived "connectedness" to their teacher (Gregory and Weinstein, 2004).

When we attempt to *control* challenging student behavior rather than *relate* to the needs their behaviors are communicating, students will continue, through their behavior, to let us know we need to change our approach. Listed below, an excellent video demonstrates how one teacher struggled to control his students' behavior. Once he focused on connecting with the same students, everything changed for the better. He became attuned to their needs and expressed through different verbal approaches that he was attuned, and they reciprocated by responding positively. The approach he adopted was relational.

Classroom Management Strategies to Take Control of Noisy Students
www.youtube.com/watch?v=u086rr7SRso.

Beliefs Shape Our Interactions

The nature of our interaction is shaped by our beliefs. I define a mindset as an entrenched belief. If the teacher in the above video had not succeeded in altering his belief about trying to control his students' behavior to one of relating to their need to feel connected and valued, his problems with control would have continued. Our beliefs about teaching and interacting with anxious and traumatized students matter greatly. Therefore, we begin with trauma-sensitive teacher beliefs about the learning capacities and needs of anxious and traumatized students. Following this, we address trauma-sensitive teacher beliefs about their students' behaviors and then focus on brief non-verbal and verbal connections that matter in developing a teacher–student relationship that helps teachers help students regulate their reactions and improve their performance. (The next chapter addresses the growth mindsets that are specific to sustaining the motivation to learn and are among the most basic processes for successful learning effort.)

Teacher Beliefs about Teaching Anxious and Traumatized Students

Beliefs, both old and new, can either support or prevent optimal learning outcomes (Connors and Smith, 2009). Our beliefs drive our behaviors. For example, if we believe anxious and traumatized students have limited learning capacity, we will not challenge them, introduce them to new experiences, or interact in ways that promote curiosity, creativity, and an eagerness to learn. Unfortunately, when asked, teachers often cannot define the core learning beliefs of their schools. Similarly, they are often unable to identify their schools' core values.

In the year prior to writing this resource, I trained over 1,500 educators in trauma-sensitive, brain-based classroom practices. They represented seventy schools. I asked participants at each training session to write down the name of their school and then list three of the school's core beliefs related to teaching/

learning. During lunch, I would group the responses by school and then review what each participant had listed. All struggled with this task and few agreed on their core beliefs.

This signaled that their environments were fractured. There was no consistency from one class to another, one teacher to another; each brought their own set of beliefs into the classroom. This is not to say that some of these beliefs were not beneficial for the students; however, when there is such variance among staff, not only is the overall performance and outcome of those in that environment weakened, but stress and conflict increase (Collins, 2009; Connors and Smith, 2009). The Goldenbergs (2013) discuss that sharing positive beliefs is critical for developing the strength and resilience of families.

To maximize the use of brain-based, trauma-sensitive learning processes and realize improved learning and behavior, it makes sense for our behaviors to be governed by a core set of beliefs that meet the psycho-social, physiological, and learning needs of sensory-challenged, anxious, and traumatized students. A few of the brain-based, trauma-sensitive beliefs derived from previous chapters are listed below:

- We believe that the learning outcomes of anxious and traumatized students are directly related to our knowledge and use of trauma-sensitive, brain-based practices. (So we engage those practices.)
- We believe in the neuroplasticity of the brain. (So we repeatedly present it with challenges and experiences to encourage it to grow.)
- We believe that providing students with daily opportunities to regulate their hyper- or hypo-arousal reactions and behaviors leads to improved learning outcomes and acceptable school-related behaviors. (So we provide those opportunities.)
- We believe movement is essential for effective learning. (So we provide movement activities every thirty minutes throughout the day.)
- We believe that the classroom environment enhances or limits learning outcomes. (So we make sure our classrooms address the physical elements that are conducive to learning.)
- We believe that learning is optimized only when students feel physically safe; when their feelings are safe; when their thoughts, ideas, and words are safe; and when their work—the things they make, the materials they use—are safe. (So we teach and support student behaviors that respect these safety needs.)
- We believe that the challenging behaviors of anxious and traumatized students are not willful acts, but primary survival responses to an environment, activity, or person that is perceived or experienced as a threat. (So we remain proactive rather than reactive.)
- We believe that relational responses are more likely than behavioral responses to minimize challenging behaviors and improve learning. (So we respond with care and compassion, and ask, "What has happened to you?" rather than, "What is wrong with you?")

- We believe even brief connections support sustained regulation and optimum learning outcomes. (So we engage in repeated brief connections with our students.)
- We believe in the four universal needs of every child as a cornerstone for developing resilience and desired reciprocal responses from our students—belonging, mastery, independence, and generosity. (So our interactions, our verbal and non-verbal communications, and the experiences we present to our students are all directed toward meeting these needs.)

Happy Kids Learn

This list of beliefs can be summarized with one core belief that may seem like an oversimplification. Yet it is rooted in all that neuroscience, social science, and learning science have discovered: **"Happy students learn."** It is amazing how many educators and therapists fail to focus on doing what is needed for their students or clients to experience each other and their environments happily. Instead, all too often, the focus is far too serious and cognitive.

Our beliefs about students' behaviors also shape our responses to them. Sister Joanna Mary did not try to reassure me that everything would be okay. But she did meet my need to feel valued, which made her and her classroom an okay place. It is essential that these beliefs are trauma-sensitive so we respond to challenging behaviors in ways that meet the need that students' behaviors are communicating.

Teachers' Beliefs about the Need Their Students' Behaviors Communicate

Responding to the challenging behaviors of dysregulated students in ways that are calming, not alarming, obliges teachers to respond from a core set of trauma-sensitive beliefs as to what their students' challenging behaviors may be communicating. Our beliefs relating to student behaviors matter greatly as they dictate how we will respond to those students and, consequently, how those students will respond to us.

At the beginning of this chapter you were asked to complete sixteen incomplete sentences. Now it is time to compare your answers with those that are provided below. (A number of these have been adapted from Hall et al. (2008) and TLC Focus (2013).)

1. Not "He's pushing my buttons" but "I'm lucky he's letting me know he needs something."
2. Not "She's manipulating me" but "She's just trying to tell me her needs are immediate."
3. Not "He is so oppositional" but "He is becoming independent. He is telling me he has a mind of his own."

4. Not "She thinks she'll get her way throwing a fit" but "She is telling me she has lost control and needs my help to feel safe and calm herself. What a great communicator."

5. Not "He's always afraid" but "He's dealing with a lot of new things and that is scary." (This includes new subject matter, new classmates, new expectations, and you, as his new teacher.)

6. Not "What's wrong with him?" but "What are we not doing right with him?"

7. Not "He's a bad kid" but "He's finding a way to cope."

8. Not "Look at his behavior" but "Look at his pain."

9. Not "He can't be trusted" but "He needs positive adults he can trust."

10. Not "Punishment will get his attention" but "Caring people will get his attention."

11. Not "We have the authority" but "We have his heart."

12. Not "He's disrupting the class" but "The environment is hurting him."

13. Not what my students are doing wrong but what they are doing right.

14. Every student has the capacity to learn.

15. The student is not the problem; the problem is the problem.

16. Problems are opportunities to connect with students.

While reading these you may have sensed how focusing on each of the responses changes the way we might otherwise respond. They also clearly tell us what we can do at that moment to meet that student's need. Once the need is met, the behavior changes. Number 1 needs us to be curious. Number 2 needs our undivided attention immediately. Number 3 needs us to empower the student through creative opportunities to experience his capabilities. The need for number 4 is stated. Number 5 needs our help with transitions and consistency. Number 6 demands we try something different, and number 7 needs our help with support and new ways to cope.

Statements 8–11 reflect beliefs that keep us more attuned to the subjective needs of students and how they are experiencing themselves and their environment, especially when dysregulated. They help us keep in mind the fear and pain the students endure and have never been taught (or even encouraged, in some cases) to learn how to regulate. Number 12 directs our attention to who or what in the environment may be activating a student's behavior. Number 13 has been mentioned several times already in this resource. The last three statements speak to students' need for us to teach them how to approach problems as well encourage their attempts to find solutions. This will be discussed in more detail in Chapter Six.

These beliefs about behaviors slow down our reactions. They help us to be less reactive and redirect our responses to our students' need for our engagement in an action that helps them return to calm and safety, which is comforting and regulating. Once this happens, what we have to say is easier to process.

It is essential to accept that right-brain, relational limbic interactions between teachers and sensory-challenged, anxious, and traumatized students are often more important than cognitive efforts to help such students with regulation (Steele and Malchiodi, 2012). This leads us to our first task.

Boston 247: **Sensory Connections Matter**

Let's return to the *Boston 247* video. What did you identify as the one sensory action or intervention that might have prevented this student from losing control and putting his fist through the glass panel? I have heard many different suggestions during training sessions, but participants rarely identify the best one. This is because it takes time for our beliefs to shift from old paradigms and for us to realize that, in this case, the student's limbic region (feeling brain) and nervous system were in desperate need of a calming sensory action (on our part) and a sensory connection (on his part) in order to regulate his intense reaction. Efforts at a cognitive level rarely accomplish this as quickly as a sensory response.

Initially, participants tend to talk about how the teacher clearly had issues with this particular student, as he confiscated only his hat and none of the others that were also on the lunchroom table. They point out that he singled out the student in front of his peers, which is likely to trigger shame, anger, and a variety of other reactions. They mention that the teacher was not open to listening to the student, as he said, "Look, this is the way it is." This slammed the door on any possible two-way communication. Participants also mention that the principal initially appeared to have some calming effect on the student. The student followed the principal into his office, sat down, and engaged in a brief conversation. The principal indicated that he was aware that this was not about the student's hat, but about respect. Unfortunately, though, he did not give the student any opportunity to express himself further. Immediately after acknowledging that this was about respect, he forced the student straight back into a state of anxiety, fear, and arousal by saying, "Come on. Follow me. I want you and your teacher to work this out."

Participants generally point out that it was unwise for the principal to connect the student with this teacher at a time when both were upset. Others mention that, given the student's initial positive responses to the principal, the principal would have been wise to stay in the room with the student. They suggest that any meeting between the teacher and the student should have been held in a neutral room (such as the principal's office), as the environment is important. A few suggest that the principal should have given the student a few minutes to walk around and try to regulate his reactions. Some mention that, as the student was on his feet and yelling at the teacher, his reactions were probably intensified when another adult came into the room and grabbed his elbow, which was sure to cause a knee-jerk/pull-away reaction. The student did indeed pull away immediately and left the room yelling, "Do not put your damn hands on me." Shortly thereafter, he put his fist through the glass panel.

These are all excellent observations and suggestions. Any one of them may have prevented the student's escalation. However, very few participants suggest what would probably be the most effective non-verbal, sensory intervention—simply giving the student his hat. On numerous occasions he pleaded, "Just give me my damn hat," but it is often difficult for participants to appreciate the power of a simple, sensory, non-verbal intervention, especially when their focus is on controlling a student's behavior rather than regulating his nervous system/limbic responses by connecting with him at a limbic level, where there is no reason or logic. Remember that the principal tried to reason with the youth when he said, "I know this is not about the hat. It's about respect," and that this verbal/cognitive approach did not help. This verbal acknowledgment would have been a good start if the youth had not been held hostage by his limbic region response. But he was, so first he needed his hat.

Brief Non-Verbal Connections That Matter (CTMs) with Dysregulated Students

In Chapter One we learned that a message's meaning is derived from three sources: 20 percent from spoken/written words; 25 percent from tone of voice and expressed attitude; and 55 percent from body language or non-verbal communication. Remember that sensory-challenged, anxious, and traumatized students rely heavily on non-verbal cues and resources to navigate their environment. When dysregulated, reason and executive functioning are not readily available to them. **So making a helpful connection with dysregulated students needs to begin at the non-verbal level.**

In Chapter One we also briefly discussed the use of non-verbal communication to co-regulate and mirror those reactions and behaviors that can help dysregulated students. The example used was the *Still Faces* video, which showed how quickly a frightened, fearful, frustrated infant responds positively to her mother's non-verbal gestures. If you did not watch this video when reading Chapter One, it would help to do so now, because we are going to expand on the value and power of non-verbal interactions or mirroring with dysregulated students.

Before looking at non-verbal approaches, however, it is important to review the scientific research into mirror neurons in order to reinforce the importance of non-verbal actions and expressions when trying to make connections that matter with students.

Mirror Neurons

The discovery of mirror neurons is one of the prime advances in recent neuroscience (Ramachandran, 2011). It seems that they are among the greatest drivers of human progress.

We first connect to others at a celluar level, through the function of these mirror neurons. Researchers recently identified them in the brain and started to learn how they cause us to mirror what we see, feel, and sense about others. There are many non-verbal behaviors that can mirror our sincere interest in our students, keep us as a safe person who is aware of and respectful toward the subjective needs of our anxious and traumatized students, and promote co-regulation with those students. One of these is greeting students with a smile and a handshake every morning, or with high-fives, fist taps, or other agreed interactions.

The fourteen-minute video listed below presents additional support as to why and how our non-verbal expressions and behaviors help with co-regulating students' reactions and positive responses to our efforts to connect.

Nova Science Now: Mirror Neurons
www.youtube.com/watch?v=Xmx1qPyo8Ks

Children read our facial expressions (Levine and Kline, 2008, p. 16). The goal is to minimize, not compound, any feelings of fear, shame, embarrassment, or confusion our students may be experiencing. How we non-verbally present our selves makes a profound difference to how students respond to us.

The Smile

The most effective facial expression for encouraging positive connections with students is the smile. A genuine smile causes others to experience us as empathetic and easygoing, approachable, and trustworthy (Detweiler, 2016). In his blog *Don't Smile 'til Christmas: A Teacher's Worst Advice*, Chase Mielke (2015) argues that smiling is "the most impactful non-verbal expression humans can use in social situations [as teachers]." He also states that smiling makes us safe and approachable, and "that we wish to share positive emotion." As is demonstrated in the video on mirror neurons, a smile socially engages others; it creates an immediate connection that is non-threatening. Smiling feels good, too. Neuroscience confirms this. In his book *Brainstorm: The Power and Purpose of the Teenage Brain*, Dan Siegel (2014) tells us that our limbic region responds to a neutral face as a threat perhaps because it hides true emotions. It responds far more positively to a smile, which immediately fires up our mirror neurons. Soussignan (2002) reported that a genuine smile is one in which we see crow's feet wrinkles around the eyes, and this triggers favorable autonomic responses in others. Research reported in the *European Journal of Social Psychology* (Reis et al., 2012) also found that people who smile are "attributed greater degrees of sincerity, sociability, and competence."

The first link below provides additional reasons for teachers to start and end every day with a smile. The second link is to Annette Breaux's response to the aforementioned article *Don't Smile 'til Christmas*. Breaux is also the author of *101 Answers for New Teachers and Their Mentors*. The third link explains how smiling benefits our own physical and mental health. All three articles are very persuasive, and they provide useful links to additional articles for creating positive connections with students.

The Power of a Teacher's Smile
http://teaching4achange.blogspot.com/2010/03/power-of-teachers-smile.html

Response: Don't Wait 'til Christmas to Smile
http://blogs.edweek.org/teachers/classroom_qa_with_larry_ferlazzo/2012/08/response_dont_wait_until_christmas_to_smile.html

Surprising Reasons Why You Should Smile More
http://inspiyr.com/9-benefits-of-smiling/

SOLER Non-Verbal Connections

Just as a simple statement ("Happy children learn") can be profound, past practices can still be our best practices today. The SOLER acronym was developed by Gerald Egan in 1986 to describe five key components of active listening (Musson, 2015). These are especially useful when approaching students who are presenting challenging behaviors. Although these practices have been taught for years in residential and other child-care settings, teachers are not generally familiar with them. Unfortunately, their apparent simplicity and our reliance on *talking through a problem* frequently lead to the minimization of such critical non-verbal approaches. They are critical because they help to slow down the dysregulated state as well as communicate that we are there to help the student, not fight them.

Egan used the acronym SOLER to classify the basic non-verbal behaviors that are best suited to begin de-escalating unwanted behavior. Each letter represents a specific non-verbal approach: Square; Open posture; Lean forward; Eye contact; and Relax.

Square to the Person

We engage with someone else by facing them, but directly face to face can be experienced as confrontational. Therefore, it is best to remain at slight angle while continually facing someone to show you are listening and interested in what they have to say. It is also important to maintain some distance, especially to someone who is dysregulated—an arm's length is usually sufficient. If you move in too close, the student will let you know through their behavior. With dysregulated students, there is always a chance that they will let you know *physically*. If they tell you to "Back off, get out of my face," do so, apologize, and ask if the new distance is okay. Finally, always approach the dysregulated student slowly and slightly to the side, rather than head on. This will be safer for both you and the student.

Open Posture

An open posture significantly increases positive feelings in others. It helps others feel more relaxed with us and encourages them to perceive us as someone who is relaxed with them. This is equated with a sense of safety, which is necessary to bring about a positive response. An open posture is one in which our feet are on the floor with toes pointing forward. Neither legs nor feet are crossed. We are looking toward the other person's face, and our palms are showing (as opposed to showing the backs of our hands, which is more of a closed position). Open palms signal that we are receptive or open to what others are saying.

Lean Forward

Most people are familiar with leaning forward while sitting to show that they are listening intently. Another slight but powerful gesture is to tilt the head slightly to one side. This tiny movement conveys that we are working hard to understand. It says, "Help me. Tell me more," and encourages students to share more details. Affirmative nods are also important, as they indicate that we are listening, interested, and agreeable.

Eye Contact

It is important to move our glance back and forth every few seconds, rather than stare intently. The student will not be aware we are doing this, yet they will feel more comfortable. By contrast, a stare can be experienced as invasive and threatening. Keep in mind that dysregulated students rarely look us in the eye, unless we have approached them too quickly or are invading their space. When this happens, they are likely to stare angrily, sending the message "Back off!" More often, though, they will look away, but at some point will quickly glance in our direction. If they do not see us looking at them at that moment, they will feel as if we are not concerned or interested, despite what we might say. Therefore, it is important to maintain focus on their facial area, so when they do take that glance, they see us looking their way.

Whenever possible, it is also important to remain at the student's eye level, as this is the safest position for them. Being forced to look up tends to trigger a fear response that can become confrontational. A concerned look, with eyebrows raised and making eye contact while leaning forward, conveys that we are truly interested.

Relax

To remain relaxed in confrontational situations, we must use what we have learned to regulate any anxiety that the student may trigger in us. If we are uncomfortable, the student will become more uncomfortable. Remember that what helps us to remain relaxed can also be used to co-regulate the student's reactions.

Non-Verbal Summary

Before connecting with dysregulated students, we should:

- Take a deep breath.
- Wait ninety seconds—the time it takes for sudden reactions to begin to subside.
- Remind yourself that . . . (insert a statement that works for you to keep you proactive).
- Know your calm facial expression.
- Approach slowly, unless the student or others are in danger.
- Stand/sit at eye level and at a slight angle.
- Do not stare. Briefly shift your focus from their eyes to another part of their face.
- Maintain an appropriate distance.
- Use a soft and low tone unless a loud voice is necessary to draw the student's attention to you.
- Attempt to engage the student in a sensory action as quickly as possible if the student is unresponsive to our initial verbal efforts to communicate and connect.

These non-verbal actions, coupled with a sensory action, will generally help students to regulate their reactions. However, it is important that we also respond immediately.

Responding Immediately

Ainsworth (1967) found that when parents or carers promptly and successfully responded to infants' cries, the infants cried less by the end of their first year than those who did not receive similar caring responses. **In brief, most infants (and students) quickly learn that the adults who expediently respond to them are reliable and safe.** To respond immediately, we need to be aware of the behaviors that students exhibit to tell us they need our attention. These include: agitated body; loud voice; breaching personal space; verbally teasing; accusing; blaming; interrupting; easily distracted; unable to sit; avoiding others; unable to stay on task; fidgeting; restless; appearing detached; and failing to respond to verbal cues. These can reflect fight-or-flight responses, hyper- or hypo-arousal, or sensory challenges, so regulation is necessary.

The first question is: what sensory intervention will be most helpful? Hopefully, as stated earlier in this chapter, we have already taken the time to be curious with the students, so we have some idea of what they find helpful. The second question is: what verbal effort will be most helpful?

Verbal Connections

Name It to Tame It

Whatever problem may have triggered a student's reactions, they become secondary to first connecting with the student about what their experience was like. If we try to go straight to problem-solving, we miss a wonderful opportunity to connect and better appreciate what they are struggling with, provide them additional time to regulate, and identify what might help them better regulate their reactions next time. Neuroscience researchers have found that when we help dysregulated students to name what they are experiencing or feeling, this activates the prefrontal cortex, the thinking brain, and helps to calm the dysregulated reactions. Siegel (2014) calls this process "Name it to tame it."

To accomplish this, we need to be curious. Helpful questions might include:

* What was it like when that was happening?
* What did your body feel like it wanted to do but could not?
* On a scale of one to ten, how bad was it?

Once we have assisted students with naming their sensation or feeling, we can try to determine what might be most helpful now as well as in the future. Helpful questions might include:

* Have you ever felt this bad before?
* What did you do then?
* Did it help or make it worse?
* What did others do for you that helped or made it worse.
* What do you wish someone had done to help you?
* Have you ever tried . . . (provide several sensory options)? We could practice a few of these to see which feels best for you. Would you like to do that? So next time you are struggling, you can try . . . If you are in class, I can help you until we find what works best.

It can be fun to practice expanding an emotions vocabulary. For instance, in one video, a four-year-old girl takes the lead in showing her mother a variety of feelings faces (www.youtube.com/watch?v=ZQDgEkooGTg& feature=youtu.be).

Several approaches may be used to help children identify their feelings as well as the gradations of each feeling. These are especially effective when integrated with paying close attention to the facial expressions that are associated with various feelings. This allows children to make connections at a cellular level, *mirroring* facial expressions with feelings, which in turns supports regulation. One such approach is Barb Dorrington's REST: Reading to Enhance Self-regulation Tasks (Dorrington, 2016). She explains the process in Box 5.1.

Box 5.1   REST: Reading to Enhance Self-Regulation Tasks—Taming the Feeling (by Barbara Dorrington)

Why is it that we connect so deeply when we watch other people? As humans, we respond to other people's facial expressions and body language. Some scientists refer to this as mirror neurons, the special circuitry in our brain that allows us to feel emotions in a similar way, whether we are doing something or simply watching something. Just think about how we get caught up in a sports game, or watching a movie.

We know that emotions matter and we often react to conflicts and upsets in typical and habitual ways. When we are happy, we tend to be wide-eyed, with the corners of our mouths raised in a smile. When we are angry, our eyes narrow and we have lowered eyebrows with clenched fists. We do this without thinking about it, because we are reacting with the lower part of our brain and are in fight/flight/freeze mode. It may only be later, when we are calm once again, that we think about other ways we might have responded.

REST, as a brain-based reading strategy for young children, allows any connected adult to teach an expansion of feelings vocabulary to children. Many young children can name the feelings of mad, sad, happy, and scared, but cannot name the gradations of these feelings, such as how mad might be furious in one instance but irritated in another. **Research shows that if we can name the feeling, we have a greater chance of taming that feeling.** Dan Siegel coined the "name it to tame it" phrase and notes that storytelling reaches both the analytical and creative sides of our brains. Reading together and using picture books which focus on a pair of cartoon-like characters, the adult encourages the child to think about the feelings of the characters, how we can tell what the characters are feeling, and to think about times that the child may have felt that way. With shared picture book reading, the child is able to act out the gestures and body postures of each character as well as the associated tone of voice without being in the "danger zone" of actually feeling that feeling. Children can practice how the eyebrows, eyes, and mouths should look and where the hands and arms should be placed to convey a certain feeling. It helps the child to think and imagine. We know that when children can be creative like this, they are calm and regulated. When children are aware of how their own bodies look, they more accurately interpret the emotions of others.

As part of REST, children love to create a feelings word list with the adult and to identify if the newly added feeling word is pleasant or not, and whether it requires higher or lower energy from the person. Many feelings lists are available on the internet to help the adult reader get started. Examples of helpful questions while book reading include:

- This is how this character is feeling. What might he be thinking?
- How does this character look right now? What are his eyebrows doing? What are his arms doing? How do you think he is feeling?
- His teeth are clenched. I wonder what that means …
- How would this other character be feeling right now? Sad? Could he possibly be worried? How would we know?
- I see that his eyebrows are pointed down. How can you tell when someone is sad?
- Do you think this character likes that? How can you tell?
- Can someone be mad and disappointed at the same time?
- Can you tell me a time when you felt happy?
- Show me your sad face. Look in the mirror at your eyebrows and your mouth. What are your hands and arms doing?

How can the adult reader help? Reading should always be a calm and connected activity. Children will invariably go off topic with the story. Embrace the child's unique contribution and make it work within the context of the reading. As with anything else, a child will pick up on the non-verbal cues of the adult reader's tone of voice and body language. It isn't important that the story gets finished; what is important is that the adult and child have fun practicing the feelings and enjoying the story and how the characters act. It is all about connection.

www.coachingtocalm.com

Sandwich Script It

Keep your comments reassuring and directed at the choices that are available to the student to self-regulate. State what you want clearly. For example, "I want to help. We need to try to figure this out. Before we do, though, can you first … [insert the choices the student has to regulate]." Teachers should become familiar with the "sandwich" technique.

A sandwich script begins with a positive statement, makes a request to correct the behavior, and ends with another positive statement. Before viewing the video below, ask yourself which single word diminishes the power of the following request: "I'm glad you are able to let me know you are upset, but you know that kind of language is not acceptable in our class. Please tell me what it is you need right now so we can solve this together."

The sandwich technique motivates students to do what we need them to do. Watch the following video to hear Dr. Susan Fletcher's advice on how to use the technique.

The Sandwich Technique
www.youtube.com/watch?v=WY3csVZvPk8

Only after students are able to regulate their reactions can we attempt to break down the problem that triggered those reactions and determine how to resolve and or prevent future issues with the same problem. This is discussed further in Chapter Six.

Connecting with Respect and Compassion

Words Matter

All of our interactions must be guided by respect and compassion. This is especially true with our verbal communication. Words do more than hurt. If heard frequently enough, as is often the case with traumatized children, they can lead to troubling behavior, impoverished relationships, attachment issues, poor grades, delayed or impaired socialization, depression, and a self-view that leaves children far more vulnerable to victimization.

Read each of the following statements slowly. Pause after each one, being mindful of the way it makes you feel, what it makes you think, and what it makes you want to do. Once you have gone through the list, sit quietly and pay attention to the cumulative effect.

- That's stupid.
- You can't be serious.
- That's silly.
- You can't mean what you are saying.
- You don't know anything.
- You'd better watch what you say.
- That mouth of yours . . .
- Be careful what you say.
- If you say any more, I'll . . .
- If you tell anyone, I'll . . .
- You said it. There is no taking it back.
- You don't know what you're talking about.
- That's ridiculous.
- Don't talk to me until you have something useful to say.
- It's better to be seen than heard.
- What am I supposed to do?
- Talk is cheap.

- Shut up. Speak only when you're spoken to.
- You are embarrassing yourself talking like that.
- You never make any sense.
- If you had any respect, you would know better than to talk like that.
- I don't want to know. I don't want to hear any more.
- You never get it right.
- Don't ask so many questions.
- Don't you dare say another word.
- You sound just like . . .
- Quit whining.
- If you were smart, you wouldn't open your mouth.
- Come and see me when you have something worthwhile to say.
- I don't care what you say, it doesn't change a thing.

Pause. Take a moment to think about the overall impact of these words on what you feel, think, and feel like doing. If this were your world . . .

- Would you keep talking?
- Would you dare raise your hand in class?
- Would you look for ways to be noticed?
- Would you think you had any value?
- Would you be angry but afraid to say anything?
- Would you try to find a way to hide your feelings of inadequacy?
- Would you trust the words of other adults?
- Would you wonder what's wrong with you?
- Would you find it hard to listen?
- Would you feel safe?

Living in an environment where these phrases are heard over and over again will do more than simply hurt a child. Learning is compromised in environments or cultures of disrespect. Even the best teacher–student relationships will find it difficult to flourish in such an environment. Environments that fail to nurture respect, including classrooms, experience arousal and as a result more frequent emotional brain-dominant responses (heightened survival responses). This limits access to the cognitive processes that are necessary for positive learning outcomes and regulation. This goes well beyond physical safety. Beyond a student knowing, (1) that their body is safe, they must know that (2) their feelings are safe, (3) their thoughts, ideas, and words are safe, and (4) their work—the things they make, the materials they use—is safe (Levine and Kline, 2008).

We do the greatest harm to students when we neglect numbers (2) and (3), and attack their feelings, thoughts, ideas, and words, even if such attacks are not always conscious. Irwin Hyman, former head of the School Psychology Division of the American Psychological Association, has documented how experiences in schools can create enduring trauma in many students (Hyman and Snook, 1999). He found that 60 percent of the most traumatic events reported by students were related to peer ridicule and mistreatment. But he was astounded to find that 40 percent of these destructive encounters were with school staff. For example, one student reported:

> One day in Spanish class, I told the teacher I was lost and didn't know what was going on; in reply he said, "There is a place for people like you to go and it's called the lost and found." The whole class laughed but to me it wasn't funny and I was embarrassed.
>
> (Brendtro, Mitchell, and McCall, 2009, p. 83)

Encouraging respect is best accomplished by anchoring our expectations of teachers' and students' non-verbal and verbal interactions to the four factors of safety mentioned above.

Spirit of Collaboration/Cooperation

Furthermore, it is important to conduct even brief connections within a spirit of collaboration and cooperation, as this reinforces the value of being connected to supportive others and teaches students that

- there are many different ways to accomplish something;
- others have ideas, experiences, and unique skills that benefit me;
- more can be accomplished together than alone; and
- I have value.

It is especially critical for teachers to embrace this practice of cooperation/collaboration, as it is directly related to teacher satisfaction, effectiveness, and retention (see Chapter Eight for more details).

What change did the new principal at one of the worst-performing schools in Kansas make with the teachers to turn the school into one of the best? In 2007, the incoming principal of Ware Elementary at Fort Riley brought the teachers together to work collaboratively in planning the best teaching approaches with each of their students. Prior to this, the teachers had been fairly isolated, doing the best they could on their own. The new principal altered the school schedule to accommodate time for teachers to meet collaboratively and "team" the needs of each student. By focusing on collaboration/cooperation, the entire school climate and culture changed. In subsequent years, this also became the focus/process for working with families and communities. Ware Elementary continues to "make a difference" to this day. Watch the video below to hear the school's story.

Kansas School Team Teaching Collaboration
www.youtube.com/watch?v=HVxRz5NOVt8

Collaboration leads to curiosity, which leads to discovery, which leads to practice and mastery. This holds true for students as well as teachers.

Teacher Compassion

Compassion runs through all we have discussed to this point—looking into and understanding the subjective world of anxious and traumatized students; reframing our thoughts about them and their ability to learn; becoming attuned to them; and attending to their various needs in order to encourage positive connections that are conducive to learning and regulation. Compassion is directly related to teacher effectiveness and student outcomes.

Principal Kafele—recipient of the National Alliance of Black School Educators' Hall of Fame Award, the New Jersey Education Association's Award of Excellence and the prestigious Milken National Educator Award—believes that student skills and outcomes are directly related to care, compassion, and the connections teachers make with their students. He has demonstrated this repeatedly. As an elementary teacher in East Orange, NJ, he was selected as the East Orange School District and Essex County Public Schools' Teacher of the Year. As a middle and high school principal, he led the transformation of four different schools in urban New Jersey, including "The Mighty" Newark Tech, which went from a low-performing school in need of improvement to national acclaim (*US News and World Report* magazine hailed it as one of America's best high schools). Listen to what he has to say about compassion in the video below. You are also encouraged to read Chapter Ten, which focuses on how to create a compassionate school.

Care and Compassion Determine Student Outcomes! Message to a Teacher
www.youtube.com/watch?v=WERHEEujpIs

Compassionate teachers give students value and empowerment. This is translated into a reduction in emotional dominance, while promoting the eagerness and capacity to learn. In turn, this translates into improved academic outcomes. However, sustaining this compassion is essential to student outcomes and to teachers' good physical and mental health, their viability, and their value to students. Should our compassion begin to diminish, this leads not only to adverse reactions from students but to adverse consequences in our professional and personal lives. Remaining compassionate demands consistent self-care. See Chapter Seven for details of how this can be maintained.

Summary

This chapter has explained that even brief connections matter because they help students achieve optimal learning outcomes and regulation of behavior. Making these connections can be challenging and stressful, yet it is well worth making the effort. Simply doing so tells students we care. Using the strategies outlined in this chapter and throughout the rest of this resource will make a difference for you and your students.

Now that we have learned how to help students regulate their reactions to the stress, anxiety, trauma, and/or sensory challenges they experience, accomplishing this through the ways we connect and interact with them, they will be better able to engage in the cognitive processes that are needed for optimal learning experiences. The next chapter examines growth mindsets for learning—those cognitive thought processes that support the sustained motivation to learn and the practices that help improve the ways in which students learn.

References

Ahnert, L., Milatz, A., Kappler, G., Schneiderwind, J., and Fischer, R. (2013). The impact of teacher–child relationships on child cognitive performance as explored by a priming paradigm. *Developmental Psychology*, 49(3), 554–567.

Ainsworth, M. D. S. (1967). *Infancy in Uganda: Infant Care and the Growth of Attachment*. Baltimore, MD: Johns Hopkins University Press.

Brendtro, L., Mitchell, M., and McCall, H. (2009). *Deep Brain Learning: Pathways to Potential with Challenging Youth*. Albion, MI: Starr Commonwealth.

Cathcart, B. (2012). Early prevention in childhood anxiety disorder. *American Journal of Psychiatry*, 167, 1428–1430.

Collins, D. (2009). *Essentials of Business Ethics: Creating an Organization of High Integrity and Superior Performance*. New York: John Wiley & Sons.

Connors, R., and Smith, T. (2009). *How Did That Happen? Holding People Accountable for Results the Positive, Principled Way*. New York: Penguin Group.

Detweiler, A. (2016) *Surprising Reasons Why You Should Smile More*. Retrieved March 6, 2016 from http://inspiyr.com/9-benefits-of-smiling/.

Dewar, G. (2016). *Student–Teacher Relationships: The Overlooked Ingredient for Success*. Retrieved March 5, 2016 from www.parentingscience.com/student-teacher-relationships.html.

Dorrington, B. (2016). *REST*. Retrieved March 22, 2016 from www.coachingtocalm. com/overview-of-services.html .

Goldenberg, H., and Goldenberg, I. (2013). *Family Therapy: An Overview*. Belmont, CA: Brooks/Cole.

Gregory, A., and Weinstein, R. S. (2004). Connection and regulation at home and in school: Predicting growth in achievement for adolescents. *Journal of Adolescent Research*, 19(4), 405–427.

Hall, N., Dip, C., Kulkami, C., and Seneca, S. (2008). *Your Guide to Nurturing Parent–Child Relationships: Positive Parenting Activities for Home Visitors*. Baltimore, MD: Brookes Publishing Co.

Hughes, R. (2009). Attachment focused treatment for children. In M. Kerman (Ed.), *Clinical Pearls of Wisdom*, pp. 169–181. New York: Norton.

Hyman, I. A., and Snook, P. A. (1999). *Dangerous Schools: What We Can Do about the Physical and Emotional Abuse of Our Children*. San Francisco, CA: Jossey-Bass.

Levine, P., and Kline, M. (2008). *Trauma Proofing Your Kids*. Berkeley, CA: North Atlantic Books.

McGonigal, K. (2011). *What Does Compassion Look Like?* Retrieved March 10, 2015 from www.psychologytoday.com/blog/the-science-willpower/201111/what-does-compassion-look.

Mielke, C. (2015). *Don't Smile 'til Christmas: A Teacher's Worst Advice.* Retrieved March 5, 2016 from www.weareteachers.com/blogs/post/2015/04/15/don't-smile-'til-christmas-a-teacher's-worst-advice.

Musson, J. (2015). *Copy of Egan's SOLER Principles.* Retrieved September 30, 2016 from https://prezi.com/cxqj6cwh7uv7/copy-of-egans-soler-principles/.

Pattison Professional Counseling and Mediation Center (2016). *How to Break through in Your Relationships: The Secret of the Two Ts.* Retrieved January 5, 2016 from www.ppccfl. com/how-to-break-through-in-your-relationships-the-secret-of-the-two-ts/.

Ramachandran, V. (2011). *The Tell-Tale Brain: A Neuroscientist's Quest for What Makes Us Human.* New York: W. W. Norton & Company.

Reis, T. et al. (2012). *What Is Smiling Is Beautiful and Good.* Retrieved March 5, 2016 from http://onlinelibrary.wiley.com/doi/10.1002/ejsp.2420200307/abstract;jsessionid=043CB0220B92F7DC323E561860FC225A.f04t04.

Shelden, D., Angell, M., Stoner, J., and Roseland, B. (2010). School principal's influence on trust: Perspectives of mothers of children with disabilities. *Journal of Educational Research,* 103, 159–170.

Siegel, D. (2014). *Brainstorm: The Power and Purpose of the Teenage Brain.* New York: Penguin.

Soussignan, R. (2002). Duchenne smile, emotional experience, and autonomic reactivity: A test of the facial feedback hypothesis. *Emotion,* 2(1), 52–74.

Steele, W., and Malchiodi, M. (2012). *Trauma Informed Practices for Children and Adolescents.* New York. Routledge.

TLC Focus (2013). *Reframing Children's Behaviors.* Retrieved March 5, 2016 from www. starr.org/tlc.

Wassmer, A. (1978). *Making Contact.* New York: Dial Press.

6 Growth Mindsets for Learning

Effective Effort

Emily Diehl

As the Director of Professional Learning and Curriculum Design for Mindset Works®, I have the privilege of meeting with educators across the country. With sixteen years' experience in K–12 schools as a teacher and later as an instructional coach, I was constantly looking for ways to motivate my students to learn. The educators I work with today have the same "tell me more" response I had years ago, when first introduced to Carol Dweck's work on mindsets. It made a significant difference to the way I taught and related to my students, and the outcomes continue to be amazing. Students who move from fixed mindsets about learning to growth mindsets show greater motivation for learning, better grades, and higher test scores.

Carol Dweck, a psychologist and Stanford University professor, developed the concept of a growth mindset. Her work has had a far-reaching impact on students and teachers worldwide. What students and teachers think about learning, intelligence, and their own abilities has a significant effect on their learning progress and academic improvement. Dweck's research has shown that moving from a fixed mindset response to a growth mindset response helps teachers become more effective and students more successful in their learning environments. That certainly has been my experience with the schools and teachers I work with and learn from for the purpose of creating growth mindset schools, classrooms, and students.

In Chapter One you read about the significant learning outcomes resulting from just one growth mindset (Dweck, 2006). Students who were praised for their effort outperformed those who were praised for their intelligence. If you did not view *A Study on Praise and Mindset* (www.youtube.com/watch?v =NWv1VdDeoRY) earlier, watch it now.

Learning mindsets matter. Yeager and colleagues (2013) found that low-achieving students at thirteen California high schools failed 7 percent fewer courses and improved their GPAs by .18 grade points after a one-period class designed to boost growth mindset. Blackwell and colleagues (2007) found that when a group of struggling seventh grade students in New York City (1) learned to think of their brains as muscles that grow with exercise, and (2) visualized new connections developing within their brains, their motivation and math scores improved at a time when math achievement typically declines (during adolescent transition). Mindsets matter. Unfortunately, students often respond to academic challenges with a fixed mindset ("I cannot learn to do this"). And many educators do the same.

What Is a Growth Mindset?

A growth mindset is an incremental view of intelligence. It is the core belief that we can grow, get better, and improve in a real way in whatever it is we are learning or striving to do. Growth mindsets are not inherent; they need to be taught and reinforced through our responses to students' efforts, and to their fears about failing, not being perfect, and not living up to expectations. These fears are the result of fixed mindset responses that are often triggered by our focus on learning outcomes versus learning processes. For example, the fixed mindset says, "Smart people succeed." Therefore, "if you succeed, you're a smart person. Therefore, pick the easier problem so success is more likely, and you validate your smartness. Pick a hard problem and you may fail, revealing your stupidity" (Vermer, 2012). To cultivate a growth mindset, it is important to focus on effort. For example, the growth mindset says, "People can get smarter and do so by stretching themselves and taking on challenges." Therefore, "pick the hard problem—who cares if you fail!" (Vermer, 2012). Utilizing and sustaining effective effort produces desired results for students at that moment and well into the future. Again, I refer to the long-term outcomes in the *Study on Praise and Mindset* presented in Chapter One.

A number of links to invaluable tools for creating and sustaining growth mindsets are provided in this chapter. I believe you will be curious to learn more if you do nothing other than follow the links and look at these tools. They will be discussed briefly for the purpose of translating theory into practice so that you can cultivate growth mindsets in your students.

A core concept of a growth mindset is that *effective effort* pays amazing learning dividends for students and teachers alike. The key word here is "effective." Many students have no real awareness of what effective effort is and how it works. Moreover, many teachers have never been taught how to interact with students in ways that build and sustain the effective effort that will serve students well into their adult lives as they are presented with an increasing number of challenges. For this reason, the majority of this chapter will discuss effective effort—what it is and what it is not, the strategies that cultivate such effort, and the improved learning outcomes students experience when they learn how to use their effort effectively. First, though, I shall briefly discuss fixed mindsets versus growth mindsets.

Fixed Mindsets and Growth Mindsets

BELIEFS → BEHAVIORS → RESULTS

Learners' beliefs regarding intelligence are shaped by their experiences at home and at school. We all have some fixed beliefs about learning, and some of us still harbor the old belief that our capacity to learn is somehow predetermined and fixed. However, research into neuroplasticity (see Chapter One) has confirmed that our brains continue to develop and learn throughout our lives. Both cognitive psychology and neuroscience confirm what research into developing growth mindsets demonstrates—that intelligence, learning capacity, and performance are malleable.

What, then, are the principal differences between fixed beliefs (or mindsets) about learning and growth mindsets, and how do they influence behavior and outcomes? The video below compares growth mindsets with fixed mindsets.

Growth versus Fixed Mindsets
www.youtube.com/watch?v=brpkjT9m2Oo

A fixed mindset response to challenge impedes learning outcomes and the motivation to learn, whereas a growth mindset response allows students to reach higher, achieve more, and remain motivated to learn, even when solutions are not immediately available. This has been confirmed at the neurological level. So we see that a fixed mindset response to challenge impedes learning outcomes and the motivation to learn compared to a growth mindset response, which allows students to reach higher, achieve more, and remain motivated to learn, even when solutions are not immediately available.

Cultivating Student Effort

We cultivate student effort by defining what "try" means, by utilizing the *Effective Effort Rubric* and *Growth Mindset Framing* (see links below), and by recognizing what triggers a fixed mindset. The limits of space preclude a comprehensive discussion of these processes and their associated tools, but a brief overview is provided below.

Define What "Try" Means

At the most basic level, effort means you are trying. In my experience, though, students always claim that they are trying, and they may even believe that they are, but they are unaware of the behaviors that are associated with *effective* effort or what trying effectively truly entails. For too many students, trying is merely obtaining answers from a friend or the internet. For example, many students have a hard time understanding the difference between doing math and copying someone else's math, or between helping someone with a task and just giving them the answer. They think they did their homework even though they copied most of it directly from the board or from a friend. To these students, I say: "What you did is like tracing a picture. You traced your homework. You didn't 'do' it."

I had this problem with my own children when I signed them up for a swim team. My children had less experience than the other children on the team, who had all been swimming for several years. I told my children, "You aren't going to win any races this year. You won't win anything. Those kids have been swimming for five years, and this is your first year, so you're not going to win. But that is okay, because you're going to learn how to swim and it'll be fun."

Everyone thought I was a mean mom, right? But then we went to the first swim meet, and guess what happened? They gave my children ribbons, even though they didn't win a single race. My children started laughing and said, "Ha, Mom, look! You said we wouldn't win anything, but we did." I was disappointed. I didn't want the organizers to hand out the ribbons, because my kids hadn't earned them. If the ribbons had said "Participant," that would have been fine. Better yet, if they had earned the ribbons for improving their times—in other words, if their effort had been rewarded—I would have been delighted. But instead they learned that they don't have to put in any effort to receive a reward. Many of today's students give up when they do not succeed right away at a learning challenge because they have never learned the value of—and what constitutes—effective effort. We really need to have this discussion with students because it is at the core of successful learning. It is also the foundation for overcoming the challenges they will face as adults.

Sometimes students don't really try because of a fixed mindset. They remember a time in the past when they tried, using the strategies they had available, but did not improve. So why put in the effort now? A new challenge can create immediate fears about failing. If they have a fixed mindset response to failure or to lacking the skills to compete with other students, they give up easily and avoid the challenge. To overcome this fixed mindset response, they need growth mindset encouragement via growth mindset feedback. For example, you might say, "Of course it's tough. School is meant to make our brains stronger, so let's break down what you tried so we can see what we need to change," or, "Tell me what was difficult for you. Once I know that, we can fix it."

Engaging in Effective Effort

Effective effort is purposeful and targeted. It's focused and metacognitive. When I am trying effectively, I am doing *a lot*! I pause and think quietly. I problem-solve. I research. I tinker. I figure out what isn't working and change my strategy. I furrow my brow. And I don't stop until I've figured it out. Then I feel amazing!

How, then, do growth mindsets support effective effort? The document below identifies specific learning processes and then compares the responses with fixed, mixed, and growth mindsets. It provides an excellent description of effective effort for each learning process and the outcomes of that effective effort.

> *Effective Effort Rubric*
> www.mindsetworks.com/websitemedia/resources/effort-rubric-for-students.pdf

Who Needs Effective Effort Training?

We can teach people how to employ effective effort. Ever more schools are coming to understand that there is a place in our classrooms for this direct instruction, and for using the tools that are available to support students' adoption of effective effort strategies and practices. Many teachers have already found ways to provide guidance and instruction in effective effort. Unfortunately, more attention is still paid to meeting set standards and testing. However, if we don't support these academic mindsets and learning strategies, many students will not learn to be effective learners, so they will ultimately become adults who continue to struggle.

The link below identifies the four key beliefs or mindsets that influence learning success, student motivation to learn, strategies, and the perseverance (regulation) needed to complete learning challenges.

> *Academic Mindsets for Learner Success*
> www.mindsetworks.com/go/academic-mindsets/

Mindset Works® consultant Jennifer Maichin, an educator in Mineola, NY, asks, "We tell students to study, but do we teach them how?" Students spend much of their homework time thinking about how frustrated they are, and doing more of what's not working, instead of engaging actively with their tasks. Partly this is due to the fact that many of them know that they can simply copy answers from the board, from a friend, from the pages of a book, or from the internet. Hence, they usually do not have effective effort strategies for those times when copying is not an option.

To determine if kids have effective learning strategies, Maichin suggests watching what they do when they don't know an answer. If they give up, choose easy or superficial responses, or resort to copying, then they do not have the growth mindsets, strategies, and drive (motivation/regulation skills) to achieve on their own. With our help and through the use of growth mindset processes, they need to experience how great it feels to discover answers for themselves and learn through effort. Unfortunately, though, to make our kids feel good, we reward them in ways that do not encourage them to engage in efforts to achieve.

Getting Started: Strategies to Teach Effective Effort

First, we have to define what effective effort is and convince learners how amazing it feels to use it to achieve something for themselves. Second, we have to be persistent and effortful ourselves in cultivating these learning strategies in our students. Two strategies to get you started are outlined below.

The Mindset Works® Effective Effort Rubric

The *Effective Effort Rubric* (see link above) is a terrific place to begin the conversation with students. The rubric places effort in the context of a growth mindset and defines explicitly what we mean when we say, "Try harder." Presenting it to a learner, a teacher might ask, "When you are trying, which of these things are you doing? Highlight in each box what trying 'looks like' for you."

Teachers can also use the rubric with families who are struggling to help their children finish their homework and complete long-term tasks. The parents can learn how to communicate the message that challenges are exciting, mistakes tell us what we need to improve, and setbacks are normal parts of learning anything new.

The rubric is also a tool for setting growth goals. Students can revisit it to identify an area in which they would like to improve, and continue to use it over time to assess their progress.

As you begin to use the rubric, the class can begin to discuss the "strategies" and how to share and acquire new ones that work for them. Asking, "What do you do when you get stuck?" and encouraging the students to share is one way to shed light on the difference between sharing strategies and answers. This helps them to realize how many strategies are available, what did and what did not work, how one strategy may work for one student but not for others, and that a strategy that failed to work for a specific challenge may be more useful for another.

Trying Hard in Your Context

Additionally, you can work with your class or professional team to define what working hard means in your context. Your context might be a content-area classroom, a professional learning community, a third grade classroom, a team of administrators; the options are endless. You need to define the daily behaviors you will agree to learn, and then practice to improve them. These behaviors must be things your team feels will help them to meet their designated goal(s) effectively.

In an elementary school in Massachusetts, a fifth grade teacher wanted to define what it meant to try in band practice. She agreed with her students that they had to do a number of things in order to learn a middle school level piece:

- Isolate the tricky bits.
- Practice carefully, so they don't learn it wrong.
- Don't practice the whole piece at once.
- Use a metronome (a tool) every time.
- Listen to the piece and follow their individual parts.

- Take a moment to mark missed notes and beats.
- Go slowly.

This list is a useful framework or outline of effort for pursuing any learning task.

Growth Mindset Languages and Messages

Educators can have an enormous influence on students' motivation simply through the messages they communicate. It is best to begin growth mindset classroom transformation by utilizing messages and the language that is used with students to communicate accepting challenges and working persistently to learn new concepts and skills. The link below presents numerous mindset statements for introducing a new concept, topic, skill, or class assignment. These statements embody the key elements that develop student motivation to learn and not to fear challenges. One of my favorites is: "After we do this, I am going to ask you all to share one mistake you made so we can all learn from it." The mindset established in this process is that mistakes are gifts to treasure, because they teach us what does not work and highlight that it is time to look for another strategy.

Growth Mindset Framing
www.mindsetworks.com/websitemedia/resources/growth-mindset-framing-tool.pdf

---

This tool shows educators how to adjust their messages in order to cultivate growth mindsets. It helps teachers to communicate learning goals and high expectations. When students are not being effectively effortful, the statements can steer them back onto the right track. Other messages about paying attention to and learning from errors, about learning and being inspired by successful peers, and about setting stretch goals can also be highly effective in helping young people appreciate how great it feels to accomplish something difficult. The *Growth Mindset Feedback* tool (see link below) provides numerous statements that will help students who are struggling despite their best efforts, when they need alternative strategies, when they are making progress, and when they have succeeded through strong effort (or with little effort).

Growth Mindset Feedback
www.mindsetworks.com/websitemedia/resources/growth-mindset-feedback-tool.pdf

---

We can all support one another by being transparent about our efforts and sharing our stories of effort. Tell your students and colleagues about a time when you did something difficult that you weren't sure you could do. Legitimize effort. Admit you aren't "a natural." You did not just wake up this way. These trust-building conversations will have several effects. First, they will inspire others to try new strategies in order to achieve ambitious goals. Second, they will allow students the precious self-reflective time we all need to reinforce the choices that work and identify those that do not reflect effective effort. Finally, they remove shame from the conversation about having to try really hard to achieve something significant. That is perhaps the greatest gift we can give each other.

Recognize Your Triggers, and Help Students to Do So Too

What triggers a fixed mindset response? Everyone is different. For some, it's when things get harder than they thought. For others, it might be when someone else does well. Carol Dweck talks about several triggers that commonly cause students to back away from trying to meet the learning goals they have been set.

Trigger: Stepping Outside of Your Comfort Zone

One trigger is stepping outside of a comfort zone. When we are outside our comfort zone, we have to work harder and use more effort than when we are doing something familiar. When we, or our students, step outside our comfort zone, we must abandon the belief that we must look smart and capable at all times, and accept that we are in a learning zone. So, of course, we won't be perfect right away. We have to remind ourselves and students that we are not a natural at this, but that is okay; and that our performances, while in a learning zone, do not define us. In schools, we can use self-reflection and goal-setting to help students improve at this. Reflective prompts help them analyze how far outside of their comfort zones they are, and whether they are truly lost or just a little disoriented. The prompts listed below can communicate how to develop behaviors that reflect a growth mindset. They can also give educators "just-in-time" insights into the current thinking of each learner.

1. How difficult was this task for you? What did you do when the task became difficult?
2. Which strategies did you use to meet your goal? Were any of them new?
3. What worked for you in this case that you might want to use in some other area of your life?
4. What did not work or is not working? Why do you think it failed?
5. What do you need to help with this that you are not getting at the moment?

Taking the time to pause and reflect should not be seen as lost time. It ignites learning and self-awareness that involves the learner in his or her own process. It is another way to help students integrate a growth mindset into their everyday thoughts about and responses to learning challenges.

Trigger: Experiencing a Setback

When young people experience setbacks, they worry that these issues are unique to them. They worry they are happening because they simply don't have what it takes to succeed. This trigger can cause them to give up on themselves early in the learning process. It can even cause them to quit on things in which they have previously excelled.

How do we help students to deal with setbacks in a productive way? First, it is helpful to communicate that setbacks are normal. Students need to hear that other people have struggled with similar challenges yet continued their effort to find new strategies that led to success. The students can do the same. Share your own setback stories or show students the *Famous Failures* video (see link below). Walt Disney was once bankrupt. Abraham Lincoln suffered from depression. Oprah Winfrey was told she would never make it on television. All of these stories help to debunk the "natural talent" myth and normalize challenges and setbacks.

Famous Failures
www.youtube.com/watch?v=zLYECIjmnQs

In order to have this conversation, there has to be some acknowledgment and admission of failure. When a student has a setback, normalize it. For example, explain that "The definition of learning is discovering what does not work as much as what does work." We take the shame out of setbacks by normalizing them and helping students process them so they can learn. Ask them if they want to talk about their failure. Ask them what they learned from it. Let them know that you would like to learn from their experience and pass it on to others. Provide reflective activities in which students can think about a recent setback, how they responded to it, and what they might do differently in the future. My favorite failure response to a setback is: "I made a big mistake or met a challenge I didn't know how to handle. I am so glad I made it, because now I know I need to . . ."

Trigger: Transition from Familiar to Unfamiliar Territory

A transition always involves the unknown. It can create a context ripe with the two previous triggers. Transitions can take students outside their comfort zone. The fear or fixed mindset says, "If I am new to something, I won't be good at it right away; and depending on how others react to my success, I might be inclined to give up." So, how do we help students to thrive during a transition? We again normalize a transition as something that can be challenging and may not work out immediately, but that is okay because it gives us an opportunity to learn more. Carol Dweck (2013) suggests communicating to students that we expect them to have a transitional period when they will not be perfect and that we value process and learning, not perfection.

Providing time for reflection about what a person is learning during a transition normalizes it and communicates an expectation that they should be learning something right now. If they are not, perhaps they need an additional challenge. We can assist with the reflection process by asking:

- What is challenging you today? What are you doing about it?
- What might be challenging for you today? What makes it challenging?
- What strategy or strategies are working for you right now?
- What has surprised you in the past week? How did it differ from what you expected?
- Identify a recent mistake you made? How did you deal with it? What did it teach you? What will you do the same or differently in the future?

This process also provides an opportunity to use the feedback statements cited earlier to help motivate students to continue their effort. For example, "We can always fix mistakes once we know what they were. Let's see how this will make you smarter."

Educators with a Growth Mindset

To be effective educators, we must work each day to choose our own growth mindset responses, so we can remove the notion of shame from the process of trying and failing for students. For example, students who fail at a challenge need to hear, "It's okay to be the kind of person who wants to improve. It's normal not to be perfect, not to get it right at the very first try (or sometimes even the second or third try). Just remember that you are learning more with every effort." We, as educators, need to believe in as well as practice this mindset. It is the practice that often suffers as teachers are pushed to attain immediate success from students and feel as if they have little time to process outcomes with students who fail first time around. This, in turn, communicates a very fixed mindset to the students: "If I don't get it right the first time, I will get no help, no second chance. So why even try?"

One way to support students' efforts to learn is to use "think-alouds." For example, "You know what I am feeling right now? I am worried about not knowing the answers as quickly as some of you want me to have them. It's making me nervous. Has anyone else felt this way when someone else has needed their help?" This process can relieve the pressure students might be experiencing to get everything right immediately. We learned in earlier chapters that our thinking brains do not work well when they are under stress. This process assists with self-regulation, allowing our students to engage their thinking brains. Indirectly, it reinforces the mindset that being smart is not about getting everything right immediately. It is about stretching ourselves and accepting challenges, even when we worry we might fail.

When students are given time to reflect on their efforts, it is good practice for teachers to use that time to reflect on their efforts, too. That moment or two will help both body and brain slow down just enough to allow us to focus on what mindset we want to communicate or share with students to help them when they are struggling.

Growth Mindsets: Educator–Student Resilience

To cultivate a school environment in which students learn resilience, have grit, and are engaged in learning, we must also consider whether the adults in the school model those same behaviors. How often do students witness an educator's negative response to having a bad day? How often do they notice when an adult handles a conflict well? Students see examples every day of what it means to be a resilient adult. Educators can and should implicitly and explicitly teach these skills so their students have a chance to develop a similar level of resilience and grit (Tough, 2012).

In several schools where I work as an instructional coach, we have taken on the challenge of creating a system-wide approach to supporting student resilience. These schools are building on the work of Dweck's *Mindset* (2006) and Daniel Coyle's *The Talent Code* (2009) to teach the students strategies for resilience and remaining growth minded. However, we soon realized that our own mindsets had to change if we were to help the students change theirs. We came to a conclusion that modeling grit and teaching effective effort throughout the school would give us the best chance to encourage drastic, positive changes among the students. The next step was to think about which of our mindsets, behaviors, words, and practices fostered effective effort, and which hindered it.

Once we had the two lists, we used Dweck's *Mindset* to transform our feedback and comments into language that would promote the growth mindsets associated with resilience. For example, "You may not be adept at this yet, but I am confident that you can master it with a bit more practice" and "Other students have struggled and mastered this; you can, too." As Dweck (2010) says, "Even geniuses work hard!"

Ultimately, all educators want their students to view challenges as exciting. It is in the stretch and the struggle that we grow. How else can students learn those lessons, if not from the adults in their lives? My colleagues and I used self-reflection to model how we take large challenges and break them down into smaller components that we can grapple with and eventually overcome. We reminded ourselves that a struggle does not mean that we are the wrong person for the task, skill, or experience. All it means is that we have an opportunity to grow, and we have to strive to be great at something, so why not go for it? We asked ourselves three questions:

- How do we respond to setbacks and talk about our failures?
- Where can we improve?
- Would using the language that Carol Dweck recommends for students work for us, too? If so, what might be the effective effort?

It is through us that students develop the mindset that resilience is something they can cultivate.

The effect in these schools has been striking. At Florin High School in Sacramento, California, where we applied mindset concepts and processes with the lowest-performing ninth and tenth graders, test scores on the California Standards Test rose 32 points for those students.

What a grand lesson that we continue to have an enormous influence on students and can affect them in positive ways by being the role model that we know we can be. When students see us model the behaviors we ask from them, we build trust and open the door to sincere relationships. In the meta-analyses discussed in John Hattie's groundbreaking book *Visible Learning* (2008), he identifies teacher–student relationships as having a staggeringly positive effect size of 0.72. When we use the language of growth mindsets and display their associated behaviors and processes, we can connect with the students in ways that allow us to have a more positive influence on them in many realms . . . even algebra! For example, in a study of adolescents, those who received growth mindset training outperformed counterparts who received other forms of training in both math and verbal achievement (Good, Aronson, and Inzlicht, 2003).

In Chapter One we saw how a participant's mindset can alter their biological response when drinking a milkshake. Mindsets matter, especially in education. Carol Dweck has studied, researched, and written extensively on how growth mindsets improve students' motivation to learn, their learning outcomes (including achieving better grades and test scores), and, indirectly, their regulation of their efforts. In a TEDx talk, *The Power of Believing You Can Improve*, Dweck discusses the remarkable successes of several growth mindset classrooms, including a kindergarten class in Harlem, New York (see link below). After just one year, the Harlem class scored in the ninety-fifth percentile on the National Achievement Tests. The twelve-minute video is well worth watching as it expands on the research, power, and value of effective effort.

The Power of Believing You Can Improve
www.ted.com/talks/carol_dweck_the_power_of_believing_that_you_can_improve?language=en

---

This Is a Journey

While there are several clear strategies we can initiate to cultivate growth mindsets in classrooms, it is not a linear path. There is a framework, and there are abundant tools, yet, as we read in earlier chapters, every school, every classroom, has its own personality, so we need to be flexible, not fixed, in our approach to bringing growth mindsets to our students and to ourselves. There must be a paradigm shift in how we think about learning, achievement, success/failure, and, most importantly, what we communicate to our students about learning and success. We should expect to trip up more than once as we make this transition. But that is okay because in the effort we become better and more comfortable in this exciting and rewarding journey outside our comfort zone.

Our effectiveness in all we attempt to accomplish certainly depends on our own mindsets, especially those related to our self-care and its relationship to sustained performance and resilience in the face of daily challenges and the stress they create. The next chapter presents a somewhat different approach to self-care, based on what neuroscience is teaching us about how to navigate through today's extremely stimulating world.

References

Blackwell, L. Trzesniewski, K., and Dweck, C. (2007). Implicit theories of intelligence predict achievement across an adolescent transition: A longitudinal study and an intervention. *Child Development*, 78(1), 246–263.

Coyle, D. (2009). *The Talent Code: Greatness Isn't Born, It's Grown: Here's How*. New York: Bantam Books.

Dweck, C. S. (2006). *Mindset: The New Psychology of Success*. New York: Ballantine Books.

Dweck, C. S. (2010). Even geniuses work hard. *Educational Leadership*, 68(1), 16–20.

Dweck, C. S. (2013). *The Right Mindset for Success*. Retrieved February 15, 2016 from https://hbr.org/2012/01/the-right-mindset-for-success/.

Good, C., Aronson, J., and Inzlicht, M. (2003). Improving adolescents' standardized test performance: An intervention to reduce the effects of stereotype threat. *Applied Developmental Psychology*, 24, 645–662.

Hattie, J. (2008). *Visible Learning: A Synthesis of over 800 Meta-Analyses Relating to Achievement*. New York: Routledge.

Ramsden, S., Richardson, F. M., Josse, G., Thomas, M., Ellis, C., Shakeshart, C., Seguier, M., and Price, C. (2011). Verbal and non-verbal intelligence changes in the teenage brain. *Nature*, 479, 113–116.

Tough, P. (2012). *How Children Succeed: Grit, Curiosity, and the Hidden Power of Character*. New York: Mariner Books.

Vermer, A. (2012). *Mindset by Carol Dweck: Summary*. Retrieved February 15, 2015 from https://alexvermeer.com/why-your-mindset-important/.

Yeager, D. S., Walton, G., and Cohen, G. L. (2013). Addressing achievement gaps with psychological interventions. *Phi Delta Kappan*, 94, 62–65.

7   Teacher Resilience, Sustained Effectiveness, and Self-Care

William Steele

Given what neuroscience teaches us about the effects of stress on our nervous system, our emotions, cognitive functioning, and behaviors, it could be argued that this chapter should have been positioned at the beginning of this resource. Working with anxious and traumatized students undoubtedly places added stress on teachers in an environment that is, by its nature, stressful. The rationale for positioning this chapter here is that the information provided throughout the resource provides a stronger argument for the importance of self-care as it relates to resilience, sustained effectiveness, and the optimization of the learning experience for students. It is well established that the most resilient and effective teachers are those who themselves are regulated and engage in practices that help them manage the stressors they face every day. Teachers who practice self-regulation/self-care are also far more consistently proactive than reactive to the challenges that students and our educational system present.

This book's Introduction begins, "These are extraordinary times." There is nothing ordinary about the twenty-first century, and nor will this be an ordinary discussion about stress and self-care. Reports (Neason, 2014; Hill, 2008) indicate that half of all new teachers leave the profession within five years. Stress and lack of support are cited as the primary reasons for poor retention and teacher dissatisfaction. Although some dispute the above statistic, teaching consistently ranks in the top four most stressful professions (ABC News, 2015). This is such an important element of teacher effectiveness and retention that we discuss it further in the final chapter.

Over the past thirty years, it has been my experience that all helping professionals, including educators, do poorly when it comes to self-care. This is not because we are unaware of the daily stressors in our lives; indeed, we are all too aware of them. For example, when asked, educators can effortlessly cite a dozen common stressors, such as:

- Inconsistent applications of rules and procedures.
- Rigid versus flexible leadership.
- Limited resources.
- Overcrowded classrooms.
- Lack of funding.

- Abundant paperwork.
- Limited parental support.
- Little collaboration.
- Too little time.
- Too many deadlines.
- Increases in anxious and traumatized students presenting with learning challenges and behaviors that very few of them have been prepared to manage.
- Increased safety concerns. (As an aside, I recall talking with several New York educators in lower Manhattan following September 11, 2001. One principal said, "I always knew I was responsible for my students' education. I never thought I would be responsible for their lives." Unfortunately, following the deadly massacre of twenty young students and six staff at Sandy Hook Elementary on December 14, 2012, and other student shootings since, the concerns and stress related to safety remain high.)
- Major curriculum shifts in federally mandated programs, such as Common Core, and the Every Student Achieves Act (ESSA) generate a good deal of stress.

Also consider that the many educators who are also parents face ongoing stress when they return home from a day of teaching as they try to respond to and meet the needs of their children well into the evening hours.

Slow to Embrace

Simply being aware of the stressors that we face every day does not translate into preventative self-care. Why is this? As an educated group, we tend to believe that we should be able to withstand the effects of stress. But this counterproductive mindset works against us, for the following reasons:

1. We are reluctant to let peers know of our stress because we fear that our professional competence will be questioned. Unfortunately, sometimes this fear is well founded. Telling your boss, your supervisor, or even your peers that you are having a hard time dealing with the stress of the job can change the way they think about you and your competence.
2. We become fearful of acknowledging the impact stress may be having on us because it raises the question, "Should I be doing this job?" After investing so much time and money in training to become a teacher, it is not easy to come to grips with this question.
3. The more detrimental effects of daily stress take time to manifest into physical, emotional, and behavioral problems. Coronary heart disease, heart attacks, high blood pressure, weakened immune systems, cancer, diabetes, nerve damage, and deteriorating performance and outcomes are all well-established symptoms of prolonged stress (see the video below). Yet, because these conditions are generally not experienced for several

years, or even decades, it is difficult to accept the need to engage in preventative practices *now*.

4.   Finally, it is difficult even to think about adding more to an already overloaded and demanding schedule.

Long Term Effects of Stress
www.youtube.com/watch?v=1B0PGFnYnv4

In addition to the long-term development of stress-related symptoms, traumatic incidents, such as a school shooting or a student suicide, can have an immediate and sometimes profound impact. Needless to say, the entire school suffers. I recommend *Trauma in Schools and Communities* (Steele, 2015b), in which survivors and responders from Virginia Tech, Sandy Hook Elementary School, Chardon, Ohio, and other schools that have suffered violent and non-violent traumatic events present their first-hand accounts of the stress they experienced and worked hard to manage.

The fact remains that motivating professionals to engage in daily self-care practices is a hard sell. Eric Gentry's six-minute video *Compassion Fatigue Prevention & Resiliency Fitness for the Frontline* (see below) discusses the aforementioned reasons for our slowness to embrace consistent self-care, and explains why a very old paradigm (or mindset) related to dealing with stressful situations simply does not work.

Compassion Fatigue Prevention & Resiliency Fitness for the Frontline
www.youtube.com/watch?v=RppP5z7AXLQ

New and Emerging Stressors

In 2014/2015, I presented a ten-question self-care practice survey to 1,500 professionals. Ninety percent of the respondents rated "poor" in daily Monday–Friday self-care practices. In a moment you will have a chance to take the same survey. First, though, it is important to discuss several new and emerging changes in our society, and certainly in our schools, that expose us to new worries, anxiety, and stress.

Digital Technology

Today's students are digital learners and communicators. The planned, integrated use of technology shows great promise in promoting overall academic improvement (Norris and Soloway, 2014). At the same time, however, a considerable body of research is raising concerns regarding the neurological, biological, social, and psychological stress created from consistent use of digital technology. Digital devices are rewiring our brains, and dysregulating our nervous systems. These changes are impacting how we are processing information, responding to problems, interacting with others, and experiencing the world. In 2015, in a blog titled *Addictive Screen Disorder—ASD* (Steele, 2015a), I cited the following research-supported symptoms resulting from repetitive use of digital devices:

- Difficulty with tasks and problems requiring focused attention.
- Easily distracted into off-task behaviors.
- Lower test scores compared to those limiting their screen usage.
- Weakened declarative memory.
- ADD behavior and symptoms.
- Decrease in productivity.
- Increase in depression and social anxiety.
- Compromised relationships.
- Compromised ability to empathize and be attuned to others.
- Weight gain/loss.
- Delayed sleep/difficulty falling asleep/reduction in hours of sleep.
- Addictive stimulant-driven behaviors and withdrawal reactions.

The fact is, what helps can also create additional stress.

Cognitive Changes

The research is especially strong in the area of cognitive deficits resulting from screen exposure. French scientists Sylvain Charron and Etienne Koelich have discovered that the human brain struggles to process information across more than two tasks at any given time, so while we might think we are "multitasking," our brain is actually skipping rapidly from one task to the next (Edwards, 2010). Devoting attention to a single task, especially if it's something new that we are attempting to learn, is not easy with a brain that is wired to jump rapidly from task to task.

Furthermore, learning relies on placing information in context, something the conditioned multitasking brain is increasingly unable to cope with. According to Shea Bennet (2011), at the turn of the millennium, the average attention span was twelve minutes; now it's only five seconds. Moreover, studies show that 25 percent of social media users forget the names and details of friends and even relatives (Bennet, 2011). Both short-term and declarative (long-term) memory suffer. The latter is used when applying information that was learned earlier to current situations/problems/explanations (Peneberg, 2010). These changes have a negative impact on academic outcomes. For example, studies have found that college students who use Facebook regularly have lower GPAs than those who avoid the site (Journalist's Resource, 2013).

Susan Greenfield, Professor of Synaptic Pharmacology at Oxford University, argues that because real-world experiences are inherently slower than online ones, especially the ability to process multiple streams of information across multiple networks, attention-deficit disorder (ADD) behaviors have increased in line with increased use of digital devices (Greenfield, 2015). This has significant implications for classroom practices. For example, one professor found that students who attempted to multitask during a lecture scored lower than those who did not. **Furthermore, those who had a direct view of the students who were multitasking scored lower than those who could not see what the multitaskers were doing** (Strauss, 2014). So, although the digital world has been positive in many ways and holds a great deal of promise, it has also introduced new challenges, the need for adaptive strategies, and the stress of the newness and uncertainty of future usage outcomes.

Diversity

This century is marked by diversity. The current generation is the most diverse in the United States' history. This diversity is creating complex communities, issues, and heightened conflict. Classrooms are also far more diverse than ever before. "Public schools in the USA began the 2014–15 school year with an unprecedented demographic profile: For the first time ever, white students are the minority, according to the U.S. Department of Education" (Toppo and Overberg, 2014). Teachers must learn how to apply differentiated, sheltered, and multicultural instruction within a "standards-based reform" framework. Any parent who is trying to raise three children experiences a good deal of stress. So imagine a teacher trying to teach and relate to *thirty* diverse students to help them all reach a high academic goal. This stressful task demands good self-care in order to remain physically energetic and positively proactive rather than reactive to the diverse learning styles, needs, and behaviors the students present.

Terrorism and Violence

Today, almost a quarter of the world's prisoners are incarcerated in the United States, even though it accounts for just 5 percent of the global population (Breslow, 2014). From 2000 to 2008, on average, there were five mass murders in the United States each year. From 2009 to 2014, that average tripled to fifteen each year (Greenberg, 2014). The country has been shocked by the murder of six college-aged victims near the campus of the University of California, Santa Barbara, on May 23, 2014; the 2013 Boston Marathon bombing; the murder of twelve people in a movie theater in Aurora Colorado in July 2012; and the aforementioned Sandy Hook massacre. Unfortunately, these atrocities represent only a small proportion of the total number of mass shootings that have occurred in the United States over recent years. A "mass shooting" is commonly defined as an incident in which four or more people are killed and/or injured. Using this definition, there were 353 mass shootings in the United States in 2015 alone, including the fourteen people who were killed in San Bernardino, California, on December 2. At the time of writing (2016), a further 555 US schoolchildren have been killed since the tragedy at Sandy Hook in December 2012. These horrific statistics suggest that violence and terrorism are likely to continue in the United States for the foreseeable future, and that we must remain vigilant in places and at events that were once considered safe. In other words, we are all living with a heightened survival stress response.

The war against Isis, contempt for law enforcement, massive auto recalls, unprecedented climate change, "monster storms," and many other uncertainties are undeniably adding to the stress we experience as individuals and professionals every day. Therefore, self-care is essential.

Educator Compassion Fatigue

Educators are vulnerable to compassion fatigue. Simply walk into any school and observe what is happening. Teachers will be cutting corners and exhibiting low energy and a lack of enthusiasm for their work. They are easily distracted when students are talking to them, distant, have little patience, instantly flustered by demanding students or difficult situations, far too serious, quick to give up on students, more reactive than proactive, and quick to discipline or avoid challenging students and those situations that call for empathy. Those who are compassionately fatigued feel overwhelmed or even hopeless, and they eventually engage in behavior that becomes a concern for others. Catherine Nyhan's excellent *Compassion Fatigue for Educators* presentation (see below) covers Eric Gentry's "Five Phases of the Compassion Fatigue Development Process" and a number of self-care practices. Simply reviewing Gentry's "Five Phases" will help you evaluate how you could manage your stress.

Compassion Fatigue for Educators
https://prezi.com/d1ag6s4wuz67/compassion-fatigue-for-educators/

Ten Self-Care Practices

A Survey: How Well Are You Doing?

The final slide of Nyhan's presentation states, "Compassion satisfaction comes from practicing self-care . . . keeping yourself in tune (regulated) with who and how you are in the room with your students." Hopefully, the above information has encouraged a mindset that self-care is something we all need to practice every day in order to remain resilient and consistently effective in our efforts to help students learn while regulating our own and their behavior in the face of unavoidable stressors.

Let's see how well you are doing. (Note: Because no one set of practices works for every individual, additional practices are provided for you to try in order to determine what will help you regulate your response to daily stress and provide you with the consistent energy, enthusiasm, and passion that are needed to be an effective teacher and leader.)

Simply answer "yes" or "no" to each statement. There is just one qualifier: these stress management strategies should be practiced Monday–Friday (during the school week). This is generally when teachers—and all other professionals—most often face their greatest stressors. This is not your typical self-care survey, but one that aligns itself with neuroscience, biology, and psychology in the twenty-first century.

1. I turn off my computer and cell phone one hour before retiring and do not check these devices before going to bed.
2. I engage in a mindful exercise of at least thirty minutes once during the week.
3. I have breakfast daily, consisting of either a complex carbohydrate and/or protein.
4. I have a snack midmorning and again midafternoon.
5. I engage in thirty-minute segments of physical exercise three times Monday through Friday.
6. I spend fifteen minutes once a week reflecting on at least three positive experiences and recall what I am most grateful for during this time.
7. I prepare and prioritize a "to do" list at the beginning of the week and review and adjust it as needed midweek.
8. I engage in at least two acts of generosity throughout the week outside of my work environment.
9. I read at least one professionally published article or journal or engage in researching topics specific to my teaching responsibilities at least once during the week.
10. I take part in some form of supervision (not evaluation), peer collaboration, mentoring, and/or coaching, including observation of my teaching practices at least every two weeks. These sessions relate to the challenges and stressors I have experienced during this time with students, my teaching practices, planning, and achievement of curriculum goals.

Scoring

Give yourself two points for every "yes" response, then add up your score.

• A score of 8 or less = poor stress management.
• A score of 10 to 14 = fair stress management.
• A score of 16 to 20 = well done.

As stated earlier, this is not a typical stress-related questionnaire. Rather, it is based on the strategies that neuroscience, biology, and psychology suggest will protect us against the stress that fills our lives today. Below, we explore at each of these strategies in turn.

1: Turning off Screen Devices

> Blue light, which in nature is most abundant in the morning, tells you to get up and get moving. Red light is more common at dusk and it slows you down. Now, guess what kind of light is streaming from that little screen in your hand at 11:59 P.M.?
>
> (Fishman, 2014)

That's right. Blue light is emitted from all screen devices. Rather than calming the brain in preparation for restorative sleep, we are stimulating it.

In a study of ten thousand sixteen- to nineteen-year-olds, researchers in Norway found that the longer a young person spent looking at an electronic screen before going to bed, the worse the quality of their sleep was likely to be. Those who spent more than four hours a day looking at screens had a 49 percent greater risk of taking longer than an hour to fall asleep, and they were three and a half times more likely to sleep for fewer than five hours each night (Cooper, 2015). Good restorative sleep leads to better focus, concentration, energy, and performance.

2: Mindful Activities

In Box 7.1 former principal Richard Curci, who is now Assistant Superintendent for the San Francisco Unified School District, shares his thoughts on the value of in-school meditation for himself, his teachers, and students.

Box 7.1   The Importance of Affording Students Time to Connect to Themselves (by Richard Curci)

Quiet Time Program

In 2008 I was planning on moving back to San Francisco from New Jersey to become the principal of Everett Middle School. This urban middle school is located in the heart of San Francisco. The demographics at the time were 45 percent Latino, 30 percent African American, 15 percent Asian and 10 percent other. During the interview there were many traditional questions about leadership. Toward the end of the interview one of the last questions was: "Our school will be participating in the Quiet Time Program [David Lynch Foundation, 2016] that has students meditating twice during the school day. We will use the techniques of Transcendental Mediation [TM]. How do you feel about that?" I was delighted and replied that back in 1975 I was teaching at a school in New Jersey—Eastside High School—where I was introduced to TM. I still remembered my mantra but had not

---

meditated since the 1970s, so I was excited at the thought that I might be meditating again. I was fortunate to get the job at Everett Middle School.

When I took over, Everett was the lowest-performing school in the district, with the highest suspension rate. There was very little structure and student achievement levels in both math and English language arts were under 10 percent of the students at the proficient level. At least a third of the students suffered from posttraumatic stress syndrome. They were coming from neighborhoods were there was much violence and it was not uncommon to hear about the death of a friend or a family member.

At the first staff meeting, I shared how excited I was about the Quiet Time Program and repeated my story from the 1970s. The person who created the master schedule included fifteen minutes in the morning and fifteen minutes at the end of each day for students to meditate. The program began with a letter and permission slip that were sent home to all families. Teachers and other staff who wanted to learn the technique were able to participate. These adults were instructed in the technique first. The funding for the program came from the David Lynch Foundation.

The adults' and students' first lesson involved a ceremony where a master teacher lit a candle, thanked their teacher, and gave the participant a mantra. They then assisted in the meditation process: they would meet with the students on a regular basis until they were able to meditate on their own.

At Everett, we began with teaching the eighth grade students and worked our way down to the sixth graders. There were five TM teachers who taught everyone in the community who wanted to participate. As you might imagine, several parents went online to research TM and were against the program because they felt it was religion. Despite their concerns, we continued with the program. Students would be called out of their PE classes to learn the technique and meet their TM teacher. The TM teacher stayed with their students all year and would conduct regular check-ins.

Once everyone had learned the technique, we incorporated it into the master schedule, with the two fifteen-minute meditations at the start and end of each day. The TM teachers also conducted weekend retreats for the adults, and many members of staff attended them.

As a result of Everett's involvement with TM, we began to see a calmer climate throughout the school and in the classrooms, less stress in the students and their teachers, and an increase in student achievement. In fact, we improved by 40 points on the API (Annual Performance Index) scores—the highest gain of any middle school in the district.

Before standardized testing, we meditated to relieve the stress and help the students focus. One of the eighth graders had to audition for his entrance into high school by performing a monologue. When I asked him how he did, he said, "I did fine. I meditated before I auditioned."

The adult interaction and meditation program gave students who might never have had the opportunity to calm their minds from day-to-day challenges a chance to enjoy a quiet mind. Their experience with meditation helped them focus on their schoolwork, deal with the stress of the day, and feel more able to deal with all the challenges in their lives. We had a significant reduction in referrals and suspensions.

I have meditated every day since I started at Everett. After five years as principal, I left to take up a district-level position. When I reflect on my time at Everett, I realize that TM was a tool that helped to keep me focused, calm, and energized—all of which I needed to run a school with so many challenges. Everett turned itself around and there is now a waiting list to enter. The TM program helped the school to make that change.

3 and 4: Breakfast and Snacks

As a society, today we are much more aware of the importance of maintaining a balanced blood sugar level. Stress can kick our blood sugar level "out of whack" (Share Care, 2015). When this happens, our concentration and focus diminish, fatigue sets in, headaches are not uncommon, and irritability and other sudden mood changes emerge (WebMD, 2015). Any one of these can significantly decrease our own performance and effectiveness, and have a negative impact on those around us.

5: Physical Exercise

There is abundant evidence in support of the benefits of regular exercise.

6: Being Grateful

There is also a good deal of evidence in support of the benefits of being grateful. In one study, one group was asked to write about what they were grateful for each week over a period of ten weeks. Another group was asked to write about what upset them. And a third group was asked to write about any incident that had affected them, irrespective of whether it was "good" or "bad." The researchers discovered that those who wrote about what they were grateful for were more optimistic and felt better about their lives [compared to the other two groups]. Surprisingly, they also exercised more and had fewer visits to physicians than those who focused on sources of aggravation.

(*Huffington Post*, 2012)

It takes only a few minutes a week to develop a lifetime of benefits. Most importantly, a teacher's optimism and resilience—typical traits of those who are grateful—is critical in the creation of a positive learning environment. The link below provides an excellent list of resources related to the science of gratitude.

The Science of Gratitude—Articles, Links and Videos
www.habitsforwellbeing.com/the-science-of-gratitude-links-articles-and-videos/

7: Prioritize

With all the demands that are placed on educators, prioritizing is essential for maintaining consistent desirable outcomes as well as avoiding the unnecessary stress that results when we lose sight of what matters and instead focus on tasks that do not support what is important. Angela Watson's *7 Ways to Prioritize Teaching Tasks When Everything Seems Urgent* (Watson, 2015) is an excellent starting point. Thereafter, simply Googling "teachers and prioritizing" will provide a wealth of resources related to teaching priorities, prioritizing the curriculum, the "must knows," "need to knows," and "nice to knows" for prioritizing students' learning, classroom management, and much more. Good time management is good stress management.

8: Generosity

Zak, Stanton, and Ahmadi (2007) theorized that experiencing generosity releases the hormone oxytocin. In their study, one group of individuals was given an oxytocin nasal spray while another was given a saltwater spray. Each group then played a game that required them to decide whether to give away a sum of money. The presence of oxytocin increased that group's generosity by 80 percent. Oxytocin actually calms the brain and engenders trust, which facilitates bonding with, giving to, and helping others (Carter, 2007; Ratey, 2002). Generosity helps us feel good; and when we feel good, we do good and are better able to regulate the stress in our lives.

9: Read

Staying informed in this information age helps us to make better decisions, spot opportunities, and earn the trust of colleagues through what we know and the resources we can provide. It develops our expertise, helps us adapt more easily to rapid change, inspires us, and improves our students' outcomes. This is especially critical in this digital age, when immediate access to information and to our peers and their work and expertise is quickly changing how we teach and learn.

10: Supervision, Collaboration, Mentoring, Coaching

This practice is also critical as it determines job satisfaction and employee retention. Teacher evaluations are not the focus of this discussion. Generally tied to student outcomes, an evaluation is an analysis of collected data. Of course, the students' performance in tests matters; however, most would agree that quantitative outcomes alone have little to do with improving teacher effectiveness and overall student performance. Furthermore, the content that is measured and the frequency of the evaluations differ in most states. There is no national standard.

Education relies on the term "professional development" when addressing teacher improvement. Unfortunately, this often equates to no more than the provision of a handful of training days that generally lack what teachers say they want and need the most. The term "supervision" is rarely used in education, yet teachers are well aware of what constitutes effective supervision and repeatedly request it. **Supervision is "the action or process of watching and directing what someone does or how something is done"** (Merriam-Webster, 2015). Effective teachers do this every day in the classroom, yet they rarely receive such support themselves to help them grow and improve.

Teacher supervision should be provided at least every two weeks

- by a principal or other leader identified as having expertise with that teacher's grade level and subject matter and trained to provide practical feedback;
- by a coach or mentor who is an experienced content expert and trained to provide practical feedback; or
- by peer collaboration.

Irrespective of who provides it, though, teachers should receive:

- consistent (weekly or bi-weekly) supervision;
- regular observation of teaching practices (at least every two weeks);
- coaches, mentors, or leaders with content expertise;
- the provision of relevant practices, resources, and information;
- supervision that addresses learning objectives, curriculum expectations, and standards;
- opportunities to express frustrations;
- collaboration with peers who are able to share frustrations, new ideas, and suggestions;
- the provision of interactive learning experiences; and
- debriefing around challenging student behavior.

Responses to the self-care survey suggest that fewer than 10 percent of teachers receive this level of supervision, a figure that seems to be fairly representative of the wider teaching population. The fact is that the majority of the above supervision criteria are not offered to teachers. The general absence of this self-care practice is very costly in terms of loss of talent. Alexandria Neason (2014) reports that half of all teachers in the United States leave the profession within five years, costing districts up to $2.2 billion each year, **with the lack of mentoring and professional support (supervision) cited as the main motivating factor.** Yet fewer than half of the teachers in the United States receive any form of supervision, and those who do suggest that the frequency and quality vary greatly (Darling-Hammond, 2010). In a 2014 survey of 1,300 educators, **those who taught in schools with structured, consistent teacher collaboration expressed very high satisfaction with their day-to-day work.** Unfortunately, only 7 percent of the teachers surveyed reported that their schools practiced a strong collaborative model. Moreover, intensive coaching—which can mirror the beneficial effects of regular supervision, mentoring, and collaboration—was similarly rare (Bill and Melinda Gates Foundation, 2015).

The National Association of Secondary School Principals (NASSP, 2015) reported, "we need to improve overall student achievement in the United States. To help further successfully fulfill their role, effective teacher supervision and evaluation are essential." Given the current lack of resources in this area, teachers are urged to be proactive about regular supervision, as it is clearly a key factor in job satisfaction and the prevention of stress and compassion fatigue.

Additional Self-Care Practices

The ten aforementioned self-care strategies will make a difference in sustaining your energy, your regulation, and your consistent effectiveness. However, there are several other viable and valuable practices, too.

Think Differently

Cognitive Behavioral Therapy (CBT) has demonstrated its effectiveness in helping individuals manage their stress. Rather than cite all the research here, I encourage you to watch Dr. Mike Evans' *90:10 The Single Most Important Thing You Can Do for Your Stress* (see below). The video contains lots of surprises, interesting facts, and strategies, all illustrated by a hand writing on a whiteboard. **This eleven-minute presentation is a must-watch lesson.**

> *90:10 The Single Most Important Thing You Can Do for Your Stress*
> www.youtube.com/watch?v=I6402QJp52M

Identify Your Sensory Regulators

We all have sensory learning preferences. Some are visual learners, some are auditory, and some are "hands on/whole body involvement" or kinesthetic/tactile learners. We also have sensory preferences to help relieve stress, and to reduce the effects of the stress we are exposed to throughout the week. It is important for teachers to identify these sensory preferences and integrate them into their daily routines.

One tool that can help with this is Diana Henry's Teacher's Sensory Preferences (Henry, 2015). In fact, this can be helpful for all educators. Simply replace references to "the classroom" with "the office," "my students" with "my staff," and so on.

Teacher's Sensory Preferences

1. To wake up in the morning, I . . .
2. To help me regulate throughout the day, I need . . .
3. What I like best about my classroom is . . .
4. What I do not like about my classroom is . . .
5. What I like about my colleague's classroom is . . .
6. What I like about my home that I would like to have in my classroom is . . .
7. I could make my classroom better by . . .
8. Throughout the typical teaching day, I sit approximately a total of _____ minutes.
9. When I do sit, my favorite chair in the classroom rocks/is on wheels/is high up . . .
10. When I was in college, I preferred to study in what position/where/with what . . .
11. When I have to listen at a meeting/workshop I like to doodle/eat/drink/chew gum/play with small objects like pens or paper clips/bring a media aid . . .
12. When I feel stressed during the school day what I need from other people is space/support/physical affection/a good listener . . .
13. If I could bring my favorite sensory item to school with me, it would be a . . .
14. When I prepare for bed, to calm down I take a warm shower or bath/snuggle under a blanket or quilt/read/watch TV/put on a heavy robe or light nightclothes . . .

(Printed with permission from Henry Occupational Therapy Services © 2000)

Additional Preferences

- The memories that bring a smile to my face are . . .
- The thought that best helps me regulate my response to a challenging situation is . . .

- The experience that reminds me of my ability to manage difficult situations is . . .
- The person(s) in my life who I have asked to let me know that I need to slow down when I am stressed is (are) . . .

Completing these sentences helps us identify the strategies we can practice during stressful moments to help us regulate our unwanted reactions to the stressors we face every day. As a frequent presenter, over the years I have learned that the best way to manage the anxiety of performing in front of peers is to feel at ease within the first five minutes of the presentation, and to be certain that I will pique the interest of my peers in those first five minutes. Different situations call for different strategies, so it really helps to identify what works best for us in those situations that we anticipate will be stressful.

It is also important to leave the stress of the working day behind, so identify the specific sensory action that lets your nervous system know that the working day is over. Possibilities include:

- Pay attention to the sound of your car door closing as you get ready to leave the school parking lot for the day.
- Pay attention to the movement of your hand as you pull up your driveway and reach to click the garage door opener.
- Pay attention to the sensation you feel when you put on your favorite jeans and tee shirt at home.
- Pay attention to the sensation you feel when you hug your loved one or pat your pet.

Any of these or other sensory moments could be that specific physical/sensory signal to your nervous system and brain that the working day is over and it's time to relax. Once you have experienced it, take a few minutes to deep-breathe, meditate, exercise, or practice some other relaxation technique before you begin to tackle your at-home tasks.

Given all the choices that are available, there is no good reason to neglect your self-care. In *Trauma in Schools and Communities*, school counselor Susan Connelly, from Newtown, Connecticut, describes all the ways in which the members of her community are managing their grief and stress following the tragic loss of so many promising young lives:

> Reiki, yoga, faith, a bubble bath, time with the kids, time without the kids, reading, fires in the fire pit underneath the stars, being with our pets, kayaking, comedy movies, compassionate acts, journaling, being honest with ourselves when we need to take more breaks at work, meditating. There's also play, music, making jewelry, shopping but not spending, cleaning or not worrying about keeping the house clean, gardening. We can go to church more, travel out of town more, not read e-mails before going

to bed, play more board games with the family, write poems, go dancing, jog, go to therapy.

(Steele, 2015b, pp.110–111)

The fact that you are reading this demonstrates your desire to bring your best to your classroom and your school. You are to be applauded for that, but it takes a good deal of energy and passion to put that desire into practice. In this endeavor, it is most important to remember that how you do what you do has a tremendous influence on how students perform and behave. I and many others have condensed all we have discussed in this resource into one simple yet profound statement:

Happy children learn.

Something similar could be said of teachers:

Happy teachers are resilient and effective.

Karen Buxman's video *Funny Stress Management Techniques* (see link below) will put a smile on your face and act as a transition to the final three chapters of this resource, which present **whole school approaches for creating brain-centric, trauma-sensitive schools**. Enjoy, and thank you for being such a critically important part of enriching the future of our children.

Funny Stress Management Techniques
www.youtube.com/watch?v=ybnzd4zu8xs

References

ABC News (2015). *Ten Most Stressful Jobs in America*. Retrieved June 23, 2015 from http://abcnews.go.com/GMA/be_your_best/page/top-10-stressful-jobs-america-14355387.

Bennet, S. (2011). *Is Social Media Ruining Our Minds?* Retrieved June 18, 2015 from www.adweek.com/socialtimes/this-is-your-brain-on-social-media/458276.

Bill and Melinda Gates Foundation (2015). *Teachers Know Best: Teachers' Views on Professional Development*. Retrieved January 8, 2016 from http://collegeready.gatesfoundation.org/wp-content/uploads/2015/04/Gates-PDMarketResearch-Dec5.pdf.

Breslow, J. (2014). *New Report Slams "Unprecedented" Growth in US Prisons*. Retrieved June 9, 2015 from www.pbs.org/wgbh/pages/frontline/criminal-justice/locked-up-in-america/new-report-slams-unprecedented-growth-in-us-prisons/.

Carter, C. S. (2007). Neuropeptides and the protective effects of social bonds. In E. Harmon-Jones and P. Winkielman (Eds.), *Social Neuroscience: Integrating Biological and Psychological Explanations of Social Behavior* (pp. 425–437). New York: Guilford Press.

Cooper, C. (2015). *Too Much Exposure to Smartphone Screens Ruins Your Sleep, Study Shows*. Retrieved July 29, 2015 from www.independent.co.uk/life-style/health-and-families/

health-news/too-much-exposure-to-smartphone-screens-ruins-your-sleep-study-shows-10019185.html.

Darling-Hammond, L. (2010). *Developing Powerful Teaching: What It Will Really Take to Leave No Child Behind.* Retrieved September 28, 2016 from http://slideplayer.com/slide/6634340/.

David Lynch Foundation (2016). *Quiet Time Changes Lives.* Retrieved January 7, 2016 from www.davidlynchfoundation.org/schools.html.

Edwards, L. (2010). *Brain Splits to Handle Two Jobs at Once.* Retrieved June 8, 2015 from http://phys.org/news/2010-04-brain-jobs.html.

Fishman, J. (2014). *How Your Smartphone Messes with Your Brain—and Your Sleep.* Retrieved August 1, 2015 from http://blogs.scientificamerican.com/observations/how-your-smartphone-messes-with-your-brain-and-your-sleep/.

Greenberg, J. (2014). *Mass Shootings Have Tripled since 2000.* Retrieved June 18, 2015 from www.politifact.com/punditfact/statements/2014/may/28/pierre-thomas/abcs-thomas-mass-shootings-have-tripled-2000/.

Greenfield, S. (2015). *Mind Change: How Digital Technologies Are Leaving Their Mark On Our Brains.* New York: Random House.

Henry, D. (2015). *Teacher's Sensory Preferences.* Retrieved November 16, 2015 from www.asdn.org/wp-content/uploads/teacher-sensory-preferences.pdf.

Hill, A. (2008). *Depressed, Stressed: Teachers in Crisis.* Retrieved June 23, 2014 from www.theguardian.com/education/2008/aug/31/teaching.teachersworkload.

Huffington Post (2012). *10 Reasons Why Gratitude Is Healthy.* Retrieved October 15, 2015 from www.huffingtonpost.com/2014/07/21/gratitude-healthy-benefits_n_2147182.html.

Journalist's Resource (2013). *Multitasking, Social Media and Distraction: Research Review.* Retrieved July 7, 2015 from http://journalistsresource.org/studies/society/social-media/multitasking-social-media-distraction-what-does-research-say#sthash.G4k47oZh.dpuf.

Merriam-Webster (2015). *Supervision.* Retrieved September 28, 2016 from www.merriam-webster.com/dictionary/supervision.

NASSP (2015). *Teacher Supervision and Evaluation.* Retrieved January 10, 2016 from www.principals.org/Content.aspx?topic=Teacher_Supervision_and_Evaluation.

Neason, A. (2014). *Half of Teachers Leave the Job after Five Years: Here's What to Do about It.* Retrieved May 15, 2015 from http://hechingerreport.org/half-teachers-leave-job-five-years-heres/.

Norris, C., and Soloway, E. (2014). Scaffolding synchronous collaboration: Leveraging data in support of teaching and learning. Presented at E-Learn: World Conference on E-Learning, New Orleans, LA, October 27–30.

Peneberg, A. (2010). *Social Networking Affects Brains Like Falling in Love.* Retrieved July 5, 2015 from www.fastcompany.com/1659062/social-networking-affects-brains-falling-love.

Ratey, J. J. (2002). *A User's Guide to the Brain: Perception, Attention, and the Four Theatres of the Brain.* New York: Vintage Books.

Share Care (2015). *Can Stress Affect My Blood Sugar Levels?* Retrieved October 29, 2015 from www.sharecare.com/health/stress-reduction/can-stress-affect-blood-glucose-levels.

Steele, W. (2015a). *Addictive Screen Disorder—ASD.* Retrieved September 28, 2016, from www.drbillsteele.com/2015/08/12/addictive-screen-disorder-asd/.

Steele, W. (2015b). *Trauma in Schools and Communities: Recovery Lessons from Survivors and Responders.* New York: Routledge.

Strauss, V. (2014). *Why a Leading Professor of New Media Just Banned Technology Use in Class.* Retrieved July 27, 2015 from www.washingtonpost.com/news/answer-sheet/wp/2014/09/25/why-a-leading-professor-of-new-media-just-banned-technology-use-in-class/.

Toppo, G., and Overberg, P. (2014). *Diversity in the Classroom.* www.usatoday.com/story/news/nation/2014/11/25/minnesota-school-race-diversity/18919391/.

Watson, A. (2015). *How to Prioritize Teaching Tasks When Everything Seems Urgent.* Retrieved January 5, 2015 from http://thecornerstoneforteachers.com/2015/09/prioritize-teaching-tasks.html.

WebMD (2015). *When Your Blood Sugar Level Gets too Low.* Retrieved October 29, 2015 from www.webmd.com/diabetes/guide/diabetes-hypoglycemia.

Zak, P. J., Stanton, A. A., and Ahmadi, S. (2007). *Oxytocin Increases Generosity in Humans.* Retrieved September 28, 2016 from www.sciencedaily.com/releases/2007/11/071107074321.htm.

8 In-School Neurological Reparative Therapy for Traumatized Students

David Ziegler

Children who experience extreme trauma also present with learning and behavioral challenges. Due to the closing of many residential centers across the country, many of these students are now in our educational settings. They often represent extreme examples of trauma, but millions of students with less extreme situations of trauma are in nearly every classroom in the United States. Knowing how to approach students on the continuum of traumatic experiences is critically important. This chapter is directed at those school psychologists, social workers, counselors, and educators who are seeking ways to optimize the learning experience for these students while also regulating their behaviors. Just like Ivan and his story at the end of this chapter, their learning potential is often buried by their constant efforts to survive the outcomes of their traumatic experiences. However, when we engage them in activities and interactions that help repair the brain's adaptive functions and focus on the neurological processes that support resilience and thriving, they begin to flourish.

To those who consider the population of traumatized children in our educational settings too small to receive significant attention, another look at the data is necessary. Every year it is estimated that another five million names are added to the list of significantly traumatized children (Childhelp USA, 2015). Of these children, up to 50 percent will develop long-term debilitating after-effects of the trauma, including learning problems in school. Not only is the population of traumatized children in educational settings not a small figure; trauma may constitute the greatest cause of underachievement in schools.

What is needed in education, when it comes to traumatized children, is to bring together the substantial new information on trauma, brain development, and the causes of and solutions for emotional disturbance that exists in psychology and psychiatry. This information must be woven into learning theory and progressive academic strategies for its maximal use. We need conceptual and practical applications of learning approaches and environments where traumatized children succeed rather than fail. This chapter will attempt to provide a conceptual framework leading to practical implementation in academic settings. It will discuss how traumatized children perform in educational settings and why, how the brain functions, the use of Neurological

Reparative Therapy, its five goals, and practical strategies for improving educational performance.

How Traumatized Children Perform in Educational Settings and Why

The combination of trauma and learning in school do not mix well. What a child learns from trauma negatively impacts learning in an academic setting (Ziegler, 2011b). The child learns not to trust, to be anxious around adults, and to be vigilant of the motivations of others. If the goal is for a child to come into an academic setting ready to learn and ready to experience the enjoyment and excitement of discovery, then the effects of a traumatic experience will hinder their learning in a variety of ways.

Many traumatized children fail in school. This failure can take many forms. For instance, some children externalize their difficulties in emotions/behaviors and find themselves in constant trouble and the subject of disciplinary actions. Extreme examples of this are children who actively try to get expelled from school, thus eliminating the problem of having to face the many challenges of going to school in the first place. An extreme example of an internalizing child is one who pretends to be ill, doesn't come to school, or, when they are old enough, drops out altogether. Some children sit quietly and can dissociate (daydream) in the classroom and not learn. These children are often considered unmotivated or underachievers, but the reality is much more complicated than a simple lack of motivation. Many traumatized children will avoid feeling vulnerable at all costs, so they will not take the risk of failing in learning. The child's brain can be impacted by trauma, making focused attention difficult or even impossible. The child's brain may also find that what is offered in school lacks relevance to survival in the harsh world they experience.

Hypervigilance

Trauma produces hypervigilance in children. It resets the brain's priorities from curiosity to protection and survival. Being acutely aware of the environment is a survival skill to the child in a setting where basic needs are not provided, but it is not a functional skill in school. Hypervigilance is often viewed as distracti- bility. In part this is due to the child focusing on aspects of the environment that are not part of the learning plan. On the surface, it is often difficult to distinguish "hyperactivity" and "distractibility" from the impact of trauma. The child in science class who is watching the non-verbal messages of a larger boy and wondering about safety during the coming lunch break is not engaged in the science lesson. The traumatized brain puts a very low priority on learning math facts if the primary goal is self-protection from a physically abusive, alcoholic parent after school. It has been recognized for decades that a variety of learning disabilities can ensue when foundational learning skills due to trauma are missed in early school years (Cohen, 1986).

Dysregulation

Trauma produces serious self-regulation deficiencies. Often viewed as the most pervasive result of trauma (van der Kolk, 2014), the lack of self-regulation causes these children not to have the inner understanding, inner strength, or desire to monitor emotional and behavior reactivity to events around them. This is often observed as intense emotional expression or mood disorders due to challenges in the classroom. These challenges were discussed in Chapters One and Two. Focusing on teaching students how to regulate their reactions to stressful situations in various ways is critical for optimizing their learning experience.

Putting What Is Learned into Context

For reasons that will be explained in the next section, many traumatized children have difficulty putting what they learn into context. An example of this can be seen in the child who can connect the numbered dots, but cannot see that those dots eventually form the outline of a horse. Being able to put learning into context is an essential aspect of educational advancement. It means little if a child learns that slaves in early American history were sad and oppressed if he or she does not understand that slavery was wrong and a violation of human rights. The common expression "not seeing the forest for the trees" suggests that the many facts, figures, and ideas in school must be integrated into understandable and usable information for learning to be sustained. This is one element of seeing the larger picture within the brain and using sensory input to form an overall understanding among the various parts of the brain. This is known as neuro-integration (Ziegler, 2011a). Trauma impairs the ability of the the brain's prefrontal cortex to facilitate neuro-integration.

Barriers to Social Progress

Trauma produces distrust in others and the frequent misinterpretation of social cues. Misunderstanding social interactions can cause conflicts leading to violence (fight) or avoidance (flight). One of the most important elements of success in school is social success. School is the first place, coming out of the family, where a child begins to develop a self-image, starts to understand others, and learns how to interact with the larger world. A great deal of success in school comes down to the ability to get along with others and form relationships that can help provide support. This is key in the relationship between student and teacher. If this first journey into the larger world outside the family home ends in failure and conflict, the child's view of school and the world can be quickly established in a negative context. With this in mind, some of the most important learning opportunities in school are at recess, lunch, and in the hallways, where a child learns their place in an important social structure. It is in these settings that traumatized children have the most difficulty in school and need support.

Emotions on Overload

Trauma increases heightened emotional responses, such as fear and anxiety. Expecting a traumatized child to give their full attention in the classroom is like asking someone who has just received a very disturbing phone call to go on with their day as if nothing has happened. The problem with both situations is the negative impact of anxiety on our ability to focus on the task at hand. Our emotions are ready to provide us with critical information to inform our decision-making process. However, our emotions can also run wild with fear and anxiety in situations we either do not understand or believe we cannot handle. School can produce debilitating anxiety for the traumatized child resulting in the child's lack of focus and reactivity, and hence in an inability to learn.

Expectations

Traumatized children often expect the worst, and they frequently experience exactly what they expect. In part, this comes from the child's experience that events seldom go the way they would like them to go, and many times the child is powerless and perceives that they are being victimized by events and people. This can produce a negative expectation of experiences in school and a self-fulfilling prophesy of failure. As Henry Ford once said, "If you think you can or can't, you are right." Negative expectations develop into negative self-esteem and the internal belief that internal personal power and interpersonal skills are insufficient to influence one's life for the better.

The following video presentation identifies a number of key areas for developing the "Unschool" approach, which refers to the unique needs of anxious and traumatized students that can be met in trauma-sensitive school settings.

> *Optimal Learning Environment for How Traumatized Children Learn*
> www.youtube.com/watch?v=Kt0eGib1egs

Mental Organization and the Brain after Trauma

The above issues are the result of trauma that develops and persists in the brain. Since the primary function of the brain is to promote survival, it is seriously altered by trauma. Because trauma, by definition, is a situation that an individual is unable to cope with, the brain views traumatic events as threats to its primary function of survival (Ziegler, 2011a). The brain has mechanisms to address threat, and these will directly impact the traumatized child in the educational environment. These mechanisms are discussed in detail in other parts of the text. However, one of the most important neurological deficiencies after trauma is the impact on mental organization or integration of neuronal activity.

Trauma can significantly degrade the brain's ability to collect, analyze, and use information the child learns either in the classroom or on the playground.

The human brain is the most complex organic structure known to exist, so how does a teacher or administrator help to change it to enable a child to be more successful in school? One answer is through an approach called Neurological Reparative Therapy (Ziegler, 2011a), which divides the challenge into a series of steps that can be implemented in any classroom or office.

Neurological Reparative Therapy (NRT)

All approaches that are designed to help young people must take on the challenge of facilitating modifications of the brain's negative adaptations. These adaptations take the form of cognitive patterns that get in the way of a functional life. It is the human brain that enables individuals to adapt to the world in either optimal or destructive ways. Effective teaching makes an impact at the operational level of the brain, which includes individual neurons and neuro-templates (families of neurons that together perform a specific function). Academic instruction can be said to change cognitions or what might be called *cognitive mental maps* or *internal working models*. Both of these terms describe how the brain understands the conditions of the environment in which it operates. How the brain perceives a situation says a great deal about how it responds. The brain of a traumatized child must perceive the school environment as a safe and supportive place where they can risk failing (making mistakes) if they are to learn and put aside safety concerns for the time being in favor of being curious, exploring, and having some fun while learning.

When the brain is allowed to develop optimally, it strives for positive adaptations to the challenges of learning. However, when trauma or deprivation become part of an individual's experience, the brain makes radical adaptive alterations that focus primarily on surviving rather than thriving. These negative adaptations become the symptoms of most barriers to learning: anxiety, depression, fear, hypervigilance, trouble connecting with others due to mistrust, inability to interpret social cues correctly, anger, aggression, and a large variety of behaviors that are associated with the autonomic fight or flight responses to stress in the limbic system. These adaptations are all barriers to learning and succeeding in school. How, then, might they be altered?

Successful Learning

Successful learning involves repairing the brain's adaptive functions and optimal neurological processes to put more focus on thriving and not just on self-protection and survival. Researchers have found that the malleability of the brain not only contributes to problematic symptoms due to negative adaptations but also facilitates good health and self-repair given the correct external guidance. Such external support and assistance form the core of Neurological

Reparative Therapy. This approach is based upon research into how to make positive changes in the thinking, emotional expression, and behaviors of young children, all of which are necessary for success in school.

The four pillars of NRT are Brain Development (Hariri and Holmes, 2006; Kagan, 2010), Attachment (Schore, 2001), Resiliency (Pillemer et al., 2010; Lyubomirsky, King, and Diener, 2005), and Trauma Treatment (Cohen, Mannarino, and Knudsen, 2005; Briere, 1992). NRT can be summarized as the facilitation of nerve functioning in order to optimize integrated cognitive processes. It is an approach that impacts the refocus of brain systems on positive adaptations to self, others, and the world. It is less an intervention than an orientation of the holistic, ecological, and environmental conditions that are needed to return the brain to its natural state of optimal learning. Researchers have established that, unless it has been damaged in some way, the brain wants to learn and strive for success and even happiness. What, then, are the goals that support this effort?

The Five Goals of NRT

First of all, Neurological Reparative Therapy is about promoting optimum brain functioning (neurological), and returning the brain to its natural state of wanting to learn (reparative). The therapy is simply an active process, such as teaching. NRT is a roadmap that can be used to improve educational performance among students. The video below explains how it creates positive brain changes by putting new practices in place.

Neurological Reparative Therapy—A Roadmap to Healing, Resiliency and Well-Being

www.youtube.com/watch?v=2zLp6ip8GKo

Each of the following five goals of the NRT roadmap will be explained first in brain terminology and then in more practical language.

Goal 1: Facilitate Perceptual Changes of Self, School, and the Child's Internal Working Model

The student's experience of school is directly connected to their perceptions based upon an internal working model or how they view academic settings from past experience. Based upon the individual's perceptions, their cognitive mental maps plot a course that they will take, including emotions and behaviors. The first goal is to impact perceptions by altering cognitions in order to provide a more positive and optimistic orientation, rather than a negative and depressive mindset toward learning. Learning requires a willingness to risk making mistakes, being incorrect, and reflecting weaknesses, which signals vulnerability.

Instruction must be directed toward developing a sense of self-efficacy and helping the individual view others as resources of support and assistance in the learning process.

The student must experience some success, however slight it may be at first. They must experience progress, improvement, and some level of mastery. Since school is a social setting, it also helps when the student has some positive influence on others and is helped to begin to see school as a more friendly and supportive place than they have in the past. An example would be to help a child see school as a fun place to learn rather than a scary place where social and academic problems result in personal failure that is visible to everyone.

Examples to meet goal 1:

- Make a list with the child of everything they do well.
- Ask the child for a list of their best attributes. Then tell them what you like best about them.
- Tell the child, "You have been through a lot in your life. Tell me a couple hard things you faced and how you were able to handle them."
- Ask the child, "What are the most positive changes you have made over the last year? Let's see if you can come up with at least five."

Goal 2: Enhance Neuro-Integration to Assist in Learning

Executive functions of the frontal lobes of the neocortex require integration of functions from all parts of the brain. Neuro-integration is the brain's ability to access component parts and integrate them into an understandable whole that promotes learning and good decision-making. Enhancing neuro-integration also involves strengthening the hemispheric communication between the left (logical, analytic, verbal) and right (intuitive, artistic, emotive) hemispheres of the brain.

At first, the higher-order thinking must come from the outside, provided by supportive people. The student must learn to combine the logical and emotive regions of the brain through activities that simultaneously involve both hemispheres. For example, do an activity with a child while listening to music and suggest that the child should allow the music to form mental images in their mind (right hemisphere); then ask the child to describe the mental images (left hemisphere). School is a setting that has many complex components. Neuro-integration can help a student see the pieces of the puzzle come together to understand the academic and social aspects of school and how to get help to succeed in both areas.

Other examples to meet goal 2:

- Ask the child, "How calm is your body right now? Give me a number between one and ten, with ten being very calm."
- Tell the child, "As I show you these pictures, tell me any feelings that come up inside yourself."
- Tell the child, "I will now read you a story and ask you some questions about what is going on with the girl in the story."
- Tell the child, "Today we will be drawing a couple of pictures and I want you to tell me a story about each of the pictures you draw."

Goal 3: Alter the Brain's Information ProcessingRegion

A primary goal of all learning is to promote functioning of the higher-reasoning centers of the brain. Many traumatized students primarily use the reactive, limbic region of the brain in daily life. This region contains the brain's fear center as well as traumatic memories and the emotional response system. It is in the limbic brain that all negative experiences at school are remembered. Combining these factors produces an individual reacting with fear and emotion to reminders of previous negative experiences. The much more functional alternative is for the higher-reasoning centers of the neocortex to access information from all parts of the brain and process that information to inform learning and good decision-making.

To maximize learning, the student must think first, feel second, and act third. The reactive, limbic region of the brain should not be used first. The student must learn to act rather than react in the classroom and throughout the school environment. For example, they must learn to stop, take a deep breath, and only then make a request whenever they feel frustrated.

Other examples to meet goal 3:

- Tell the child, "I am going to read out several situations and in each one I want you to tell me the best decision the student can make."
- Tell the child, "Right now there is a lot going on inside you, so slow down and tell me what you are feeling."
- Ask the child, "You look a little tense, what is your body saying to you right now?"
- Tell the child, "Today we are going to get excited and then get calm several times. It will be fun. Let's begin."

Goal 4: Facilitate Orbitofrontal Cortex Activation

Optimal learning involves activating the orbitofrontal cortex in the frontal lobes of the neocortex. It is this complex part of the brain that accesses information from all of the other parts and enables deliberative and proactive mental activity. This is the opposite of the reactivity of the limbic brain region. This region can be viewed as the chief executive officer, because it is the most complex and potentially productive part of the brain. Its processes can result in effective consideration, planning, goal setting, and accurately perceiving challenges, all of which are higher-order executive functions that assist learning.

Over time, the goal is to have the student process most of the information they receive in the most advanced area of the neocortex. It is this region that optimally provides what are called "executive functions," including goal setting and goal-directed behavior, delaying gratification, impulse control, organizing, cause-and-effect reasoning, focused attention, mental flexibility, problem-solving, abstract and creative thinking, moral and ethical reasoning, and empathy for others, among many others. Every intervention that promotes thoughtful consideration exercises the orbitofrontal cortex and enhances learning.

Examples to meet goal 4:

- Give the child a problem and several choices for a response, then ask them to pick a solution and explain why they made that choice.
- Teach the child how to break a problem down into its component parts and consider a solution based upon such analysis.
- Help the child to work toward a classroom goal, thus teaching goal setting and goal-directed behavior.
- Outline a number of social situations, then ask the child what is going on and what the situation demands.

Goal 5: Neuro-template Development through Repetitive Practice

Networks of communication in the brain are made possible by neuro-templates and their individual component parts—neurons. Neurons have a "use dependent" developmental process, in that those that are used frequently become larger and stronger, do more work, and do that work faster. In contrast, neurons that are never used may atrophy and die, while those that are seldom used gradually deteriorate. **One key goal of learning is to exercise the brain through repetition, since it is in repeated use that neurons and neuro-templates, which are composed of millions of individual neurons, become more robust and efficient.** The more we use it, the stronger and more capable the brain becomes, which in turn facilitates optimal learning.

The expression "practice makes perfect" highlights the importance of repetitive efforts to improve the results. The brain changes gradually over time through the repetitive use of families of neurons that help us perform daily tasks, such as reading, math problem-solving, remembering dates in history, playing the piano, typing on a computer keyboard, or hearing critical feedback without reacting with anger. The more practice the brain has, the more it changes.

The goal here is to explain the challenge, determine the correct course of action to address the challenge, and finally implement a practical, effective solution. In a general way, this goal can be explained by saying that academic settings must become more skilled at working with a traumatized child's brain, rather than against it.

Examples to meet goal 5:

- Tell the child, "You are becoming a good reader. Can you read that last paragraph for me again?"
- Tell the child, "You have all your spelling words correct, except for 'detour.' After you write that word ten times I will give you a chance to spell it again and get one hundred percent for all your effort."
- Tell the child, "I will let you help in class if you can tell me three times correctly what we are working on today."
- Tell the child, "Do that again, because every time you do it you get a bit better at it."

Elements to Enhance In-School Settings

Expressive Learning

Children learn best by doing, not by listening or even watching. Traumatized children bring into the classroom many fears and emotions as well as poorly self-regulated excitement and activity levels. Expressive learning channels mental, emotional, and behavioral energy into learning. This can address NRT goal 5 by repetition of learning that involves expression.

Predictable Structure

While avoiding rigidity, the optimal learning environment for the traumatized child must have a predictable and comforting structure that signals to the child that safety is assured, adults are appropriately in charge, and students can focus full time on being interested learners in their own childlike fashion. Predictability is important because although most children enjoy surprises, traumatized students often react negatively to surprises they did not anticipate, setting off their fear arousal system. Safety addresses NRT goals 1 and 3.

More Successes than Failures

When people try something new, they fail many times before they master the task. Traumatized students give up long before the mastery stage and therefore decline or even refuse to take the risk to try something new in the first place. The child must experience many more successes than failures in small and large ways. Experiencing success is reinforced by repetition in NRT goal 5.

Adult Mediated Peer Interaction

Adults must monitor what is going on among the children because, while "kids will be kids," the traumatized student will experience a lack of physical or interpersonal safety with "normal" communication among children that is negative, teasing, bullying, or demeaning. Even if these negative elements are not present, traumatized students often misinterpret the messages and motivations of others. Adults who are present can help prevent real or perceived negative peer interactions, helping NRT goal 1.

External Cognitive Structure

Instructors must overcome the brain deficits of traumatized children by providing meaning, planning, and connections from outside the child's brain. Adults must help the child understand the mental processing steps as well as the end result of higher-order reasoning. Executive functions, such as thoughtful consideration, goal setting, planning, learning from past practice, and step-by-step activity, are all necessary practices for achieving optimal learning. This is an effective way to assist with NRT goal 2 by helping the brain internally organize.

The "Unschool"

Most traumatized children have been in school before, and often it was a negative experience. Since their brain filters new experiences through past negative memories, it may be helpful to shed the trappings of "school." The *unschool* looks different, feels different, and is different. What does the child experience when walking into the environment? Color, energy, interesting things, and space to be expressive? Or rigid order, regimentation, posted rules and regulations, and constrictions on movement and activity? Active learning will capture the interest of traumatized students before inactive learning. This addresses NRT goal 1 when the child experiences a very different setting.

Encouragement through Relationship

Traumatized students need social support but seldom know how to ask for such support or accept it when it is offered. Adults cannot wait until the child is receptive to a relationship; the adult must meet the child much more than halfway. Forming a relationship with a safe adult addresses much of what the child needs in order to begin to open up to the risks of learning and trying new tasks. A positive relationship helps the child operate from the prefrontal cortex (NRT goal 4).

Teaching to the Child's Individual Learning Style

All children learn differently, and the specific learning style of each traumatized child must be identified to help overcome the many hurdles to learning. Multidimensional instructional approaches that include auditory, kinesthetic, and visual components can be very effective. This can help with neuro-integration (NRT goal 2).

Even Competition

As mentioned earlier, competition can be an energizing learning tool as long as it is even and not overdone. Even competition ensures that each of the competitors has a good chance of winning every time. Any competition with a predetermined outcome may be fair, but it is not even and it will not be a positive learning experience for the traumatized child. Even competition can help the student invest in an activity, which addresses NRT goal 5.

Internalized Goal Setting

Although mental reasoning must come from the outside initially, effort must go into the child setting reachable internal goals. Adults must insure that these goals are not only reachable but also successfully reached before the child can set additional ones. When a student with a losing attitude either wins a competition or reaches a goal, they seldom know how to handle the experience and initially can be tiresome and demand constant attention, which they need to make up for the past. They will need help to be a "good winner" and appropriately proud of an accomplishment. This helps activate the orbitofrontal cortex (NRT goal 4).

Enjoyment and Fun

Learning will be unsustainable if it is not fun for the traumatized student. The two primary jobs of a child are to learn and to have fun. Ideally, they will do both at the same time, when possible. The optimum learning environment facilitates learning in an enjoyable and fun setting. This will increase repetitive engagement, helping with NRT goal 5.

Variety of Activities and Help with Transitions

The opposite of a constricting/rigid learning setting is one that has a variety of interests and activities. Traumatized students are often poor at self-regulating high energy, so they will need outside help, even with positive emotional expression. These children will also need adults to help them prepare for and initiate transitions from one activity to another. Outside help assists with attaining NRT goal 2.

Choices in Areas that Interest the Child

Students have more investment in learning things they are interested in and have some role in choosing. With creativity, nearly any subject area can be learned through nearly any topic or interest the child has. An optimal learning environment has room for the student to pursue their chosen interests. NRT goal 1 is helped when the child perceives some control.

Group / Cooperative Efforts Promoting Teamwork

Because a traumatized child lives in a solitary world, positive social experiences are critically important. Such a student may not initiate or even willingly participate in group learning at first, but this is a very potent and important way to gain social success and support. Group efforts must be monitored closely by adults, who should also encourage all of the participants to achieve a successful outcome if the student is to receive the optimal gain. Positive social engagement helps to change perceptions (NRT goal 1).

Ivan: A Case Study

In a rural part of Siberia, in the foothills of the Ural Mountains, Ivan was born to a troubled, unemployed, alcoholic mother. She agreed with the local authorities to place Ivan in an orphanage for his well-being. After thirty months of poor institutional care, Ivan was adopted by an American family. Over the next six years he and his adoptive family struggled and he was failing at home and at school. Some of his problem areas were: violent tantrums, aggressive and intentionally hurtful behavior, hypervigilance, oppositional behavior, and continual arguing. He was in and out of school and had missed out on basic academic skills in addition to the long-term psychological and physical (extremely poor coordination) impacts of his early trauma. He was referred to our trauma treatment center and school, which uses Neurological Reparative Therapy.

A plan for Ivan was developed to work with all of the components of his complex needs in a holistic and integrated approach. In other words, all of his treatment and academic interventions were coordinated. A case plan was developed to meet all five of the NRT goals in his residential and classroom settings. Listed below are some of the components of Ivan's plan.

Goal 1: Alter Perceptions of School

Ivan lacked basic academic skills but was smart in other ways. We encouraged Ivan to choose some topics he could teach to the other children, making him "the expert." He loved this idea and was excited to do it.

Goal 2: Improve Neuro-integration

Ivan liked to draw, so he was encouraged to draw pictures and develop stories about the pictures. He loved to make up stories, and when doing this he engaged his brain's right hemisphere (artistic expression) while also inventing and telling a story with his left hemisphere (linguistic expression).

Goal 3: Help Ivan React Less (Limbic Brain) and Use His Thoughtful Brain (Prefrontal Cortex)

We made Ivan's school day very predictable and let him know a few minutes in advance of each transition. When he began to react, we taught him approaches to relax, encouraged him to calm down, and then discussed the issue (but only when he was calm).

Goal 4: Enhance Development of Orbitofrontal Cortex

We worked on one executive function at a time: setting goals, self-regulation, and planning what Ivan would say in a school debate, since he loved to argue. We just added the thoughtful component.

Goal 5: Encourage Positive Brain Change through Repetitive Practice

Ivan practiced everything multiple times. For example, he seriously lacked coordination, so we gave him physical drills that he did hundreds of times. We made these fun, and his coordination gradually improved.

There are no easy interventions with difficult children, but there are many success stories, including Ivan. There was significant improvement in all five goal areas over a full school year (we implemented many other approaches in addition to those mentioned above), and Ivan successfully graduated from our treatment program and school. He showed significant growth during our program and his improvement continued at an accelerated pace with his adoptive family. Five years after leaving the treatment and academic program, he was on the honor roll of his public high school and was entering college to study mechanical engineering a year early. Moreover, his coordination had improved to such an extent that he was competing in high school sports. While Ivan's progress may seem remarkable (and it is), it is not particularly unusual from our experience of brain-based interventions with learning.

School as the Doorway to Social and Personal Success in Life

Success in school carries more weight for the traumatized child than for other students. For those who have suffered trauma, attending school can merely confirm that the world is filled with unresponsive, threatening adults and peers.

On the other hand, it can also reveal that some places are safe, stimulating, and even fun. Given the vast numbers of traumatized children in modern society, it is time to take a very close look at how we might facilitate learning for these students. One size does not fit all in education, particularly the education of traumatized students. Putting the requisite effort into developing an optimal learning environment can reap huge rewards for children who deserve the very best education we can provide for them. We may need to start small in this endeavor, with limited experiments; but until we reach all of these students, we will continue to struggle with large numbers of them failing in their academic and social efforts. And traumatized children cannot afford to suffer more failure.

As every teacher and school administrator knows only too well, there is nothing easy about working with troubled children. But they also know that having a positive impact on a child and opening the doors to a better future generates the greatest satisfaction in education and in life.

How Traumatic Experiences Change the Brain
www.youtube.com/watch?v=lSQvFd8tyuE

The Critical Elements of Healing and Rebounding from Trauma
www.youtube.com/watch?v=mHqOPpBIHw4

References

Briere, J.N. (1992). *Child Abuse Trauma: Theory and Treatment of the Lasting Effects.* Thousand Oaks, CA: Sage.

Childhelp USA (2015). *Child Abuse Statistics and Facts.* Retrieved September 28, 2016 from www.childhelp.org/child-abuse-statistics/.

Cohen, J. (1986). Learning disabilities and psychological development in childhood and adolescence. *Annals of Dyslexia*, 36(1), 287–300.

Cohen, J.A., Mannarino, A.P., and Knudsen, K. (2005). *Treating Sexually Abused Children: 1 Year Follow-up of a Randomized Control Trial.* Pittsburgh, PA: Drexel University College of Medicine.

Hariri, A.R., and Holmes, A. (2006). Genetics of emotional regulation: The role of the serotonin transporter in neural function. *Trends in Cognitive Science*, 10, 182–191.

Kagan, J. (2010). *The Temperamental Threat: How Genes, Culture, Time and Luck Make Us Who We Are.* New York: Dana Press.

Lyubomirsky, S., King, L., and Diener, E. (2005). The benefits of frequent positive affect: Does happiness lead to success? *Psychological Bulletin*, 131, 803–855.

Pillemer, K., Fuller-Rowell, T.E., Reid, M.C., and Wells, N.M. (2010). Environmental volunteering and health outcomes over a 20-year period. *Gerontologist*, 50, 594–602.

Schore, A.N. (2001). The effects of a secure attachment relationship on right brain development, affect regulation, and infant mental health. *Infant Mental Health Journal*, 22, 7–66.

US Department of Health and Human Services (USDHHS), Administration on Children, Youth, and Families (2007). *Child Maltreatment 2005*. Washington, DC: US Government Printing Office.

van der Kolk, B. (2014). *The Body Keeps the Score: Brain, Mind, and Body in the Healing of Trauma*. New York: Viking.

Ziegler, D.L. (2011a). *Neurological Reparative Therapy: A Roadmap to Healing, Resiliency and Well-Being*. Jasper, OR: Jasper Mountain.

Ziegler, D.L. (2011b). *Traumatic Experience and the Brain: A Handbook for Understanding and Treating Those Traumatized as Children* (2nd ed.). Phoenix, AZ: Acacia Publishing.

9 A Vision for a Trauma-Sensitive School

Susan F. Cole, Anne Eisner,
Michael Gregory, and Joel M. Ristuccia

Having stated the very big challenge before us in the prior chapters, we now move to action. The nature of trauma is that it can cause feelings of disconnection from the school community that undermines students' success. Experts explain that a welcoming, supportive community can help children overcome these feelings and diminish the severity of the trauma response. In recent years a broad range of programs have been developed to address a variety of discrete issues. Many good programs and services can be employed in the process of creating a trauma-sensitive school. However, no program by itself can make a school trauma-sensitive, and overly prescriptive instructions cannot address the difficulties of making changes in a complex school ecosystem and culture. For programs and services to be helpful, they need to "fit" the school's culture and support its capacity to tailor solutions to priorities identified by its educators. They need to foster the growth of a trauma-sensitive learning community. Thus, we offer tools —not instructions— to equip schools with the ability to select their own trauma-sensitive approaches to meet the particular needs of their students and families. School-wide thinking and planning must grow from within rather than be imposed from the outside. This allows schools to become trauma-sensitive learning communities that ignite a process of dynamic change.

Each school will implement trauma sensitivity in its own unique way. However, a shared definition of what it means to be trauma-sensitive can bring educators, parents, and policymakers together around a common vision that can help them meet ongoing challenges. A trauma-sensitive school is one in which all students feel safe, welcomed, and supported and where addressing trauma's impact on learning on a school-wide basis is at the center of its educational mission. It is a place where an ongoing, inquiry-based process allows for the necessary teamwork, coordination, creativity, and sharing of responsibility for all students, and where continuous learning is for educators as well as students.

Figure 9.1 Kids in Classroom

For schools to achieve trauma sensitivity, it is important to clarify this vision to show what trauma-sensitive ways of responding to students can look like at school. Based on our past eight years of work in schools, and with the input of our partners, we have distilled six distinct but interrelated attributes of a trauma-sensitive school that are described in the first section of this chapter. A set of questions based on these attributes serves as a tool to help keep the vision of trauma sensitivity in the foreground as educators carry out the multiple daily demands of the modern education system. The attributes and associated questions help schools evaluate which efforts will lead the school toward the trauma-sensitive vision. Ultimately they help the school identify which efforts are successful, and which need more work, as they pursue the kind of change they are seeking.

Sustaining trauma-sensitive ways of thinking and acting will require a shift in the culture of a school, and the key elements of school operations need to work together to support this shift. The second section of this chapter introduces the Flexible Framework for identifying how school operations can be brought into alignment to achieve the vision of trauma sensitivity. A second set of questions, based on these school operations, provides a tool schools can use to develop effective Action Plans that integrate trauma sensitivity into the daily school experience of its students, staff and families.

Attributes of a Trauma-Sensitive School

No single attribute of a trauma-sensitive school can be viewed as an isolated fragment; they are all interrelated, adding up to a whole that is greater than the sum of its parts. Together they define ways to empower schools to understand and realize a shared vision.

Leadership and Staff **Share an Understanding** *of Trauma's* *Impacts on* **Learning and the Need** *for a* **School-Wide Approach**

Awareness is the critical first step in creating a trauma-sensitive school. All staff—educators, administrators, counselors, school nurses, cafeteria workers, custodians, bus drivers, athletic coaches, advisors to extracurricular activities, and paraprofessionals—should understand that adverse experiences in the lives of children are exceedingly common and that the impact of these traumatic experiences on child development can play a major role in the learning, behavioral, and relationship difficulties faced by many students. These difficulties can include perfectionism, withdrawal, aggression, and inattention, as well as lack of self-awareness, empathy, and self-regulation. They can also include problems with spoken and written language and executive functioning.

Educators in a trauma-sensitive school understand that one of the most effective ways to overcome the impacts of traumatic experiences is to make it possible for students to master the school's academic and social goals. Children often interpret lowered standards as a validation of their own sense of worthlessness, a self-image created by their experiences. For many children, however, their trauma-related challenges cannot be addressed separately from learning goals; their reactions become intertwined with the learning process itself, acting as a barrier to academic success. Therefore, trauma sensitivity is critical to high quality instruction. Addressing trauma's impact on learning at school does not require specialized curricula or programming, although planning and supports for individual children who are struggling will continue to be very important. Rather, trauma-sensitive approaches must be infused into the curricula, the school- and district-wide philosophy, the way educators relate to children, and all the daily activities of the classroom and school.[1]

The School Supports All Students to Feel Safe *Physically, Socially, Emotionally, and Academically*

A child's traumatic response, and the associated difficulty in learning, is often rooted in real or perceived threats to his or her safety, undermining a funda-mental sense of well-being. Therefore, it is important to ensure that students feel safe in the classroom, on the playground, in the hallway, in the cafeteria, on the bus, in the gym, and on the walk to and from school. Physical safety is clearly important, but so is social and emotional safety. Critically important as well is that children feel a sense of academic safety. That is, children need to feel safe enough to make mistakes as they are learning, rather than cover up any gaps through distracting behavior or withdrawal. Educators in a trauma-sensitive school understand that helping students undertake what may feel like a risk, such as volunteering an answer to a math problem, can happen only in a classroom where every child knows that his or her contribution will be respected by adults and peers. And they recognize that students with seemingly unquen-chable needs for attention may not respond to approaches that merely ignore the behavior because these students may in fact be looking for reassurance that they are safe.

Children can feel unsafe for a host of reasons. They may bring with them to school traumatic effects from past experiences—some of which they may have been too young to remember—or have pressing fears related to what they are currently experiencing in school, such as bullying. They may also have fears related to ongoing events outside of school—for example, an unsafe home or neighborhood—or be preoccupied with worry about the safety of a family member or friend, reinforcing the notion that their own security may be threat-ened. Structure and limits are essential to creating and maintaining a sense of safety for all students and staff at school, but that does not mean having rules that are followed and enforced no matter what.[2] We are referring to structure and limits that provide a sense of safety through predictable patterns and respectful relationships, with adults in charge who convey confidence—through tone of voice, demeanor, a calm presence during transitions, and in other subtle and overt ways—that they will maintain each student's feeling of safety in the school. With careful planning, all of the adults in the school can work

Figure 9.2 Child on Bench

together to provide a blanket of safety comprehensive enough to cover every space and every person in the school.

The School **Addresses Students' Needs in Holistic Ways,** *Taking into Account Their Relationships, Self-Regulation, Academic Competence, and Physical and Emotional Well-Being*

The impacts of traumatic experiences can be pervasive and take many forms, and a traumatized child's presentation may mask, rather than reveal, his or her difficulties. For example, a middle school student who pushes adults away may in fact long for their help but be afraid of betrayal. A high school student who appears lazy and not interested in completing work may actually be afraid to follow through out of fear of making mistakes. Approaches that address only the behaviors that appear on the surface often do not respond to a student's real needs. A broader, more holistic approach is required to understand the needs that underlie a student's behavioral presentation and to provide supports and build skills that respond to those needs.

Educators maximize children's opportunities to succeed at school, despite the adversities they may have endured, by bolstering them in four key domains: strong relationships with adults and peers; the ability to self-regulate behaviors, emotions, and attention; success in academic and nonacademic areas; and physical and emotional health and well-being.[3]

In reality, skills in these four areas are inseparable; there is a complex and systemic interaction among them. Academic competence is connected to

Figure 9.3 Girl Writing

self-regulation and fewer behavior problems; relationships help children modulate their emotions and foster success in both academics and self-regulation.[4] Physical and emotional health is the overall foundation for learning.

A trauma-sensitive school recognizes that these domains are inextricably linked and understands the critical role they play in helping students be successful. A trauma-sensitive school bolsters *all* children in these four areas, knowing that many of them will need a great deal of support in building these skills, which must be practiced in context, meaning in the classroom, the hallways, the lunchroom, and elsewhere. Applying this holistic perspective both at the school-wide level and on behalf of individual children requires time for educators to meet and brainstorm creative solutions that address student needs. Schools have found that this time can be integrated into existing planning blocks, not necessarily requiring yet another set of special meetings. The point is to be sure that a holistic approach based on these four core domains is part of how the school is run on a day-to-day basis and that children needing extra help developing these skills will receive that assistance.

The School Explicitly Connects Students to the School Community *and Provides Multiple Opportunities to Practice Newly Developing Skills*

Helping children build skills addresses only part of what is needed to help them learn. The loss of a sense of safety caused by traumatic events can cause a child to feel disconnected from others. Typically, the child is looking to those at school to establish or restore feelings of security and connection with the school community. Too often we respond negatively to a child who is seeking attention or whose behavior is confusing or oppositional, when the child may be desperately in need of connection to peers and adults. We too easily discipline students for an inappropriate response to an adult, labeling it disrespect, rather than recognizing it as the student's halting or awkward effort to relate.[5] It is essential for staff to understand that all students have a need to engage actively in the school community, even those who may seem to be pushing us away.

Helping students make positive connections to other members of the school community, providing opportunities for them to use their newly developing skills in context, and supporting them as they become fluent in participating fully in the community are essential elements of a trauma-sensitive school. Equally important is creating a culture of acceptance and respect in this community of learners, focusing on building a school and classroom culture where everyone is seen as having something significant to offer and is encouraged and supported to do so.

For many students, their sense of connection to school is enhanced when their parents feel welcomed and respected in the school community. A trauma-sensitive school makes deliberate efforts to engage parents and caregivers and help them connect to the school community in meaningful ways. As their parents become involved, students can begin to feel that they and their families are truly part of the school community.

The School **Embraces Teamwork** *and Staff Share Responsibility for All Students*

Expecting individual educators to address trauma's challenges alone and on a case-by-case basis, or to reinvent the wheel every time a new adversity presents itself, is not only inefficient, but it can cause educators to feel overwhelmed. A trauma-sensitive school moves away from the typical paradigm, in which classroom teachers have primary responsibility for their respective students, toward a paradigm based on shared responsibility, requiring teamwork and ongoing, effective communication throughout the school. In a trauma-sensitive school, educators make the switch from asking *What can I do to fix this child?* to *What can we do to support all children to help them feel safe and participate fully in our school community?*[26] Otherwise, the positive impacts one teacher might have made in his or her classroom can too easily be undone when a child gets in line for the bus, walks into a chaotic hallway, or enters the lunchroom. Opportunities for adults to share effective strategies are lost. Trauma-sensitive schools help all staff—as well as mental health providers, mentors, and others from outside the school who work with staff and students—feel part of a strong and supportive professional community that shares responsibility for each and every child and works as a team to address the impact of trauma on learning.

Figure 9.4 Classroom with Hands Raised

Addressing the impacts of trauma takes the solidarity of a whole community. Acknowledging the harmful experiences many children endure can be unsettling; for some educators it can also evoke uncomfortable memories of adversities they experienced in their own childhoods. The human need for safety and security is so powerful that at times even the most caring adults may feel the urge to turn away from facing the impacts of trauma. If they raise the issue of trauma when discussing students' needs, educators must trust that they will be supported by their colleagues and leaders. They must also feel confident that a structure will be in place to address a struggling student's needs holistically and that their colleagues will join together in this difficult work.[7]

This focus on teamwork extends to partnering with families. By providing meaningful, confidential ways for parents and caregivers to share their knowledge of, and insight into, their children, educators can help them gain a sense of trust in the school. As this trust deepens, it becomes possible for parents and teachers to discuss a child's strengths and interests, openly share concerns, and work together to address sensitive issues that might be affecting a student's school performance. These may range from everyday ups and downs to more serious concerns, such as medical needs, divorce, adoption, foster care, homelessness, or other losses. Students will benefit greatly from the consistent approaches that can be forged through the strong home-school partnerships that result from this teamwork.

Leadership and Staff **Anticipate and Adapt** *to the Ever-Changing Needs of Students*

Research describes the endless number of experiences that can have traumatizing impacts on children. A whole community can be adversely affected by an episode of violence or other tragedy that may reverberate particularly strongly for students in the school. Sometimes a troubling event may occur within the school. On top of this, we know that children bring dramatically different experiences into school from year to year as the surrounding community changes due to economic pressures, immigration patterns, and other factors. Often these changes can result in large turnovers in the school population, even within the same school year. Likewise, there might be high levels of staff turnover from year to year, creating a sense of instability. When schools and classrooms are constantly confronted with changes, the equilibrium of the classroom or school can be upset.

Educators and administrators in a trauma-sensitive school do their best to adapt to such challenges flexibly and proactively so that the equilibrium of the school is maintained despite inevitable shifts and changes. They try to plan ahead for changes in staffing and policies. And taking the time to learn about changes in the local community can, in some cases, help them to anticipate new challenges before they arise. Of course, many disruptions to a school's equilibrium are simply not predictable, and it is important to be aware that, whether expected or not, they may leave the staff extremely unsettled. A school can spend much time, resources, and energy feeling "thrown off." A trauma-sensitive school is prepared for these reactions and views them as opportunities to stop and reflect on goals and successes, but then moves quickly ahead, making plans to accommodate any new needs or issues that have arisen.

Trauma-Sensitive Vision Questions

The Trauma-Sensitive Vision questions, based on the above attributes, are offered to encourage active reflection and thoughtful inquiry on ways to achieve the vision of a trauma-sensitive school. They serve as a touchstone or reminder to keep the vision in clear view as schools identify priorities and plan, implement, and evaluate their action plans. An example of using the Trauma-Sensitive Vision questions might be to ask,

How will addressing a given priority or taking a specific action:

- deepen our **shared understanding** of trauma's impacts on learning and the need for a school-wide approach?
- help the school effectively **support all students to feel safe**—physically, socially, emotionally, and academically?
- **address students' needs in holistic ways**, taking into account their relationships, self-regulation, academic competence, and physical and emotional well-being?

- **explicitly connect students to the school community** and provide them with multiple opportunities to practice newly developing skills throughout the school?
- support staff's capacity to **work together as a team** with a sense of shared responsibility for every student?
- help the school **anticipate and adapt** to the ever-changing needs of students and the surrounding community?

The Flexible Framework

Schools sometimes take on new initiatives with a sense of excitement that can keep them from taking the time to consider all the pieces that need to be in place and anticipate the institutional barriers that might hinder effective implementation. In order to support the culture change required to make progress toward the trauma-sensitive vision, it is important for schools to "cover the bases" and make sure that trauma sensitivity is infused into each aspect of the school. The Flexible Framework, which was first introduced in Volume 1 of *Helping Traumatized Children Learn*, is based on six familiar and important school operations that schools should keep in mind as they implement trauma sensitivity on a school-wide basis:

1. **Leadership** by school and district administrators to create the infrastructure and culture to promote trauma-sensitive school environments
2. **Professional development** and skill building for all school staff, including leaders, in areas that enhance the school's capacity to create supportive school environments
3. **Access to resources and services**, such as mental health and other resources, that help students participate fully in the school community and help adults create a whole-school environment that engages all students
4. **Academic and nonacademic strategies** that enable all children to learn
5. **Policies, procedures, and protocols** that sustain the critical elements of a trauma-sensitive school
6. **Collaboration with families** that actively engages them in all aspects of their children's education, helps them feel welcome at school, and understands the important roles they play[8]

Flexibility is key in addressing the role of trauma at school. While the six components of the Flexible Framework remain constant, the *content* of Action Plans will not look the same at any two schools. Each school has its own strengths and challenges. The idea is to ensure that every critical area of operations is taken into consideration when generating ideas, considering actions, and tailoring solutions that fit the school's own community and the prioritized needs of its students. Using the Flexible Framework helps avoid a situation in which staff are left wondering why sufficient professional development, connections to mental health services, or policies to cement new approaches into place were not included in an Action Plan, why the initiative did not withstand inevitable changes in leadership, or why many students and parents felt left out.

Flexible Framework Questions

The Flexible Framework questions help educators ensure that their Action Plans take into account all the important elements of school operations. The questions also help identify institutional barriers as well as strengths that may become relevant as the school works to achieve its intended goals. The Flexible Framework questions lead educators to inquire:

- What role does school and/or district **leadership** play in implementation?
- What **professional development** is necessary for implementation?
- What resources, supports, or **services** need to be in place for students, families, and/or staff?
- What classroom **strategies**—both **academic and nonacademic**—support implementation?
- What **policies, procedures, or protocols** do we need to review, revise, and/or develop?
- What do we need to do to ensure that **families** are active partners in helping with implementation?

Using the Trauma-Sensitive Vision Questions and Flexible Framework Questions

The Trauma-Sensitive Vision questions and the Flexible Framework questions, used together, are essential to the process of making whole-school trauma sensitivity an ongoing and familiar part of how the school is run. The two tools do not substitute for the process a school engages in to determine its own priorities and select the actions it will take to address them. Rather, their purpose is to assist the school, during the course of this process, to keep the focus on the whole-school vision while developing an Action Plan that infuses trauma sensitivity into the daily operations of the school.

The more often staff use the Trauma-Sensitive Vision questions and the Flexible Framework questions, the more it will become second nature to identify priorities that call for trauma-sensitive approaches and to plan and implement school-wide actions to address them. As successes grow and understanding deepens, regular use of these tools will become an integral part of the school culture and begin to organize the thinking behind identifying priorities and solving problems. Based on the experiences of schools we have observed, the key to success is a willingness to engage in the kind of process described in the Guide in Chapter 2 that includes a large portion of the staff, harnesses their creativity and professional wisdom, and fosters excitement about working in interdisciplinary ways to address the needs of all children, including those who have faced adversity.

Note from the Authors

We recommend reading Chapter 2 of *Helping Traumatized Children Learn*, Volume 2: *Creating and Advocating for Trauma-Sensitive Schools* (downloadable at no charge from www.traumasensitiveschools.org). Titled "Guide to Creating a Trauma-Sensitive School," this chapter describes an inquiry-based process where the new awareness about trauma's impact on learning can become a primary motivator for making trauma-sensitivity a regular part of the way a school is run. The process begins with an individual's or small group's sense of urgency about the need for trauma-sensitive approaches. Through more learning and reflective conversation, this sense of urgency grows into a deeper awareness of the pervasive role trauma plays at school and how addressing it can improve students' educational accomplishments. From this foundational awareness, a small coalition can engage the entire staff in trauma-sensitive action-planning. The process described in Chapter 2 empowers educators to look holistically at their school's infrastructure and gain greater clarity about the ways in which its school operations may be encouraging or hindering success. It describes a process for overcoming these barriers so that the school can address its priorities in trauma-sensitive ways. The goal of using this inquiry-based process is for schools to become trauma-sensitive learning communities where new ideas and expansive thinking are nurtured and where synergy and teamwork make it possible for complex issues to be explored.

Notes

1   Approaches to trauma sensitivity do not require specific programs, but rather embedding approaches throughout the district's curriculum. Cole, S., Greenwald O'Brien, J.,Gadd, G., Ristuccia, J., Wallace, L., and Gregory, M. (2005). *Helping Traumatized Children Learn, Volume 1*. Boston, MA: Massachusetts Advocates for Children, pp. 47–76. This publication is available on www.traumasensitiveschools. org. For many helpful strategies, see Craig, S.E. (2008). *Reaching and Teaching Children Who Hurt: Strategies for Your Classroom*. Baltimore: Brookes Publishing. Additionally, the Washington Office of Superintendent of Public Instruction has published its own handbook, Walpow, R., Johnson, M., Hertel, R., and Kincaid, S. (2009). *The Heart of Teaching and Learning: Compassion, Resiliency, and Academic Success*. Olympia, WA: Office of Superintendent of Public Instruction.

2   Often, schools rely on behavior plans to reinforce structure and limits. However, behavior plans for traumatized students that are based solely on providing external consequences for observable behaviors are often ineffective. An excellent resource for developing behavior plans and contracts that avoid this pitfall by merging a deep clinical understanding and best practices for students within a behavioral construct is Minahan, J. and Rappaport, N. (2012). *The Behavior Code: A Practical Guide to Understanding and Teaching the Most Challenging Students*. Cambridge, MA: Harvard Education Press. Bruce Perry has explained why traumatized children's underlying concerns about safety often render consequences alone ineffective and why it is so important for a clinical understanding to guide the development of behavioral approaches for them: "The threatened child is not thinking (nor should she think) about months from now. This has profound implications for understanding the cognition of the traumatized child. Immediate reward is most reinforcing. Delayed gratification is impossible. Consequences of behavior become almost inconceivable

to the threatened child." Perry, B. (2002). "Neurodevelopmental Impact of Violence in Childhood." In D.H. Schetky and E.P. Benedek (Eds.), *Principles and Practice of Child and Adolescent Forensic Psychiatry* (pp. 191–203, 200). Washington, D.C.: American Psychiatric Publishing. In addition to concerns about safety, Susan Craig has highlighted an additional reason why traditional behavioral approaches sometimes do not work for traumatized children: because the trauma response can undermine their understanding of cause–effect relationships, they often exhibit "resistance to behavior management techniques that assume an understanding of cause and effect." Craig, S. (1992). "The Educational Needs of Children Living in Violence." *Phi Delta Kappan*, 74: 67–71, 68.

3   The use of these four domains (caring relationships with adults and peers, self-regulation of emotions and behaviors, success in academic and nonacademic areas, and physical health and wellbeing) as the organizing structure for bolstering success at both the school-wide and individual child levels is an intellectual contribution of an interdisciplinary group of experts convened by TLPI. These conclusions are based on the work of Masten, A. and Coatsworth, J.D. (1998)."The Development of Competence in Favorable and Unfavorable Environments." *American Psychologist*, 53(2): 205–220; and Kinniburgh, K.J., Blaustein, M., Spinazzola, J., and van der Kolk, B. (2005). "Attachment, Self-Regulation, and Competency: A comprehensive intervention framework for children with complex trauma." *Psychiatric Annals*, 35(5): 424–430. They are also based on numerous studies demonstrating the educational benefits associated with bolstering each of these areas for children. On the importance of caring relationships at school, see for example Connell, J. and Klein, A. (2006). "First Things First: A framework for successful secondary school reform." *New Directions for Youth Development*, 111: 53–66, 55 (stating that "[a]ll major school reform strategies share the hypothesis that better relationships between adults and students contribute to improved educational outcomes for students"). On the importance of helping children master self-regulation of emotions and behaviors, see for example Saxe, G.N., Ellis, B.H., and Kaplow, J.B. (2007). *Collaborative Treatment of Traumatized Children and Teens: The Trauma Systems Therapy Approach*. New York: Guilford Press (reviewing literature on the importance of self-regulation skills and calling upon all adults to help children gain competence in this area). On the connection between health and academic success, see for example, California Department of Education. (2005). *Getting Results: Developing Safe and Healthy Kids Update 5: Student Health, Supportive Schools, and Academic Success*. Sacramento, CA (citing Furstenberg, F.D. et al. (1999). *Managing to make it: Urban families and adolescent success*. Chicago: University of Chicago Press [finding that students have better grades and attendance when their health needs are met]). These four domains have also been proposed as an organizing structure for a more expansive way to conduct psychological evaluations of students with traumatic histories. See Tishelman, A.C., Haney, P., Greenwald O'Brien, J., and Blaustein, M. (2010). "A framework for school-based psychological evaluations: Utilizing a 'trauma lens.'" *Journal of Child and Adolescent Trauma*, 3(4): 279–302.

4   A meta-analysis of 213 school-based, universal SEL programs involving 270,034 kindergarten through high school students found an average increase of 11 percentile points in achievement test scores among students receiving quality instruction in social emotional learning (SEL) from their classroom teachers. Durlak, J., Weissberg, R., Dymnicki, A., Taylor, R., and Schellinger, K. (2011). "The Impact of Enhancing Students' Social and Emotional Learning: A Meta-Analysis of School-Based Universal Interventions." *Child Development*, 82(1): 405–432.

5   In working with schools and on behalf of individual students, a tension can sometimes exist between behavioral and relational approaches to address student behavior. As already described above, students exposed to traumatic experiences can have

particular difficulty establishing trust in relationships, and may require additional support to bolster their relationship skills and connect them to the school community. Some of the behaviors they may display stem from this lack of security in relationships. Aspects of whole-school positive behavioral interventions, such as clarifying expectations, focusing on a safe and predictable learning environment, and providing consistent positive feedback to students will be very helpful to set a positive context. However, within that context, the preferred approach with individual students is a relational approach, building on the connection between the teacher or school counselor and the student. An educator who is proactive about forming relationships with students early in the year will be able to check-in with students on a frequent basis and ensure that the student feels the teacher's positive regard. This positive regard and strong connection can form the basis for helping students articulate and cope with their feelings in the moment, for modeling how strong emotions can be effectively managed, and for engaging students in processing what has happened. Ensuring that the student feels the teacher's positive regard throughout this process is essential. However, behavioral approaches, such as planned ignoring, placing children in time-out rooms disconnected from the school community, suspending students from school—all of which intentionally withhold the opportunity to connect—may exacerbate a student's underlying fears of rejection and deprive the student of a much desired opportunity for connection. David Osher and his colleagues state succinctly that, "Behavioral approaches alone will not develop supportive relationships between and among students and adults." Osher, D., Sprague, J., Weissberg, R. P., Axelrod, J., Keenan, S., Kendziora, K., and Zins, J. E. (2008). "A Comprehensive Approach to Promoting Social, Emotional, and Academic Growth in Contemporary Schools." In A. Thomas and J. Grimes (Eds.), *Best Practices in School Psychology V, Vol. 4*. Bethesda, MD: National Association of School Psychologists, p. 6 (citing Bear, G.G. (In press). "School-wide approaches to behavior problems." In B. Doll and J.A. Cummings (Eds.), *Transforming School Mental Health Services: Population-based approaches to promoting the competency and wellness of children*. Thousand Oaks, CA: Corwin Press).

6   This shift from "I" to "we" represents what Fritjof Capra describes as a shift from "mechanistic" thinking (which focuses on parts) to "holistic" or "ecological" thinking (which focuses on the whole). Capra argues that this shift in thinking is necessary to understand the complex relationships that characterize a school community. Capra, F. (1994). *From the Parts to the Whole: Systems Thinking in Education and Ecology*. Berkeley, CA: Center for Ecoliteracy.

7   Judith Herman articulates the need for teamwork among those engaged in "creating a protected space" that can support individuals who have experienced traumatic events. She calls this work "an act of solidarity." Herman, J. (1997). *Trauma and Recovery*. New York: Basic Books, p. 247.

8   Readers of *Helping Traumatized Children Learn, Volume 1* will note that a sixth element has been added to the Flexible Framework since the original writing—Collaboration with Families—and Academic Instruction and Nonacademic Strategies have been fused together into one element. At the time of the first edition, families were not an explicit part of the Framework because we felt that families should be a part of each piece. Cole, S. et al., supra note i., p. 47. However, schools have found that families often get left out of the work unless they are explicitly considered.

10 Compassionate Schools

Responding to Kids Impacted by Adversity, Trauma, and Toxic Stress

Ron Hertel and Susan O. Kincaid

Since passing the No Child Left Behind Act 2001, school districts throughout the United States have busied themselves with the development of more rigorous outcome-based curricula, assessment plans, and coaching for standardized tests. Teaching methods were examined, and teachers and administrators were held more responsible for outcomes. In spite of these efforts, many schools have not significantly improved on-time graduation rates and test scores. This is particularly true for students struggling with challenges outside the school walls, sometimes being involved with multiple systems such as health care, legal, mental and physical healthcare, child protective, family reconciliation, and other social services.

A deeper look to determine which students were not likely to be successful in completing their K-12 school careers revealed that students who struggled most with family and economic issues topped the list (Blodgett, 2015). These struggles can reach traumatic proportions and become toxic, with significant impacts on life and learning. A new understanding of the role of the school began to emerge. If attention is not paid toward supporting these struggling students, the pattern will likely continue. The Carnegie Council on Adolescent Development (1989) stated, "School systems are not responsible for meeting every need of their students. But when the need directly affects learning, the school must meet the challenge."

In Washington State, staff at the Office of the Superintendent of Public Instruction (OSPI) felt it was imperative for school staff to understand the interconnected issues critical to the academic success of students in today's schools. In 2007 and 2008, the staff collaborated with faculty from Western Washington University to create a resource, *The Heart of Learning and Teaching: Compassion, Resiliency, and Academic Stress* (Wolpow, Johnson, Hertel, and Kincaid, 2009), that would contribute to a deeper understanding of learning and teaching, as well as the impact of adversity on learning, compassion, self-care, resiliency, and partnership. The concept of the Compassionate School was born.

The word "compassion" can seem too soft for those whose ideals are founded in academia or science. For the purpose of this chapter, it is defined as the fusion of equal parts of caring and high expectations. Without helping our students focus on high expectations, caring, in and of itself, would be insufficient to promote achievement and resilience. In order to facilitate optimal learning for students, schools must intentionally seek and promote ways for their staff to respond to and support students impacted by negative events in their lives. A compassionate rather than punitive approach allows students to feel fully supported, empowered, able to self-correct. It allows all to become goal oriented and ready to learn. Its relational process opens doors for constructive communication between students and school staff. It promotes a culture and climate that is supportive of all students, those students impacted by trauma or adversity, and all staff.

A compassionate school articulates the relationship between learning and social and emotional health and involves more than the single efforts of the school. Schools and communities, together, can do much to improve both. They seek a deeper understanding and encourage activities and strategies that promote student and staff wellness by embracing values that meet the diverse needs of students and their families. A compassionate school and community actively partner to address the health, social, emotional, and behavioral needs of students. The Compassionate School approach promotes a paradigm that:

- focuses on whole child education and development;
- raises awareness of the effects of stress, adversity, and trauma on children and families;
- utilizes data to build strategies that mitigate the negative effects of adversity and trauma;
- creates a context for change in the school and community environment;
- makes teaching more enjoyable and successful; and
- informs relevant policy revision and development that affects the culture and climate of the school.

Working in a school has both rewards and costs. The work can often be overwhelming and impactful. Compassionate Schools acknowledge that it is not just teachers who shape the lives of students, but the entire staff of the school. Many adults can look back at their school experiences and recall the significant, positive impact of someone who worked in food services, someone who drove the bus, someone who swept the floors, or someone in the front office. Therefore, a Compassionate School considers a team approach involving, at a minimum, everyone who comes into contact with students.

Successful Compassionate Schools create a context for learning through tailored principles that focus on the whole child; maintain high expectations; and empower *all* students to self-regulate emotions and behaviors, develop executive functions, and, as a result of connections with others, increase individual and community resilience. In this chapter, we will discuss: (a) neurodevelopment and the impact of trauma; (b) the development of the Compassionate School model; (c) piloting the Compassionate School model; (d) what teachers and staff need in order to succeed; (e) a description of the Compassionate School model;

(f) specific strategies for initiating and sustaining change toward becoming a Compassionate School; and (g) our conclusions.

Neurodevelopment and the Impact of Trauma

The Adverse Childhood Experiences (ACEs) study quantified, for the first time, the impact of life challenges on health, wellbeing, and cognitive functioning (Felitti et al., 1998). When the study was first launched, nine adversities were identified: physical abuse, sexual abuse, emotional abuse, neglect (later divided into emotional and physical neglect, to create a tenth adversity), mental illness, drug-addicted or alcoholic family member, witnessing domestic violence against the mother, loss of a parent to death or abandonment (including divorce), and incarceration of any family member. There is a dose/response correlation between the number of ACEs a person experiences and the level of impact on wellbeing: the higher the number of ACEs, the greater the impact. The total number of ACEs a person suffers is more significant than the severity of a single ACE.

In 2002 and 2006, data was collected from tenth and twelfth grade students in Washington public schools through the Healthy Youth Survey and cross-referenced to the original nine adverse childhood experiences (Longhi, 2010). Forty-three percent of the students were found to be dealing with three or more ACEs. Therefore, the prevalence of adversity was much higher than expected in Washington State classrooms. How we respond to students who are struggling can mean the difference between engagement and disengagement, between graduation and dropping out, between a fulfilling life or a life of unrelenting and irresolvable challenges.

Trauma and toxic stress occur when intense, regular, and/or long-term adversity is experienced in one or more areas without employing or having access to adequate resources and supports. Trauma is not the event itself but rather the perception of and subsequent reactions and responses to significant challenges. We may ask ourselves why one person can easily glide through a challenging experience whereas another may be incapacitated by it. The stress response system is woven into our bodies as a means to survive. It is engaged by our perception and reactions. If we perceive something as a threat, whether it is or not, our stress response system kicks in, along with the production of hormones that trigger our bodies to take action: freeze, fight, or flight. The body's trauma response system fires whether the threat is real or perceived, and the hormones are dispatched in the same manner. The hormones, along with internal reactions and responses, ignite external behaviors—behaviors we mobilize, as needed, to survive. Reactions to trauma in the lives of our students (and sometimes adults) often manifest as behavior, especially in young children. Educators are often ill-equipped to respond to extreme behaviors that can result from threats perceived by children.

Although helpful for immediate survival in the presence of real danger, triggering our body's trauma response system is very taxing on bodily functions.

Prolonged engagement of the stress response system and the repeated flood of hormones can disrupt development or even damage the brain and eventually impair cognitive functioning. Some students entering our schools develop perceptions and/or come from environments where vigilance for their own safety is a daily occurrence. They come to school with brains that are wired for survival, regardless of the circumstance. For these children, survival supersedes learning.

Neurological development is dictated by the experiences and reactions to those experiences we have throughout our lives. Our brains are highly adaptable, and have evolved for survival in very individual and distinctive ways. Therefore, the wiring of each brain is akin to the uniqueness of fingerprints; but, unlike fingerprints, the brain's wiring changes over time in order to adapt to the environment (Medina, 2009). Additionally, there is a relatively new term that is exciting those who work with students who have endured years of deprivation and abuse. That term—"neuroplasticity"—has overturned the doctrine of the unchanging brain. We now understand that the brain is truly malleable, changeable, and modifiable throughout our life spans, but most notably in younger years (Doidge, 2007). Compromised brain processes can be overcome by building new bridges between neurons in order to allow us to work around deficits that have occurred (Cozolino, 2013). Neuroplasticity has provided much hope for educators in reaching students who have experienced arrested brain development through their life experiences.

Recent and compelling research suggests that social emotional health is foundational to cognitive development (Cozolino, 2013). Therefore, a student whose social and emotional wellbeing is negatively impacted by trauma and/or toxic stress cannot learn in the same way as a person without similar constrictions. The traumatized student is simply too busy focusing on survival. Therefore, toxic stress can rob them of a fulfilling life and successful academic pursuits. Educators can perceive students who experience these barriers to learning as difficult to manage or disengaged when they are really just doing their best to survive without the necessary skills and support (Cole, Eisner, Gregory, and Ristuccia, 2013). The best approach to dealing with students impacted by trauma is never "one size fits all." If educators have a deeper understanding of the body of knowledge related to trauma and the underpinnings in the lives students, it often allows them to see and approach students differently, demonstrating more understanding and supporting them in becoming resilient. Resilience is the counterbalance to adversity, toxic stress, and trauma, and schools can do much to promote resiliency skills in their students.

Resilience is a powerful force in fostering positive student growth. It can be difficult or nearly impossible to foster within children who grow up with chronic internal and external adversities in environments that lack nurturing adults who genuinely care about them. How we structure our school environments by paying attention to the climate and culture that surround staff and students can do much to support the development of resilience. "A resilient community can be described as having social competence, problem-solving capacity, a sense of identity and hope for the future" (Benard, 2004, p. 104). These same traits are present in resilient individuals, necessary to overcome trauma, and essential for academic success. School provides an opportunity to teach and nurture them in individual students, contributing to the resilience of the community in general. There is a reciprocal relationship between individual and community resilience.

Educating children today includes far more than academia. It is holistic. The physical, emotional, and cognitive functioning of students must be addressed for learning to take place. Maslow's motivational hierarchy identifies physiological, safety, belonging, love, and esteem needs as necessary foundations for cognitive functioning. Schools are challenged with understanding why some students succeed while others do not, given the invisible nature of the experiences the latter students endure outside of the school environment. Often, they fail to make the connection between how students' social and emotional needs are interdependent with cognitive function. They must be ready to adapt and respond to the ever-changing constellation of events and circumstances in the lives of individual students and families, and utilize their own resources and those of the surrounding community.

Development of the Compassionate School Model

The development of trauma-informed education began in Washington State in 2008 with a focused study to understand the impact of adversity on students and the development of a pedagogical framework and professional development on strategies to mitigate that adversity. A supportive structure across the school culture was designed and introduced for students impacted by trauma, but also to support all students and all staff who interact with students (a tier 1 approach). Thus, the Compassionate School benefits not only children impacted by trauma but *all* students, including those who are at risk. It has a significant impact on the culture and climate in the school. Focusing on all students facilitates the identification of individual students whose need for additional support may not be immediately apparent. Creating a safe and friendly environment for all students allows the modeling of compassion and the building of resilience. The school system is similar to the narrow passage at the center of an hourglass. Students come from all parts of the community (the top part of the hourglass) to enter the school system (the narrow passage of the hourglass), where they learn the academic, cognitive, behavioral, and social skills required for life, before returning to the community (the bottom part of the hourglass) when they leave the school system. This has a profound effect in that the principles learned in a Compassionate School will, on an ongoing basis, impact the wider community and society as a whole.

Similar research and educational shifts have occurred in other areas of the country. In 1969, the Massachusetts Advocates for Children (MAC) formed an advocacy initiative called the Trauma and Learning Policy Initiative, a joint program with Harvard Law School. The trauma-informed work in Washington

State was ignited by the work of this group, particularly the publications of Cole and colleagues (2005), and continues to be influenced by a follow-up publication (Cole et al., 2013). As with the Washington Compassionate School model, the MAC model uses specific principles in a process for developing a trauma-sensitive learning environment that is unique to each school and benefits all students.

The ARC framework (Kinniburgh and Blaustein, 2005) also strongly informed the Compassionate School model. The ARC model is based on three domains: attachment, self-regulation, and competency. Each domain is organized around a target area, with an additional target area of integration of the skills from the three domains. The ARC model is designed to be flexible and has been successful with diverse populations and age groups (Arvidson et al., 2011).

Another model, City Connects (Boston College Center for Optimized Student Support, 2014) has been in use since the 2001–2002 academic year. In this model (which focuses on elementary school children), a multi-discipline team reviews the strengths and academic, social and emotional, physical, and family needs of every student identified by the classroom teacher and then develops a specifically tailored plan for that student. Although this model focuses on issues of poverty, teams are unlikely to miss services for individual students experiencing trauma because of the student review process.

Clearly, this is not an exhaustive review of the numerous models and programs that have emerged over the past decade. It simply highlights a few of the successful models that informed the development of the Compassionate Schools initiative.

Piloting the Compassionate School Model

An initial pilot of Compassionate Schools was done in 2008 as a part of the Substance Abuse and Mental Health Services Administration's (SAMHSA) Mental Health Transformation grant. Eleven schools were identified to implement the training, concepts, and strategies that were outlined in *The Heart of Learning and Teaching: Compassion, Resiliency, and Academic Success* (Wolpow et al., 2009). The schools were chosen in two culturally distinct areas of the state. All eleven that implemented the program reported positive results in a summary of the project's outcomes (Hertel, Frausto, and Harrington, 2009). Comments from Compassionate School staff reflected a variety of changes in perception that ultimately affected their ability to respond rather than react to student trauma-related behaviors that had previously been a challenge to them. These comments included:

*   "A compassionate focus creates a shift in thinking for school staff, from 'What's wrong with you?' to 'What's happened to you?'"
*   "Our frequent discussions have helped us to reflect on the possible reasons for some students' behavior."

- "I believe we are looking at our students through different eyes—realizing there might be a reason for their 'outbursts.'"
- "Thinking differently about kids' behavior, teaching skills rather than punishing when kids misbehave."
- "Compassionate Schools helped us look at how we view kids and how we treat them individually. Staff started to show more understanding of what might be happening to their students."

What Teachers and Staff Need in Order to Succeed

Education can be a noble vocation, and it often demands an investment from teachers to meet the needs of all those who enter their classrooms. Many students come to school with seemingly monumental challenges that impact learning and their overall ability to flourish. A student weathering life storms can make teaching the most challenging and, at the same time, if approached properly, the most rewarding profession. The primary obligation of schools is to help children achieve academically; however, there are times when traumatic events and toxic stress become barriers to academic achievement and a thriving life.

One of the key aspects of the Washington State Compassionate School initiative is its emphasis on self-care. It is an ethical obligation for those who work with others in supportive roles (Wolpow et al., 2009). As indicated in the ACEs study (Felitti et al., 1998), the majority of adults go through life with their own constellation of ACEs. Awareness is the key to changing our approach to others through the recognition of how ACEs manifest in one's own life and of the resilience that is needed to weather them. If staff do not take care of themselves, they are not able to care for others effectively. When working with students, it is not uncommon to empathize so strongly that the emotional content of their lives results in symptoms of secondary trauma, which can cause someone to internalize the stress of others. This secondary trauma can take its toll on educators in a way that impacts their personal lives through added stress, particularly when they feel helpless to resolve the issues of students. An intentional and well-designed self-care plan is therefore essential if we are to be at our best, maintain positive health and wellbeing, and avoid burnout.

For teachers and school staff, understanding ACEs and becoming mindful of the potential reasons for specific behaviors (including their own) are vital components of becoming a Compassionate School and also point to the need to develop a self-care plan. Through professional development, teachers and staff gain an understanding of a comprehensive approach and develop strategies and infrastructure that authentically support students through positive responses and an optimal learning environment. Research demonstrates that there are fewer classroom discipline issues when the principles of a Compassionate School are instituted (Hertel et al., 2009). In that way, a Compassionate School contributes to the self-care of teachers and staff by reducing stress and increasing resilience.

Teachers and other school staff are extremely busy, so it is unreasonable to suggest that they should become therapists to traumatized students. The Compassionate School teaches skills of observation. This approach is designed to bolster awareness and familiarize staff with strategies and tools to utilize with students who may be challenging and when nothing else has worked. The ethical obligation to engage in self-care allows staff to be fully engaged with students and to model healthy behaviors and attitudes for them. In general, educators are keenly aware of readiness—that the basic needs of the student have been met—before learning can take place. However, it is imperative that staff are able, first, to recognize and address *their own* stresses and adversities. It is only then that they can be truly open to being aware of the condition of their students' lives in order to help them prepare a solid foundation for learning and develop healthy and functional social and emotional skills. Educating the whole child requires educators be aware of their students' personal gifts, needs, and related barriers to learning, and to regard their social and emotional development as well as the academic skills that are necessary to prepare them for their future lives and careers.

Everyone has physical, emotional, social, cognitive, spiritual, and economic attributes, and a good self-care plan addresses all of these areas. Self-care hinges on a commitment to be constantly mindful of each area of our lives, self-monitoring our wellbeing in each area. Lipsky (2009) likens the mastery of trauma resilience to five steps:

• asking ourselves why we do what we do and whether it is working for us;
• choosing to focus on strengths and positive outcomes and controlling our mental investment in negatives;
• building social networks nested in compassion and actively participating in the community in all aspects of life;
• intentionally creating a balance between work and social activities, and between positive and negative thinking; and
• starting each day becoming centered by reflecting on why we do what we do.

Self-care does not happen accidentally. It requires forethought and routines. Plans for self-care are as unique as the individual who makes the plan.

Physical exercise can include doing things individually or in groups, and it can be as varied as walking, aerobics, snowboarding, yoga, pilates, soccer, skating, and jogging. According to Medina (2009), exercise is not only good for body functioning but also promotes brain function through the release of neurotransmitters and substances that mitigate the effects of stress hormones. A good plan includes activity that fosters pleasure and enjoyment. Physical exercise is part of—and a precursor to—balance in other aspects of life.

Mental engagement is not necessarily academic. It can involve other cognitive activities, such as reading, playing challenging games, watching documentaries or movies, analyzing news stories, and stimulating conversation. It might also include crafts, following or creating recipes, redecorating, planning vacations, gardening, or remodeling. If all mental engagement is related to work, we lose the balance that we so badly need to process secondary trauma. As with physical activity, mental engagement should foster pleasure and enjoyment.

Drafting a plan for emotional wellbeing may prove difficult for some people. Time for reflection, journaling, and confiding in a trusted friend or therapist can be helpful to emotional health. For most, emotional wellbeing is tied to culture, worldview, and spirituality. It is also tied to narrative, the stories we tell ourselves, and the family and societal stories in which they evolve (Beier, Cannadine, and Rosenheim, 1989). We assign meaning to events through the stories we form. If we change the story, we can change the meaning. This is a critical skill for processing trauma. Mental engagement and emotional wellbeing are integrated, making it difficult to achieve balance in one area without balance in the other.

Lastly, professional ethics contribute to self-care. An understanding of professional boundaries, mandated reporting, and the professional role each school staff member plays in assisting students with trauma allows each to separate his or her individual responsibility from the overall responsibility. Educators are generally responsible for the academic growth of thirty or more students, making it impossible to focus on the needs of a single child. Hopefully, other members of staff, such as school counselors, behaviorist paraprofessionals, and resident human service professionals or social workers, may be able to connect with the family or provide individual time to the traumatized student. It is also helpful to reach out to the surrounding community in partnership to meet the needs of students. The teacher who feels helpless is likely to experience compassion fatigue and burnout. That is why a team approach to Compassionate School development is critical to its success.

Description of the Compassionate School Model

No two individuals are alike, and no two schools are alike. There is not a "one size fits all" program for Compassionate Schools. In fact, it is not even a program. Rather, it is a process that continues and builds over time. The intent in developing the Compassionate Schools framework was to equip educators with information, specific tools, and approaches to help them respond compassionately to the needs of students impacted by trauma in more positive, productive, and supportive ways (Wolpow et al., 2009). It is individualized and tailored for each school and community on the basis of their specific assets and needs. Each Compassionate School is developed through a long-term goal process that involves a careful scaffolding of events, staying focused and methodical so as not to become overwhelmed. It is a comprehensive process and, given an open and inviting platform on which to participate, there will be no shortage of ideas about how to improve the school. Creative ideas are important and should be actively solicited from families and the wider community. The plan for how they should be implemented—and who should implement them—becomes critical. Full, meaningful, and authentic partnerships with families and communities to realize school-based goals create an environment where people feel ownership and vital to the process.

The process involves six principles of "How We Teach" and three domains of "What We Teach" (see Table 10.1).

In the "What We Teach" domains, first and foremost, there must be a safe and supportive environment for learning. Students must feel a sense of their own wellbeing, created by connectedness and a nurturing environment. Second, there is a focus on emotional and behavioral self-regulation. Most elementary school principals we have worked with state that the most important element in the early years of learning is self-regulation—the ability to modulate reactions to challenges. Third, there is personal agency and executive function—the ability to make and follow through with plans and goals in life that will shape the future in positive ways. Having these skills will be foundational for students toward achieving their academic goals. The *Common Core* (2016) articulates three skills for success in college, career, and life: an analytical approach; critical thinking; and problem-solving. These skills are also key elements in building resilience, which is so vital for survival.

In order to achieve the "What We Teach," it is important that we understand the "How We Teach." To design a set of guidelines to inform "How We Teach," Wolpow et al. (2009) spent significant time researching the components of resilience. What kind of environment and interaction are needed to foster

Table 10.1 Principles and Domains of Compassionate Schools

How We Teach Compassionate Teaching and Discipline Principles	What We Teach Compassionate Curriculum Strategies	
1 Always empower. Never disempower.	Domain One	Safety, Connection, and Assurance of Wellbeing
2 Provide unconditional positive regard.		
3 Maintain high expectations.	Domain Two	Emotional and Behavioral Self-Regulation
4 Check assumptions. Observe. Question.		
5 Be a relationship coach.	Domain Three	Competencies of Personal Agency, Social Skills, and Academics
6 Provide guided opportunities for helpful participation.		

Source: Wolpow et al. (2009) © Washington State Office of Superintendent of Public Instruction. Reproduced with permission.

and develop the skills of resilience for students (in actuality, for everyone)? The authors arrived at six principles. When these are consistently applied in work with students, regardless of the situation from where they originate, they bolster the development of resilience in their lives.

The first principle, *Always empower–never disempower*, promotes a sense of control that is crucial to decision-making. If we feel as though we do not have control, our motivation for moving forward is often compromised. Therefore, it is crucial for students to have a sense of control in their lives. Providing them with choices and allowing them to make decisions in their lives helps them to learn the concepts of cause and effect; they learn responsible decision-making and the potential consequences of those decisions. Sometimes, in a rush to maintain tight teaching schedules and academic requirements, teachers rush to make decisions on behalf of their students without considering the implications and the outcomes. But whether a student is in elementary school or high school, the teacher could offer a number of viable alternatives and ask the student to choose one of them. That decision should be made in terms of its implications for, and impact on, the student's life. This empowers the student while also building a relationship and trust.

The second principle, *Provide unconditional positive regard*, reminds us to avoid mental models that lead to negative judgments about others. Such mental models result in messages that the other person is *less than*, and the student can easily interpret them as discouragement. We repeatedly hear from our most challenged students that the one thing that helped them to become resilient was having someone (an adult) who believed in them. During our training sessions, several people have indicated that the person who believed most in them was an educator.

The third principle, *Maintain high expectations*, is a very important component of compassion. High expectations reflect the belief that the student is capable of meeting those expectations, and it takes positive regard to a more precise level of confidence in the student's ability. It may be a common perception that compassion means going easy on students; however, the opposite is more accurate. *True* compassion means that we believe that students have the ability to learn and achieve in all areas of life. When a teacher does not believe that a student can achieve, that teacher has diminished the student's potential for high achievement, resulting in lower confidence, lower performance, and lower resilience.

The fourth principle, *Check assumptions–observe–question*, reminds us to investigate before reaching conclusions that may temper our ability to respond. Taking thoughtful time to step back and understand the situation and intentions will help to shape a thoughtful and constructive response rather than a reaction. This principle allows teachers and other staff to cross cultural and other barriers to understand others' situations and world views, especially if they intently observe and listen to the answers that are provided to their questions.

Regardless of culture, gender, orientation, ability, or socio-economic class, people respond to the combination of unconditional positive regard, genuine open questions, and keen observation and listening. The idea of cultural competence is related to this set of skills, rather than to knowledge of the depth of information regarding a particular culture. As Attneave (1982) pointed out, there are multiple possibilities in every culture. To ignore a person's self-disclosure because of preconceived ideas regarding his or her background is anything but cultural competence. Information about various cultures has been generalized and categorized, and while it may reflect the worldview and attributes of a group as a whole, it does not necessarily reflect the worldview and attributes of a particular member of that group.

Be a relationship coach is the fifth principle. Siegel (2010) focuses on the three Rs of learning that are essential for success: relationship, rigor, and resilience. He takes into account the absolute importance of relationships, as school staff become role models for learning to navigate relationships in constructive ways. Teachers and other staff have a huge influence on students through their own relationships with them and their peers. All eyes are watching.

The sixth and final principle, *Provide guided opportunities for helpful participation*, suggests that teachers should go beyond the mundane to provide exercises and events that involve deep and meaningful learning for participants. This is vital to engagement for staff, students, families, communities, and anyone else who comes into contact with students. Doing so in meaningful ways taps into the gifts and talents of everyone, which in turn improves self-esteem and a sense of purpose and leads to greater resilience.

Compassionate Schools serve as an *up-stream* (prevention-based) strategy for students. It is designed to create a climate and a culture within the school that support students who may struggle with mental wellness, as well as students who are poised to turn to drug and alcohol addiction, delinquent behavior, or even suicide. The work is proactive and preventative rather than reactive, and development follows a continuous quality improvement process, always remaining mindful of improvement strategies.

It is important to reemphasize that Compassionate Schools is not a program. It is a systemic process and framework that is tailored to the strengths and needs of each student, family, school, and community. It is a strength-based approach that, first and foremost, asserts that all problems are solvable and all students are capable of learning and achieving.

The benefits of Compassionate Schools are presented in Table 10.2.

Implementing the Compassionate School Model

To begin the journey toward becoming a Compassionate School, there has to be a foundational agreement of values amongst school staff and what goals and outcomes, collectively, the school wishes to achieve. It is essential that the school leadership is fully supportive of the motivation and direction in order for it to succeed. Ideally, the principal will designate a team of four to six individuals—known as a "Compassionate Learning Team"—who will hold the vision of this path. Rather than relying on a single person to lead the effort, this group will share roles and utilize the collective strength they have as a team

Table 10.2 Observed Benefits of Compassionate Schools

For Students	For Staff	For Schools	For Communities
Improved test scores	Increased knowledge of learning architecture and pedagogy	Improved climate and culture	Increased school connection and sense of belonging and purpose
Reduced discipline referrals	Improved fidelity of evidence-based programs	Improved strategies for responding to ACEs	Increased investment in producing thriving citizens
Reduced special education referrals	Improved understanding of SEL and academic success	Increased family and community partnerships	
Reduced anxiety	Improved ability to apply trauma-informed teaching	Improved student outcomes in all areas	
Improved social/emotional skills	Increased compassion and resilience		
Improved attendance and graduation rates	Increased self-care and wellbeing		
Improved self-regulation, resilience, cognitive skills, and executive function	Increased job satisfaction and performance		

to reach out and gather information from other school staff and community members. As stated earlier, the Compassionate School training is not only for teachers but for every member of staff, classified and certified, who touches the life of a student, as well as stakeholders within the community. Therefore, in creating a Compassionate Learning Team, representation from various disciplines within the school and the community will create a more inclusive and eclectic environment from which the new infrastructure can be launched.

After interest and commitment have been established, training can begin. This training should include information toward building a base of knowledge that involves basic understanding of the neuroscience of brain development, adverse childhood experiences (ACEs) and their impact on a student's ability to learn (especially through early childhood and adolescent years), the need for self-care as an ethical obligation for everyone who interacts with students, strategies for the whole school and individual classrooms to promote a compassionate learning environment (including the promotion of healthy living, which includes nutrition, sleep, and the importance of exercise), and the development of meaningful partnerships with students, families, and community stakeholders as a part of school operation. Providing opportunities for students, the community, and family members to review school policies for consistency with compassionate practices can provide an outside look into the operation of the school and uncover potential archaic and undermining rules that are working against establishing a compassionate and nurturing environment.

Implementation of a Compassionate School framework varies widely, depending on the assets and needs of the community. As it is not a "one size fits all" program, it is developed through a process that is unique to each school and community. The school must begin by developing a broad-based understanding of what the students need to be successful and the obstacles to achieving that. A climate that ignites inspiration is vital. This requires a series of activities and conditions that support student achievement and cultivate an overall positive culture and the climate that the school is able to maintain. Although it is predominantly a tier 1 strategy, it is a universal approach that also supports students who are in the targeted and tertiary categories of needed support. It manifests as paying attention to how we treat one another in our interactions, be they teacher–teacher, student–student, or teacher–student. The atmosphere created in the school by paying attention to those interactions can often ignite inspiration rather than a continuation of stagnated or stunted operation.

It can be easy for a caring staff member to become overly engaged with a particular student's hardship. Therefore, it is vital to pay attention to maintaining appropriate boundaries while treating each student compassionately. If a staff member begins to overidentify with a student, that staff member's effectiveness in the student's life is significantly compromised and can end up being more destructive than helpful. This is not to say that staff should not display appropriate feelings of empathy; however, it is essential to maintain a balance between healthy empathy and overidentification, not only for the student but for the health and wellbeing of the adult. This is where the need for self-care may be most evident. Overidentification does not help the student as much as create a burden to become a care-giver for the staff member. Therefore, creating and maintaining a structure both internally and externally is important in terms of remaining attuned to the students' needs.

Transitions are difficult, be they between home and school, kindergarten and first grade, elementary school and middle school, middle school and high school, or high school and adulthood. They can be a challenge, and all students require a significant amount of support to negotiate them. And this need for support is even more critical for children who are impacted by trauma and toxic stress. Across the United States, we see high recidivism rates for children who have been incarcerated or held in treatment facilities. Plans for returning a child to the community after a lengthy stay in such a facility are often not well thought out in terms of providing support either prior to or after their return. Some of our schools in Washington State take special note of these children and establish internal, school-based support groups during the school day as safe havens in which returning students can talk with and receive support from peers who have been through similar experiences. These groups support them personally and allow them to adjust to being back in the mainstream school environment. Schools must develop internal, specific protocols, procedures, and policies that address the stigmatization of students who have been excluded from the community. Paying attention to their needs and concerns on their return is a prerequisite for their successful reintegration.

Students also need opportunities to learn and practice social and emotional competencies. Schools and pre-schools are often the best environments for this to take place. Interactions with peers are practiced and monitored through the school setting and the climate and culture that are established. Relationships are participated in and monitored by teachers and other members of staff. Establishing relationships can be the most expedient pathway to learning social cues. Neurodevelopment is a continuous process throughout a child's involvement in the school setting. Guidance and modeling for social interactions during this period is one of the highest forms of learning a child can accomplish.

Some aspects of classroom and school structure are essential ingredients in the successful development of a compassionate school:

- Each classroom should have a specific and designated space where students can go to self-regulate when they feel the need. Utilization of that space can be at the student's or the teacher's discretion. Helping students to recognize when they are stressed and need some "space" is a part of teaching that is vital in a compassionate school.

- Greeting students at the door of the classroom invites each child into the class and helps them to feel welcome, respected, and a vital member of the class. Teachers are recommended, to the best of their ability, to recognize and provide personal comments of interest to each student. This encourages the belief that they are cared for and that the teacher is genuinely interested in their wellbeing. In our training sessions, numerous participants have told us that they were positively impacted by a simple gesture from one of their teachers or other school staff. The effects of these interactions often stick with people throughout their lives. Indeed, one moment of interaction can change the course of a life. Even seemingly insignificant actions can have a profound effect.

- Promoting activities that help students self-regulate. These activities might be called mindfulness activities, centering activities, or breath-based activities. Regardless of the label, scientific research (Lipsky, 2009; Mindful Schools, 2016) has proven that developing internal ways to calm an adrenalized system can be the difference between a child who can self-regulate and one who cannot. Students report that they often use mindful, centering, and breathing practices in the classroom on their own initiative when they are feeling stressed. In a similar manner, stretching activities, such as yoga, or other physical exercises can help to get a child out of their stress and into their brains through increased blood flow and the production of substances that mitigate the effects of stress hormones (Medina, 2009).

- Predictability is important. Students impacted by trauma benefit from having predictability in their lives. That predictability in the school can be accomplished in one clear way by posting schedules in places where students can readily view them. Communication from staff to students about expectations, including behavioral expectations, should be as clear as possible. Some classrooms begin the school year by establishing classroom rules and expectations that students themselves help create.
- Support during transitions is critical. It is important to provide some structure for transitions between classes, and between the school and the school bus, and to help students find their own structure for supporting those transitions in a calm and efficient manner. One elementary school in Washington State stopped using the traditional bell between classes; instead, it played classical music to signal the move from one class to the next.
- The students' own affirmation messages can serve as constant reminders of the strengths and assets that abound in every school, especially if they are displayed on the walls of classrooms and hallways.

Conclusions

A recent bipartisan act of Congress that replaced No Child Left Behind—the Every Student Succeeds Act (ESSA)—affirms and empowers the movement toward trauma-informed education, including a requirement for Congress to provide sufficient funds for implementation. The act was signed on December 10, 2015.

Elizabeth Prewitt is a community manager and policy analyst for the ACEs Connection Network. In a January 2016 blog post (Prewitt, 2016), she reviewed the trauma-informed requirements of ESSA that directed state and local school districts to implement programs to address the academic, social, and emotional needs of all students. Prewitt suggested that trauma-informed/sensitive advocates will need to engage further with policy-makers on these issues as the act is implemented.

The ESSA and associated authorization to design strategies specific to each community are congruent with the six principles of Compassionate Schools and support the notion of designing unique programs that are tailored to each school and community, rather than imposing a rigid, universal model. The positive benefits of the Compassionate School and similar models have been researched and documented. The benefits to children and society are enormous, particularly in the long-term context of an educated populace who are better citizens. The ESSA sets the stage (and guarantees the funding) to make each and every school a place where all children can thrive.

Schools are the only public places where we have the opportunity to interface with such a diversely concentrated and impressionable group of young individuals. Embracing whole child education as the assumed expectation of student support becomes the strategy to support students toward becoming excellent analysts, problem-solvers, and critical thinkers. For some, it may be their last opportunity for such development. We cannot afford to squander that opportunity.

References

Arvidson, J., Kinniburgh, K., Howard, K., Spinazzola, J., Strothers, H., Evans, M. . . . Blaustein, M. E. (2011). Treatment of complex trauma in young children: Developmental and cultural considerations in application of the ARC intervention model. *Journal of Child and Adolescent Trauma*, 4, 34–51.

Attneave, C. (1982). American Indians and Alaska Native families. In M. McGoldrick, J. K. Pearce, and J. Giordano (Eds.), *Ethnicity and Family Therapy* (pp. 55–83). New York: Guilford Press.

Beier, A. L., Cannadine, D., and Rosenheim, J. M. (Eds.) (1989). *The First Modern Society: Essays in English History in Honour of Lawrence Stone*. Cambridge: Cambridge University Press.

Benard, B. J. (2004). *Resiliency: What Have We Learned?* San Francisco, CA: WestEd Regional Educational Laboratory.

Blodgett, C. (2015). *No School Alone: How Community Risks and Assets Contribute to School and Youth Success*. Report prepared for Washington State Office of Financial Management in response to the Legislature's Directions in Substitute House Bill 2739. Retrieved September 29, 2016 from www.erdc.wa.gov/briefs/pdf/no_school_alone.pdf.

Boston College Center for Optimized Student Support (2014). *The Impact of City Connects: Progress Report 2014*. Boston, MA: Boston College Center for Optimized Student Support. Retrieved September 29, 2016 from www.bc.edu/schools/lsoe/cityconnects.

Carnegie Council on Adolescent Development. (1989). *Turning Points: Preparing American Youth for the 21st Century*. Washington, DC: Carnegie Council on Adolescent Development. Retrieved September 29, 2016 from www.carnegie.org/media/filer_public/45/4c/454cd6fa-9aae-4e2e-8155-6c243909f7e0/ccny_report_1989_turning.pdf.

Cole, S. F., Eisner, A., Gregory, M., and Ristuccia, J. (2013). *Helping Traumatized Children Learn*, Volume 2: *Creating and Advocating for Trauma-Sensitive Schools*. Boston, MA: Massachusetts Advocates for Children.

Cole, S. F., O'Brien, J. G., Gadd, M. G., Ristuccia, J., Wallace, D. L., and Gregory, M. (2005). *Helping Traumatized Children Learn*, Volume 1: *Supportive School Environments*. Boston, MA: Massachusetts Advocates for Children.

Common Core State Standards Initiative (2016). *Common Core*. Retrieved September 29, 2016 from www.corestandards.org/.

Cozolino, L. (2013). *The Social Neuroscience of Education: Optimizing Attachment and Learning in the Classroom*. Norton Series on the Social Neuroscience of Education. New York: Norton.

Doidge, N. (2007). *The Brain that Changes Itself: Stories of Personal Triumph from the Frontiers of Brain Science*. New York: Penguin.

Felitti, V. J., Anda, R. F., Nordenberg, D., Williamson, D. F., Spitz, A. M. . . . Marks, J. S. (1998). Relationship of childhood abuse and household dysfunction to many of the leading causes of death in adults. *American Journal of Preventative Medicine*, 14(4), 245–257.

Hertel, R., Frausto, L., and Harrington, R. (2009). *The Compassionate Schools Pilot Project Report*. Olympia, WA: Washington State Office of the Superintendent of Public

Instruction. Retrieved September 29, 2016 from http://k12.wa.us/Compassionate Schools/pubdocs/CompassionateSchoolsPilotProjectReport.pdf.

Kinniburgh, K. J., and Blaustein, M. (2005). *Attachment, Self-Regulation, and Competency: A Comprehensive Framework for Intervention with Complexly Traumatized Youth.* Brookline, MA: The Trauma Center at JRI.

Lipsky, L. v. D. (2009). *Trauma Stewardship: An Everyday Guide to Caring for Self While Caring for Others.* San Francisco, CA: Berrett-Koehler.

Longhi, D. (2010). *The Relationship between Two Kinds of Adverse Experiences (AEs) and Academic, Behavioral and Physical Health among Youth in Washington State and the Promising Effects of Higher Community Capacity.* Olympia, WA: Family Policy Council, Washington State.

Medina, J. (2009). *Brain Rules: 12 Principles for Surviving and Thriving at Work, Home, and School.* Seattle, WA: Pear.

Mindful Schools. (2016). *Why Mindfulness Is Needed in Education: The Impact of Toxic Stress on Communities.* Retrieved September 29, 2016 from www.mindfulschools.org/about-mindfulness/mindfulness-in-education/.

Prewitt, E. (2016). *New Elementary and Secondary Education Law Includes Specific "Trauma-Informed Practices" Provisions.* Retrieved September 29, 2016 from www.acesconnection.com/blog/new-elementary-and-secondary-education-law-includes-specific-trauma-informed-provisions.

Siegel, D. J. (2010). *Mindsight: The New Science of Personal Transformation.* New York: Bantam.

Wolpow, R., Johnson, M. M., Hertel, R., and Kincaid, S. O. (2009). *The Heart of Learning and Teaching: Compassion, Resiliency, and Academic Success.* Olympia, WA: Washington State Office of Superintendent of Public Instruction. Retrieved September 29, 2016 from www.k12.wa.us/CompassionateSchools/pubdocs/TheHeartofLearningand Teaching.pdf.

Appendix

Additional Sensory Processing Strategies

Lindsey Biel

Start the Day off Right

In addition to self-regulation techniques such as mindfulness meditation prior to school, pre-school sensory diet activities may include a firm massage or squishy hugs while still in bed; playing favorite music; jumping on a mini trampoline; taking the stairs instead of the elevator; biking, riding a scooter, or jogging to school rather than taking the bus or subway; or another activity that helps wake up the body and brain to help set the tone for a good day at school. Some kind of protein to feed the nervous system before school will help, though food battles should be avoided. It does not have to be traditional breakfast fare. If the child loves chicken nuggets with cheese, that's fine. Something like a fruit smoothie with some protein powder could work well, too.

Many schools have staggered drop-off and pick-up times to minimize mayhem when children arrive in the morning and leave at the end of the day. This can really help students who feel overwhelmed by crowds. If students first assemble in a certain location, such as a cafeteria, the student should be permitted to go to the classroom early.

Unstructured Time

Some students appreciate the freedom of choice time, gravitating toward favorite toys and activities, whether it's building with blocks, doing dress-ups with classmates, pouring and mixing at the sand table, or drawing with markers and crayons. However, many students with sensory issues become anxious and quickly overstimulated by all the sights, sounds, and movement in the classroom and struggle with purposeful exploration of toys and equipment. Instead, they may simply play alone on the sidelines. They may seek out the same doll or toy truck each time, engaging in repetitive and self-absorbed play in a quiet area of the room. They may skip around from one exploration station to the next, looking at what others are doing without participating, or simply wander around the periphery of the room. They may refuse to help at cleanup time because they cannot tolerate the noise and activity.

Children who are hyposensitive or sensory cravers tend to seek out movement and deep pressure, grabbing heavy blocks and hurling them, crashing into other kids, pounding on toys. They may need frequent reminders to be gentle, keep hands to themselves, and look where they are going. They may play with one toy for just one or two minutes before jumping to the next. During cleanup time, they may have trouble following directions and become overexcited and overstimulated.

It usually helps to create some structure for the student who doesn't know what to do with herself during these times. A parent or teacher may help the child who is "lost" to make a game plan for what she is going to do. The student may benefit from a written list of activities, perhaps with a drawing or photo of the toys or equipment she will use. Then she can cross off each item once she has completed it.

For the sensory-seeking child, such a list should include organizing, self-regulating activities that satisfy the craving for sensory input. This may include intense movement and proprioceptive work, such as jumping on a trampoline or doing jumping jacks, somersaults, wall and floor pushups, animal-themed yoga stretches, or other activities.

Another visual timer is the Time Tracker (available from http://learning resources.com), which works like a traffic light to tell students at a glance whether they have plenty of time (green light), need to start winding down (yellow light), or that it's time to stop (red light). There are accompanying tones for each color. Old-fashioned egg timers can also work well.

If children are not too startled by sudden sounds, preferred alarms on iPhones and other mobile devices can be quite helpful.

Floor Time and Desk Time

Many students struggle to sit still and pay attention at circle time or meeting time on the floor for several reasons:

- Low muscle tone (the state of the muscle *at rest*) means they cannot fight the force of gravity, while decreased muscle strength (the state of the muscle *in use*) results in rapid fatigue when attempting to maintain an unchanging position.
- Poor body awareness due to poor proprioceptive processing results in difficulty managing body position.
- Difficulty processing auditory and visual input makes looking at and listening to the teacher while filtering out other sounds increasingly tiresome as time passes.
- Tactile issues make sitting on a hard floor or thin carpeting painful, and sitting close to classmates poses a risk of unwanted touching.
- Finally, of course, anxiety and learning issues compound these problems.

Cross-legged sitting is especially difficult for a student with low muscle tone, loose ligaments, poor body awareness, and other issues. He seems to melt into the floor, with his spine forming a C-curve, and his neck hyperextended so he can see what is going on. This position results in back ache and neck ache, and it interferes with respiration and digestion.

Most students will compensate by changing body position frequently or by sitting on pelvic bones, hips, legs, knees, ankles, or feet. While this can be quite stable, it interferes with proper development of muscles and ligaments. Other children will switch from cross-legged to long-legged sitting to ring-sitting to kneeling to flopping around on their backs or tummies so that different muscles are engaged and no one set of muscles gets fatigued. Moving around also helps the child receive more sensory input in order to stay alert.

Schools should consider at what age and for how long students sit on the floor. Toddlers should not be required to sit in circle time until they are thirty-six months old (Copple and Bredekamp, 2009). Circle time for preschoolers should run about ten–fifteen minutes, yet some preschool circle times run for thirty minutes or more. Meeting time for older students may also last much longer than many students can comfortably tolerate. A few strategies might help:

- Teachers can help students organize their bodies in space with visual place markers that identify where their bodies belong, such as laminated paper mats with the child's name or photo attached. Carpet squares work even better to create boundaries on the floor and give nice sensory input when students carry them from one part of the room to the floor. Most will appreciate the added cushioning under their bottoms on the hard floor, and fidgeters can fidget with their own squares. Teachers can add ribbons or fabric tabs to the edges if needed.
- Children who are anxious or have difficulty with visual or auditory attention should be positioned thoughtfully, most likely close to the teacher. At the same time, a child who dislikes casual, unexpected touch may need to be situated with nobody behind her. Positioning a student who is hyper-alert by the wall or a bookcase will add a sense of security about what is happening in the room.
- Some students are better able to self-regulate if they are given the oppor-tunity to move (Pfeiffer et al., 2008; Pontifex et al., 2012). These students will benefit from a lightly inflated seat cushion that is designed to improve sitting posture. One such cushion that is very popular in some schools is the Disc "O" Sit, which lets students remain seated while they subtly wiggle. For kids who slouch, a lightly inflated, wedge-shaped cushion called the Movin' Sit Jr. can help correct the position of the pelvis and spine when the wide end is placed toward the back. Both are available at www.gymnic. com. Do not overinflate these cushions, because that will destabilize the student just when he needs added stability. Another option is a vibrating sitting pillow which provides tactile input that may help a child sit still comfortably (available from http://senseez.com).
- Children who have significant difficulty with floor sitting may need postural support. Students can sit on yoga blocks or specially designed floor sitters that provide back support, such as the BackJack chair (available from

http://backjackinc.com), often with a Movin' Sit Jr. cushion placed within it. Kids who seek out tactile and proprioceptive input by leaning against others, lying down, or rolling around on the floor may benefit from sitting in a beanbag chair or wearing a homemade Lycra wrap, which snugly swaddles the student while he sits and provides sensory feedback as he makes postural adjustments. A HowdaHug chair (available from http://howdahug.com) is another good option.

- Some students will participate better if they do not sit on the floor at all. With its convex base and soft foam padding, the Hokki Stool (available from http://kaplanco.com) lets students move in all directions while remaining seated. Other kinds of seating, such as regular classroom chairs, ball chairs, rocking chairs, plastic cube chairs, low benches, and other chairs should also be considered if they enable students to stay focused and organized.

- Circle time or meeting time may be the perfect time for a student to wear a weighted vest, lap pad, shoulder wrap, or other item if it helps them feel more organized and comfortable. As detailed in *Sensory Processing Challenges* (Biel, 2014), while there are duration and weight recommendations for the use of weighted wearables, the student should be allowed to wear the weighted vest or lap pad for the duration of any given activity. Never interrupt a focused, productive child to put on or remove a weighted wearable. Compression garments that can provide reassuring proprioceptive and tactile input, such as the SPIO vest, shirt, or leggings (available from http://SPIOworks.com) may be worn all day.

- Hand fidgets and oral comforts often help kids stay tuned in during sitting time. Teachers may provide a basket of hand fidget tools for the entire class, such as squeeze balls, Silly Putty, and so on. Students may be allowed to bring their own fidget tools from home. Remember: these are tools, not toys, and they should be treated as such.

- We all comfort ourselves orally, starting at birth. Oral comforts can include sipping water from a cup or a bottle with a sports nozzle. Crunchy and chewy snacks, such as carrot sticks, pretzels, dehydrated string beans, fruit leather, and chewing gum, help satisfy and meet oral sensory needs. Chewing gum provides great proprioceptive input into the jaw and mouth, increases alertness, reduces chronic (although not acute) stress, and boosts cognition (Allen and Smith, 2011). Therefore, it is well considering lifting a ban on gum in school.

- When seated, the student's forearms and hands should rest comfortably on the tabletop so he does not have to hike up his shoulders in order to work on the surface. Hips, knees, and ankles should be at more or less right angles, with feet flat on the floor. Chair depth should match the distance from the student's back to a few inches behind the knees when seated. The front edge of the seat should never dig into the soft area behind the knee. At the same time, the child should be able to gain postural support from the back of the chair. If the seat is too deep (too much space between the child's back and the back of the chair), a cushion that provides lumbar (lower back) support should be provided.

- A student may benefit from a hand fidget tool at his desk. If the child sits at the same desk each day, textured materials, such as stick-on Velcro, can be attached on the under surface. Hand fidgets can be attached to desk legs so that they are always available and can be used without distracting classmates.

- Upon entering a classroom, it may be hard for a sensitive student to find an acceptable seat while the other kids are talking, walking, and jostling each other. Therefore, the student with sensory issues may greatly appreciate having an assigned seat, even if he travels to different rooms throughout the day. The preferred seat location is often at the front of the classroom, where the student's view is unobstructed and he has fewer distractions. Often it is reassuring to sit by a wall and away from the glare of daylight streaming in through windows. It should also be away from clanging radiators and whirring air conditioners. It may take some trial and error to find the best seat for an individual student.

- For the older student who travels from room to room, individual teachers can save a preferred seat in each one to make the transition into each classroom easier. The science teacher, for example, can stack workbooks or graded papers on the student's table, reserving the seat without advertising the fact to the entire class.

Easy Movement Ideas for the Classroom

Frequent movement breaks boost learning and mood by stimulating sensory receptors, increasing oxygen intake, and releasing excess energy in a beneficial way. Here are a few additional ideas:

- "Heavy work" using large, deep muscles includes pushing, pulling, and carrying tasks, such as moving furniture, pulling a wagon full of books, carrying a heavy bag, playing tug-of-war, catching a weighted ball, climbing stairs, wheelbarrow walking, and commando crawling.

- Structured movement games, such as card decks available from http://superduper.com, include: Move Your Body, Upper Body and Core Strength, and Yogarilla.

- Assign special errands, such as carrying a note to the office or distributing worksheets or supplies.

- Use a high-quality mini trampoline or rebounder with a stabilizing safety bar for younger students (available from http://needak.com or http://purefun.com) or a Bouncy Board (available from http://rehabmart.com) before moving onto focused work.

- Mindfulness meditation is increasingly used in schools to help student self-regulation. It is best taught by someone who regularly practices meditation. Yoga can be very helpful as well. Regardless of whether a teacher is experienced with meditation or yoga, he or she can teach students to breathe deeply and slowly, focusing on exhaling rather than inhaling. Younger kids can use straws, blow toys, and whistles or roar like lions. Or they can exhale forcefully through a straw into a bowl of soapy water to make "bubble mountains."

- Singing, especially loudly, opens up the diaphragm for deep breathing. Find music that students will enjoy singing along with, whether it's Barney, Bowie, or Beyoncé.

Some Recommended Brain Gym Activities

- Brain buttons: These are the soft connective-tissue pockets beneath your right and left collarbones. Place one hand on your belly while you massage these points with the thumb and middle finger of your other outstretched hand for twenty to thirty seconds. Reverse hand placement and repeat.
- Cross crawl: Start with "unilateral" (same side) movements (e.g., alternate right hand to right knee, then left hand to left knee) and then do "contralateral" (opposite side) movements (e.g., alternate right hand to left knee, left hand to right knee; elbow to knee; hand to foot in front of body; hand to foot behind body; and other variations).
- Lazy 8s: This activity loosens up arm muscles while focusing the brain. It is especially helpful when preparing to write. Make a fist with your thumb straight up and extend your arm in front of you. Draw the infinity sign in the air (a sideways 8) using large arm movements, keeping the center at the center of your body so your arm has to cross your midline. Repeat ten times. Then do the same with your non-dominant hand. Finally, interlace your fingers and do it with both hands, allowing yourself to twist your torso and hips as needed.

Visual Considerations

Lighting

- If fluorescent fixtures cannot be replaced, turn them off and use floor lamps that can be bolted to walls for safety, if necessary. If no modifications to lighting fixtures are possible, ensure the lights have fresh fluorescent tubes that flicker less and add a diffuser to soften the light. Several light diffusers that comply with fire prevention guidelines are available, including inexpensive single-color Classroom Light Filters (available from http://educationalinsights.com), color-balancing Cozy Shades Softening Filters (available from http://schoolspecialty.com), and the pricey but attractive US Sky Panels (available from http://usaskypanels.com), which come in designs such as cherry blossoms and blue sky with fluffy clouds.
- Curtains, shades, or sheers should be hung over windows to filter out glare, which can range from annoying to blinding. Installing dimmer switches is also a good idea, so brightness can be adjusted as needed to accommodate incoming light from outdoors.

Visual Overloading

Today's classrooms are frequently packed with visuals that some students find overstimulating. Teachers can provide visual respite for sensitive children by taking the following steps:

- Cover mandatory wall decorations with plain paper during key times, such as lectures, in-class essays, and so on.
- Allow students to wear caps in class if they are disturbed by overhead lighting.
- Use a small area of the room as a reading or relaxation nook, with reduced visuals and reduced lighting.
- Provide a clear work surface: that is, no unnecessary papers or books on the child's desk.
- Remind parents to provide a quiet, well-lit workspace at home for homework and other activities that require the student to focus.
- Incorporate individual study carrels to reduce distraction and boost concentration.

Vision and Reading Issues

- A comprehensive vision examination should be conducted if there is any concern about the child's visual system and especially if the child is struggling with reading, ball skills, or maintaining visual attention. This should be done by either a developmental optometrist (also called a behavioral optometrist) or a pediatric ophthalmologist, who specializes in the development of children's functional vision, as opposed to just diseases and surgery of the eyes. A vision screening by a parent volunteer, school nurse, or even a pediatrician is not a comprehensive vision examination. Visit http://covd.org and enter your zip code to locate the closest developmental optometrist.
- Double-check that all written materials are printed clearly and cleanly since copies of copies of handouts and worksheets become increasingly hard to read.
- Simplify worksheets if they are overcrowded, enlarging font size as needed.
- Good, comfortable lighting is obviously quite important whether a student is just learning to read or poring over texts for hours. Even with good visual acuity, some visually sensitive students may struggle with contrast sensitivity. Their eyes and brains cannot deal with the sharp contrast between the white paper and the black typeface. Some students will benefit from using colored acetate overlays (available from http://reallygoodstuff.com) or handouts printed on colored paper which reduce contrast and relax the eyes.
- Children who struggle with reading often become self-conscious or anxious. The Tail Waggin' Tutors reading program from Therapy Dogs International (available from http://tdi-dog.org) may be an excellent solution. Spending

time with a gentle therapy "literacy dog"—petting and reading to him—makes it pleasurable and fun while building self-esteem and motivating a student to read without the fear of being judged by other people.

Dealing with Noise

Due to large class sizes and avoidance of sound-absorbing fabrics, such as carpeting, due to sanitary concerns, many of today's classrooms can be way too loud for everyone. Teachers may need to raise their voices to get attention. A sensitive child may feel like the teacher was yelling at the class when she was simply trying to be heard. Here are some ways to manage noise level in the classroom:

- Teachers can turn lights on and off or play a certain piece of music to get students' attention, rather than raising their own voices.
- If chairs make scraping noises when moved on a bare floor, add tennis balls with an X-shaped cut to the bottoms of the chair legs.
- To help students block out the distracting sounds of scratching pencils, sniffles, coughs, and talking, it may help to use white noise machines, white noise CDs, or a white noise iPhone app. Even the sound of a fish tank's filtration pump can help mediate more challenging sounds.
- Designed to look like a traffic light, the Yacker Tracker monitors noise levels in the classroom, cafeteria, or elsewhere and alerts students when noise has reached an unacceptable level (as defined by the teacher). Available from http://yackertracker.com.

Writing Time

Handwriting is a basic skill students must acquire to satisfy basic scholastic demands in elementary school. When you analyze the components of handwriting, it is easy to see why so many students struggle with learning how to write, putting their thoughts down on paper, and taking notes. A continuous interaction between cognitive and emotional skills, fine motor, perceptual, language, and sensory components makes this a very complex task. *Sensory Processing Challenges* (Biel, 2014) has dozens of writing strategies, hand exercises, suggestions for handwriting, and links to keyboarding apps to improve handwriting and written communication.

Before asking students to write, have them:

- Drink water and eat something crunchy or chew gum.
- Engage in upper-body warm-ups, such as shoulder shrugs, shoulder rolls, chair push-ups, or karate finger flicks (with arms straight out, palms down, alternate between making a fist and fully extending fingers quickly ten times, then turn palms upward and repeat then times).
- Pop strips of bubble wrap with fingertips or tape large pieces to the wall and have the students pop the bubbles by pushing against them.

- Depending on age, have students use Play-Doh, Sculpey, Silly Putty, Theraputty, or Crazy Aaron's Thinking Putty.
- Some good preparatory games and toys are: Lite Brite; Perler or Fun Fusion beads (with tweezers for a greater challenge); ZooSticks and other connected tongs to pick up small items, including snacks; Lakeshore Learning's Feed the Dog; dot-to-dots and mazes; Tic Tac Toe and Connect Four (teaches diagonals); Don't Break the Ice; Sneaky, Snacky Squirrel; Alex's My Tissue Art or My Clay Pictures; Color by Number (markers or colored pencils), Shrinky Dinks, Kumon books for scissor skills; among many others.
- Most students benefit from a multisensory approach and practice. Rolling out Play-Doh into "snakes" to form letter shapes, painting letters, writing them with a finger in pudding, tracing them on a carpet square, or writing them with a stick in mud are all fun, tactile ways to learn letter formation. One of the best and most popular structured, multisensory handwriting programs is Handwriting Without Tears (see http://HWTears.com), a curriculum that includes hands-on activities for kindergarten and upwards.
- Molded pencil grips can be added to a pencils or slim markers to improve grasp and boost sensory comfort for students. It is best to start children using grips as young as possible—preschool or kindergarten—since it becomes increasingly difficult to change grasp patterns in older students. Some of the most effective ones are the Pencil Grip, the CrossOver Grip, the Grotto Grip, and the Stetro Grip.
- Chubby pencils and triangular pencils may be easier for a student to hold.
- Weighted pencils and pens add heft and give more proprioceptive feedback to a student with sensory issues. This is also something to try for the student with hand tremors. Vibrating pens wake up hand muscles and attention spans. These include the Squiggle Wiggle Writer, which is lots of fun but difficult to control. The Z-Vibe, well known as an oral motor vibration tool, has a pencil adaptor kit that includes a chewable tip. The similar Tran-Quil pen or pencil set also provides light vibration.
- Tabletops are composed of hard, durable material that makes the writing tool slide quickly over the top and reflect light. You can add an old-fashioned desk blotter or polyester desk pad to eliminate glare and soften the writing surface.
- Reconsider writing paper. Old-fashioned gray or cream paper with solid blue, red, and dotted lines can be confusing for some students, especially those with visual issues. Opt instead for simple, clean writing papers, such as those from Handwriting Without Tears, or raised line paper which uses "fried ink" to raise the lines, providing kids with tactile cues about where letters should go.

All of these grips, pencils, slant boards, desk blotters and pads, and other adaptations, are available from www.amazon.com and therapy supply sites, such as http://therapro.com.

While children should always be encouraged to improve their handwriting, studies show that handwriting development plateaus by third grade (Hamstra-Bletz and Blote, 1990) or at the very latest sixth grade, as students develop their personalized writing styles (Graham et al., 1998).

When ability to produce written work interferes with written communication, it is time to consider other ways to facilitate getting ideas on paper. An assistive technology evaluation that assesses speed and legibility of handwritten work versus typing speed and accuracy will help determine whether keyboarding and other assistive devices should be introduced and the extent to which technology should be incorporated into daily schoolwork.

Note-taking can be difficult for many students. Here are a few tips for dealing with this issue:

- The teacher can provide a set of written notes for students (may need to be included in the 504 or IEP plan).
- Teach the student not to write every word the teacher says. Practice listening for keywords as well as using abbreviations and outlining lessons.
- The student can record the lesson with a SmartPen, which has a built-in recorder and uses special paper on which the student can outline the lesson. When reviewing class notes, the student touches the pen to sections of the handwritten notes and the pen plays back that part of the lesson.

Meals and Snacks

Lunch can be an unsavory time for students with sensory issues due to embarrassing picky eating issues, plus smell and auditory sensitivity if they eat in a school cafeteria. Here are some lunchtime strategies:

- Encourage parents to send in well-tolerated snacks and meals from home.
- Encourage the student to sniff a preferred essential oil, such as sweet orange or vanilla, prior to entering the cafeteria so it is the dominant scent in their nostrils.
- Arrange to have the cafeteria cleaned with non-ammonia cleansers at the end of the school day, with all the windows open so the room is fully aired out.
- The child who is sensitive to smells should sit far away from where the food is prepared and from trash, and close to a source of ventilation, such as an open window.
- Many students would benefit from avoiding the cafeteria altogether since lunchtime can be both a sensory and a social challenge. In some schools, understanding school psychologists, therapists, teachers, or even parent volunteers host a lunch club in which a small group of students sits together in a room other than the cafeteria.

Fire Drills

Typical fire alarms ring at ear-splitting volume, which can traumatize a sensitive student.

Obviously, local fire ordinances must be followed. However, the school system does have a choice about which approved fire alarm system to install and when and how to conduct fire drills. Many modern systems can be set to a safe but lower volume with selectable, less jarring sirens. Even with a tight budget, this may be a wise investment if fire alarms interfere with students' ability to participate at school comfortably.

Fire drills are intended to teach safe behavior in the unlikely event of an actual fire. The mere potential of a fire is scary enough for many students. The element of surprise may reduce their ability to practice necessary behaviors, such as staying calm and following directions. Fire drills do not have to be unannounced interruptions. They can be scheduled for a time that works best. For example, a fire drill might be conducted five minutes before afternoon recess, so students have to walk up and down the stairs only once.

Of course, drills are intended to help students practice how they will react in the event of a fire. An announced drill will allow them to grab a coat, handbag, or ear protection. Students should have the right to wear noise-reducing earplugs, headphones, or earmuffs in the event of a fire drill. They will still be able to hear the siren and directions.

If fire drills cause severe, prolonged distress that is not alleviated by ear protection and other measures, a student should be warned in advance and allowed to leave the building a few minutes before the scheduled drill. This should be added to the IEP and staff members should be assigned to supervise the child.

Gym and Recess

Gym and recess should be times when students can play, blow off excess energy, get physically fit, and feel great. Unfortunately, this is not the case for some students as the environment can result in strong echoes as the sounds of other children, whistles, balls, and other gym equipment bounce around the room. The sensory experience is frequently magnified by a gym teacher who blows a shrill whistle. All too often, students are directed to enter the room quietly and sit while the gym teacher explains the day's activity. Sensitive students can benefit from the following strategies:

- Give students five minutes to move before asking them to sit down and be quiet.
- In elementary school, have the gym teacher come to the classroom to discuss the day's activity before leading the class to the gym.
- Eliminate the gym whistle. Instead, turn the light switch on and off if student attention is required.

- If clothing changes are required, allow sensitive students to change earlier or later than their classmates and provide private changing areas. A student should be able to change in a separate room if requested.
- Allow sensitive students to work in smaller groups, if possible.

Some students become disorganized at recess or in gym because of their intense craving for input. It will help them to make a plan before going out and to practice safe, appropriate behaviors. For example, the child who tends to run to a desired piece of playground equipment, knocking over classmates in his path, may work with a teacher or therapist to practice navigating obstacle courses, including moving people. Risk-takers may need to be reminded of safety rules to avoid impulsive sensory-seeking behaviors, such as jumping off the top of monkey bars.

Kids who tend to get overloaded are especially at risk at recess because classmates are speaking loudly, running haphazardly, and there is sound and movement everywhere. The oversensitive student may retreat to a corner and avoid participating in playground activities. Strategies that may help this student include:

- Wear ear protection, such as noise-canceling headphones that dampen sound.
- Wear sunglasses or a wide-brimmed hat or visor.
- Play with a small group of students: for example, hit a tennis ball against a wall; complete an obstacle course; play hopscotch; shoot hoops; and so on.
- Have recess time in a smaller, more contained space, such as an alcove, with supervision for safety.
- Have occupational or physical therapy sessions scheduled on the playground at this time.

Transitions between Activities and Classes

Some students have trouble with transitions between classes or activities. It may be that the student has trouble with changes—from indoors to outdoors, being in a crowded hallway between classes, or simply changing mindset. Such transitions are prime times for sensory overload. Here are a few tips:

- Keep lights low during transitions in and out of the classroom or between activities and keep the noise volume down. Encourage children to whisper as they prepare to enter the hallway.
- If children are required to stand in line and have difficulty doing so, tape an actual line onto the floor. Allow the child who avoids casual touch to stand at the end of the line, or give them a special task while the others line up.

Stairs

Climbing stairs is great for students, providing intense "heavy work" for the deep, large muscles of the body. However, going up and down stairs can be tricky for some kids due to any combination of neuromuscular and sensory processing issues, and for the trauma survivor who may not sleep well. They may feel crowded in by other students and may refuse to climb stairs, or they may push others out of the way in self-protection.

- If possible, the sensitive student should be escorted up and down the stairs discreetly, either at the end of the line or before or after the other children have ascended/descended.
- Double-check that all stairways are well illuminated with light that is not glaring.
- The edges of each step should be clearly demarcated. Reflective stair tape (available from many hardware stores or from http://seton.com) is a quick fix but may peel off and wear poorly, especially on outdoor stairs.
- Reflective paint, as is used on roads and some playgrounds, contains tiny glass beads that reflect light. It can be used as a more permanent, safer, stair-edge marker.
- If safety, fatigue, or physical challenges are an issue and there are several flights of stairs to climb several times a day, the student should be allowed to use the elevator, if one is available. This will need to be added to the IEP.

Art Class

Art projects in the student's own classroom or in a separate art room can present significant sensory offenses. The goal here is participation, and sensory issues should not prevent that. Students should be allowed to wear soft, oversized shirts from home instead of smocks (which may be unbearable because of the scratchy texture of the fabric).

- If the student cannot tolerate the smell of regular markers or tempera paint, try alternatives such as Mr. Sketch scented markers or liquid watercolor paint. Colored pencils and crayons may be best tolerated.
- If a student refuses to touch Play-Doh or regular clay, try fruit-scented Lakeshore dough, unscented gluten-free Wonder Dough, or low-residue Crayola Model Magic. Older kids might enjoy using Sculpey, which hardens when baked to make beads and other objects.

Science Class

In science classes, smell can be a challenge since malodorous chemicals may be used in the room. Remember that even if these smelly chemicals are not used during the child's own science period, the hypersensitive smeller might still have to contend with their lingering presence in the air. All chemicals and other smelly materials should be stored as far away as possible, preferably in a room that is not used by the students. The smell-sensitive student can sniff his favorite essential oil before science classes to mask intolerable odors.

Many science classes have students sit on high stools to enable them to peer more easily into microscopes, pour liquids out of beakers, and so on. This may be physically challenging for students with poor postural control and body awareness. Such students will benefit from height-adjustable stools that have back support (available from http://k-log.com).

Music Class

Music class can be pure cacophony for the auditory-defensive student. Such students should be allowed to wear noise-canceling headphones and given preferential seating far away from loud instruments. If the din is still intolerable, investigate whether requirements can be met through alternative arrangements, such as one-to-one music lessons.

End of the School Day

School dismissal may be a stressful transition.

- Consider whether a student should be allowed to leave at a staggered time— either a few minutes ahead of the other students or after they have left.
- Some kids require some down time after school. If they have expended a lot of emotional and physical energy keeping it together all day at school, they will be exhausted when school lets out. For these kids, nothing may be more beneficial than to spend a few minutes in a relaxing place—whether it's a pretty park looking at the ducks or a quiet bedroom with their books.
- For students who attend an after-school program, care should be taken to match each child's sensory and emotional needs with the program activities. Allow students who need to regroup some time to relax before engaging. Active participation in a group activity should not be demanded. After all, this is an optional rather than a mandatory program. If the child needs to take twenty minutes with a book or to listen to some favorite music over headphones before playing a game with classmates or doing her homework, this should be acceptable and clearly communicated to the people who are running the after-school program.
- Likewise, at home, parents need to recognize and respect whether the child needs down time or active time. A parent may not realize how draining it is for a child to run a series of errands after school and then sit down and do their homework. A child may first need low-stimulation time alone in a quiet, dimly lit room with cozy clothing and furniture; or soothing, reorganizing input, such as lots of hugs or a deep pressure massage; or intense movement, such as a bike ride, swimming, or a trip to the playground.

References

Allen, A.P., and Smith, A.P. (2011). A review of the evidence that chewing gum affects stress, alertness and cognition. *Journal of Behavioral and Neuroscience Research*, 9 (1), 7–23. New York: WPS, 2005.

Biel, L. (2014). *Sensory Processing Challenges: Effective Clinical Work with Kids and Teens*. New York: W.W. Norton.

Copple, C., and Bredekamp, S. (2009). *Developmentally Appropriate Practice in Early Childhood Programs, Serving Children from Birth through 8* (rev. ed.). Washington, DC: National Association for the Education of Young Children.

Graham, S., Berninger, V.,Weintraub, N., and Schafer, W. (1998). Development of handwriting speed and legibility in grades 1–9. *Journal of Educational Research*, 92(1), 42–52.

Hamstra-Bletz, L., and Blote, A.W. (1990). Development of handwriting in primary school: A longitudinal study. *Perceptual and Motor Skills*, 70, 759–770.

Pfeiffer, B., Henry, A., Miller, S., and Witherell, S. (2008). The effectiveness of Disc 'O' Sit cushions on attention to task in second-grade students with attention difficulties. *American Journal of Occupational Therapy*, 62, 274–281.

Pontifex, M.B., Saliba, B.J., Raine, L.B., Picchietti, D.L., and Hillman, C.H. (2012). Exercise improves behavioral, neurocognitive, and scholastic performance in children with ADHD. *Journal of Pediatrics*, 162, 543–551.

Trauma-Related Intervention Considerations for IEP/504 Plan

Case Example: Jane, Age Five–Kindergarten

Kathie Ritchie

The following case example presents a number of the most common challenges traumatized children, their teachers, and their parents experience. Many traumatized children are scheduled for IEP planning. The following example provides intervention considerations that are specific to traumatized children. It addresses several of the most common and most challenging areas traumatized children and the adults in their lives need to understand and respond to within a brain-centered, trauma-sensitive framework.

Parental Concerns

Jane's mother reports the family has a history of domestic violence, which is why they moved abruptly. She is concerned that Jane, now age five, has become withdrawn, and she is afraid her dad will come and take her. She does not feel safe at home or at school. She does not handle frustration well, often resulting in her crying and having a tantrum, in which she hits and kicks others and objects. Her previous teachers reported inattention and lack of focus as areas of concern. Jane is not making progress in school and her mom is concerned, since she started school late this year.

Student's Level of Functional Performance

Jane currently requires prompting to focus and complete academic tasks. When frustrated, she withdraws and/or displays verbal and physical aggressiveness. This occurs on a daily basis, ranging from five minutes up to thirty minutes per incident, depending on her frustration level. She has kicked and pushed her classmates. She is struggling with making friends. She displays inattentive behaviors during instruction and requires verbal prompting and one-to-two assistance in order to focus and complete all academic work. Visual skills are stronger than verbal skills. She seeks attention from staff and peers and often needs reassurance that she is safe.

When Jane is frustrated, she retreats to the back corner of the room, often stomping, kicking, and pushing anything in her path. Once she has regained control, she is often apologetic. She can be bossy with peers and wants to have her way, which impairs her ability to make friends. She becomes upset when students are redirected in the classroom. She does not like loud sounds, such as the fire alarm, or sudden noises, such as a book dropping, or loud voices.

Jane's behaviors have intensified in frequency and duration over the last three months. She exhibits aggressive and refusal behavior multiple times each day, ranging from saying "no" to teachers' requests to kicking, yelling, and shoving furniture. The incidents can last from thirty seconds and up to twenty minutes during attempts to return to her preferred activity.

Setting In Which Behaviors Occur

Behaviors occur primarily in the classroom or during unstructured settings, such as recess or lunch. Jane displays behaviors in the classroom, hallway, during lunch and recess, ranging from yelling at other students to kicking them during recess and lunch.

Antecedents: Events That Precede Behaviors

Jane's refusal and aggressive behaviors are triggered when she is frustrated with academic work, redirected by staff in the classroom, or perceives exclusion by peers during lunch and recess. She struggles when her peers experience academic or social success and receive praise. When non-preferred activities are required for Jane to complete or when she does not understand the concept that is being taught, she presents refusal behaviors. Her aggressive behaviors are sometimes triggered when she receives one-to-one redirection for non-compliance behaviors. She does not like group activities. Transitions to school and at the end of the day are hard for her, especially on Mondays and after holidays.

Student's Strengths

Jane loves to draw and color, and she is a good dancer. She enjoys music class and listening when her teacher reads a story. She likes to please her teacher and wants to develop friendships with her peers. She enjoys receiving praise from staff and likes to socialize with her peers. She likes it when she has positive interactions with her peers during lunch and recess, enjoys attention from staff and wants to please them. She likes dancing or any other activity that requires movement. She sometimes displays a good work ethic. She enjoys math and her skills are strong in this area.

Problem Source

Jane displays symptoms associated with unspecified trauma/stressor related disorder, which adversely affects her progress in the general education setting, including structured and unstructured settings.

Intervention Considerations

Teacher/Parent

Before briefly addressing each of these areas and possible interventions, it is important to appreciate the need for Jane's teachers and mother to be trauma-informed and trauma-sensitive in their responses and interactions with her. For example, Chapter Five listed the mindsets and beliefs that are related to what the behaviors of traumatized children may be communicating. The adults in Jane's life need to accept that her kicking, yelling, and aggressive behaviors are not willful acts but her primal fight or flight survival responses to whatever or whomever she perceives to be a threat to her wellbeing at that precise moment. At that point in time, she needs help to engage sensory activities and/or be with a co-regulating adult to help her regulate her own reactions. It would be counterproductive to attempt to verbally correct or control her behavior. The adults in Jane's life must be informed of all that is covered in the first five chapters of this resource and respond accordingly. Without this "sensitivity," they and Jane will continue to struggle.

Further Evaluation

Following the assessment of 2,000 children exposed to various traumatic situations, research conducted by the Child Trauma Assessment Center of Western Michigan University revealed that 70 to 85 percent of these children experience delays in memory, repetitive language, visual processing, attention, sensory processing challenges, rule breaking, aggression, and externalizing behaviors associated with hypervigilance. They also demonstrate limited self-regulation skills (Steele and Malchiodi, 2012). Given the conditions Jane has been exposed to at such an early age, it is likely that she is experiencing developmental delays in these—and possibly other—areas. For example, many traumatized children have alexithymia—an inability to identify emotions or no awareness of specific emotions. These areas need to be evaluated in order to arrive at the in-classroom and out-of-classroom reparative interventions that will be most helpful for Jane, her teachers, and her mother.

Bottom-up Strategies

Assuming that Jane will be experiencing the previously mentioned delays, it is recommended that intervention should reflect a "bottom-up" approach, as discussed in Chapter One. Given that she is experiencing much of her world in the lower (limbic) regions of her brain, and that her nervous system is frequently dysregulated, developing self-regulation skills needs to be a priority. In reality, several interventions are likely to occur concurrently. For example, Jane may receive help from an occupational therapist for existing sensory processing challenges, learn and practice self-regulation skills, and learn to identify or "name" her feelings.

Self-Regulation

Jane enjoys movement and music. The use of MeMoves in the classroom and at home is a natural fit, takes little time, and is something that Jane and her mother can do together. Although the focus of Chapter Three was primarily the use of MeMoves with children, adults also benefit from it. Given the frequency of her dysregulation, Jane would benefit from brief periods (three to four) minutes of integrated movement and music and other identified sensory activities or use of sensory resources in the classroom, such as the use of a safe space or a safe corner.

Given that Mondays and Fridays are the most challenging days for her, she would also benefit from access to the school's resource room and/or meeting with the occupational therapist or social worker on these days for additional self-regulation activities and support. Referencing Chapter Two, appropriate self-regulation practices across the five domains (biological, emotional, cognitive, social, and prosocial) could be included in her daily routines. Jane is easily activated by group activities. This is understandable, given that group activities lend themselves to embarrassment, shame, ridicule, and competition, all of which activate the nervous systems of traumatized students and their emotionally dominant/limbic survival responses. A number of the activities cited under the social and prosocial domains in Chapter Two would be helpful for Jane.

Jane is also easily activated during transitions. So it would be helpful to alert her to upcoming transitions and give her a few minutes to initiate the regulation skills she is learning to move to the next task, activity, or location more calmly, especially when the transitions are unstructured (during lunch and recess). Possible interventions are listed in the Additional Sensory Processing Strategies section of this Appendix.

Sensory Processing Challenges

Some of Jane's behaviors may be triggered by sensory challenges created by the classroom/school environment. An evaluation will reveal which senses experience the most challenges. For example, Jane struggles with loud noises (auditory processing). Numerous helpful interventions and resources are listed in the Additional Sensory Processing Strategies section of this Appendix. Although Jane's visual processing skills seem stronger than her language skills, some areas related to visual processing may be problematic. As was stated in Chapter Four:

Poor visual acuity and impaired ocular-motor and other visual processing skills are common, and can make tasks such as playing ball, reading, and writing difficult. A student may be hypersensitive to color, patterns, lights, movement, and/or contrast. Some students are visually distractible. Those who have experienced trauma may be triggered by visuals that are reminiscent of the traumatic experience, along with sensory annoyances such as glare, fluorescent and strobe lights, jarring patterns, and other visual inputs.

As detailed in Chapter Four and in the Additional Sensory Processing Strategies section of this Appendix, there are many intervention options to assist with this and other sensory processing challenges. Many of these activities can take place in the classroom environment and also support nervous system regulation/modulation.

Language Delays

The inability to identify or "name" and verbally communicate her reactions appropriately to others limits Jane's ability to develop supportive connections and to reciprocate in interactions with others. She needs help with "naming" her emotional reactions and should be provided with ways to express these appropriately through verbal communication and behavior. The use of visual aids, as well as adults who can help her associate her physiological reactions with her emotions, will be helpful. For example, flushing or a tightening of muscles may accompany a surge of anger, whereas there may be a sense of heaviness with sadness. Helping children associate bodily reactions with specific emotions makes it easier for them to identify what they are experiencing. Co-regulation with a safe adult will be very helpful in this effort. Chapter Five discusses the importance of helping children "name it to tame it" and other co-regulating interactions.

Memory: Executive Functioning

Trauma often leads to problems with short-term memory. Jane may be having difficulty completing tasks and may engage in frequent off-task behaviors because she has no memory related to verbal instructions she has been given or because her attention is easily diverted by other activities or environmental factors. Evaluating delays in these areas, how she's processing information, her verbal and visual processing strengths, abstract reasoning, and sequencing is critical to assigning the most appropriate remedial intervention. Although Jane is five years old she may have the information processing skills of a two-year-old. Traumatized children are often given tasks that match their chronological age but not their developmental age. Because many of the adults in their lives are not trauma-informed, they are often unaware of the cognitive delays that trauma can induce.

It is important to mention that cognitive capacity can improve rapidly when traumatized children receive trauma-directed early intervention, especially related to regulation of their emotionally dominant survival responses. We all perform better when in a state of calm and happiness than when in a state of fear or anxiety. Once regulated, the following practices specific to memory tasks can be helpful:

- Use multi-modal instruction.
- Use visual prompts for multi-step directions that are needed to complete a task (sticky notes, visual calendar-type prompt on desk).
- Practice new skills in short sessions during the day (three to four times daily).
- Incorporate advanced/graphic organizers.
- Teach one new concept or strategy at a time.
- Teach strategies including when, why, and how to use it.
- Rhymes, songs, movements, and patterns help with memorization (recommended every thirty minutes).
- Review information presented at least twice during each lesson.
- Have the student repeat verbal directions.
- Provide the student with advance warning of when they will be asked questions.
- Avoid open-ended questions.
- Color code new concepts: for example, addition problems are red; new words are green.
- Highlight parts of new words.
- Review the main ideas of previous lessons when introducing a new one.
- Use general and answer masking on assignments and tests. Provide recognition versus recall opportunities.
- Teach students to create outlines for essay tests, using keywords to expand ideas.
- Allow the use of reference materials.
- Incorporate short breaks of one to two minutes (and use movement or mindfulness activities in these periods).
- Use technology. New apps and programs are created regularly (Can Learn Society, 2013).

Additionally, particular attention should be paid to praising the effort rather than the outcome (see Chapter Six). Jane's teachers and mother need to understand the importance of this strategy and would benefit from viewing several of the videos related to growth mindsets in Chapter Six.

Attachment

Jane's exposure to a violent and chaotic environment, along with emotionally unavailable parents and multiple disruptions to her primary relationships, is consistent with the formation of insecure attachment. Insecure attachments are at the root of developmental delays in many areas. However, disruption of attachment during infancy and early childhood does not preclude the development of secure attachment later in life (Steele and Malchiodi, 2012). Trauma experts such as Perry (2009) advocate for early intervention, as a younger brain is more malleable than a more mature brain. Siegel (2003) suggests that all individuals can find emotional security, even if they experienced neglectful or violence-ridden childhoods, as long as intervention focuses on the relational aspects that involve attachment and attunement.

As discussed in Chapter Five, brief connections can have long-term benefits, especially when these connections are attuned to and respond immediately to the needs that a student's challenging behaviors are communicating. Given Jane's trauma history, right brain/limbic interactions—the non-verbal interactions discussed in several chapters—will be critical, in addition to repetitive activities and interactions that meet the universal needs of all children: belonging, mastery, independence, and generosity (see Chapter Five). Many of the sensory interventions recommended up to this point will help strengthen Jane's connections with other adults.

It would also be advisable to consider an "attachment team" approach with Jane. Assigning several adults with whom she feels safe in the school setting to take turns visiting her briefly during the school day will communicate that others are watching out for her, and that she is valued. She may also visit these adults for help with self-regulation when other interventions fail. Many of the previously recommended interventions also provide opportunities to help Jane with her need to feel connected, to experience a sense of belonging.

Summary

In this and other interactions, we begin by focusing on using Jane's strengths and what she identifies as helpful. New interventions, regulations, activities, and/or resources can be introduced slowly and repeatedly made available on the basis that Jane affirms they are helpful. Repetition and predictability are critical components of any successful effort, as is consistently checking with the child as to what is helpful or unhelpful. Patience is also important as it may take time to see which of the many interventions and resources are most helpful. Most importantly, teacher self-care remains a priority, as teachers are seeing a growing number of children with trauma histories struggle with anxiety and/or self-regulation.

References

Can Learn Society (2013). *Supporting Students with Working Memory Difficulties.* Retrieved September 30, 2016 from http://canlearnsociety.ca/wp-content/uploads/2013/03/LC_Working-Memory_N2.pdf.

Perry, B. (2009). Examining child maltreatment through a neurodevelopmental lens: Clinical applications of the neurosequential model of therapeutics. *Journal of Loss and Trauma*, 14(4), 16.

Siegel, D. (2003). An interpersonal neurobiology of psychotherapy: The developing mind and the resolution of trauma. In M. Solomon and D. Siegel (Eds.), *Healing Trauma: Attachment, Mind, Body, and Brain* (pp. 1–5). New York: W.W. Norton.

Steele, W., and Malchiodi, M. (2012). *Trauma Informed Practices for Children and Adolescents*. New York: Routledge.

Additional Teaching and Learning Resources

Kathie Ritchie

The following interventions/activities can be easily incorporated in the classroom to assist students.

One-Minute Interventions for Traumatized Children and Adolescents **(Kuban and Steele, 2008)**

These activities can be easily incorporated into the daily schedule. They are great for sensory breaks, before or after the student begins the school day, before bells, and as end-of-day activities. The interventions take place in the age range three to eighteen, and the activities are designed to be brief. These quick interventions allow the child to reduce their arousal symptoms. Among the most helpful are:

- This is a Band-Aid for My Hurt (p. 38)
- Spaghetti Arms (p. 52)
- This Is the Safest Place for Me to Be, Cell Phone (pp. 64–65)
- My Mask (p. 88)
- Breathe (pp. 96–97)
- I'm Afraid of . . .When I Get Really Scared it Helps to . . . (pp. 130–131)
- Mandalas/Coloring (pp. 99, 141–142, 145–146)
- The Good Parts of Me (pp. 148–149)

Ready . . . Set . . . R.E.L.A.X **(Allen and Klein, 1996)**

Scripted activities are designed to work in group or individual settings. They emphasize breathing and muscle relaxation, feeling good about self, academic motivation, healthy self-concept, and relationships with others (p. 47). Other useful activities include:

- Relaxing Arms, Hands, Legs, Feet, Neck, and Shoulders (p. 56)
- Cloud of Calmness (pp. 70–71)
- Fall Fireworks (p. 82)

- Hidden Heroes (p. 96)
- Finding Treasure (p. 118)
- Drawer Full of Memories (p. 148)
- Paint a Picture (pp. 168–169)

Teaching with the Brain in Mind (Jensen, 2005)

This provides varied activities to increase epinephrine levels in students who appear drowsy, decrease restlessness, and reinforce information and ideas taught in the classroom.

The Calm Classroom: Early Childhood and Kindergarten (Griffith, Luster, and Luster, 2013)

Available in English and Spanish, this book is filled with thirty-second to three-minute activities related to breathing, focus, relaxing, and stretching. It provides a script for each activity. Teachers report positive outcomes for both students and staff when these activities are incorporated with fidelity.

The Calm Classroom: Elementary and Middle School (Luster and Luster, 2013)

This book also focuses on self-awareness, mental focus, and inner calm. Once again, it offers thirty-second to three-minute breathing, concentration, relaxation, and stretching activities to use in the classroom.

The Classroom Environment

Children who have experienced trauma need a safe classroom. Establishing a consistent, safe and nurturing environment during the first week of school must be a priority for every teacher. *The First Days of School: How to Be an Effective Teacher* (Wong and Wong, 2004) presents practical, easy-to-initiate practices that help children identify the environment and their teachers as safe.

Trauma-Informed Relationships

"Teachers can play an important role in connecting traumatized children to a safe and predictable school community and enabling them to become competent learners" (PBS, 2005, p. 5). *The Language of Trauma and Loss: Teacher Guide* (PBS, 2005) presents numerous strategies and qualities of teachers who are most effective with traumatized students. It also discusses the behaviors of traumatized students, what those behaviors may be communicating and how best to respond.

"Classroom strategies for traumatized, oppositional students" (Fecser, 2015) also provides a variety of ways to respond to students' behaviors while sustaining a sense of safety for all students in the classroom.

Traumatized students are often misdiagnosed with ADHD because the effects of trauma often create similar learning challenges. ADHD is also an appropriate diagnosis for some traumatized students. Regardless of the source of the learning challenges, the **Can Learn Society's website (http://canlearn society.ca/resources/)** provides numerous learning strategies that benefit all students, but are particularly effective as targeted supports for students with learning disabilities and/or ADHD.

Web Resources for Creating Safety Spots in the Classroom

www.teachjunkie.com/management/create-a-safe-spot-classroom-setup/.
www.smartappsforspecialneeds.com/2014/08/creating-safe-places-in-classroom.html.
www.smartclassroommanagement.com/2011/11/19/make-your-classroom-a-safe-haven-for-students/.
www.teachingquality.org/content/blogs/bill-ferriter/if-we-were-going-have-safe-happy-and-fun-classroom.

Resources/References

Allen, J. S., and Klein, R. J. (1996). *Ready . . . Set . . . R.E.L.A.X.* Watertown, WI: Inner Coaching.

Fecser, M. E. (2015). Classroom strategies for traumatized, oppositional students. *Reclaiming Children and Youth*, 24(1), 20–24.

Griffith, J., Luster, J., and Luster, J. (2013). *The Calm Classroom: Early Childhood and Kindergarten*. Highland Park, IL: Learning Institute.

Jensen, E. (2005). *Teaching with the Brain in Mind* (2nd ed.). Alexandria, VA: Association for Supervision and Curriculum Development.

Kuban, C., and Steele, W. (2008). *One-Minute Interventions for Traumatized Children and Adolescents*. Retrieved September 30, 2016 from www.starr.org/training/tlc.

Luster, J., and Luster, J. (2013). *The Calm Classroom: Elementary and Middle School*. Highland Park, IL: Learning Institute.

Public Broadcasting Service (PBS) (2005). *The Language of Trauma and Loss: Teacher Guide*. Retrieved September 30, 2016 from http://westernreservepublicmedia.org/trauma/images/trauma.pdf.

Wong, H. K., and Wong, R. T. (2004). *The First Days of School: How to Be an Effective Teacher* (3rd ed.). Mountain View, CA: Harry K. Wong Publications.

Compassionate Schools Resources

Ron Hertel and Susan O. Kincaid

ACEs Connection (www.acesconnection.com/home): ACEs Connection is a social network for people working with traumatized individuals. It includes research, articles, blogs, and chat rooms.

ACEs too High (http://acestoohigh.com/author/jestevens/): Started by journalist Jane Ellen Stevens, this website reports current news on ACEs, neurobiology, and other related topics. Also includes a blog.

ARC Model PowerPoint (www.nctsn.org/nctsn_assets/pdfs/Kinniburgh.pdf): The ARC model is based on attachment, self-regulation, and competency. Slide presentation developed by Kristine M. Kinniburgh, LICSW; Margaret E. Blaustein, Ph.D.; and the Trauma Center at JRI.

Attachment and Trauma Network (www.attachmenttraumanetwork.org/): Uses trauma-informed attachment theory focused therapy to address early childhood trauma.

Centers for Disease Control and Prevention (www.cdc.gov/violenceprevention/acestudy/): Partner with Kaiser Permanente in the first ACEs study of more than 17,000 subjects in 1998. Links to numerous academic studies of ACEs.

Compassionate Schools Initiative, Washington State (http://k12.wa.us/CompassionateSchools/HeartofLearning.aspx): Home page of the Compassionate Schools Initiative at the Office of Public Instruction. There is a twelve-minute video regarding the initiative that includes interviews with the four authors of *The Heart of Learning and Teaching: Compassion, Resiliency, and Academic Success*, a handbook for developing a compassionate school. The book is available as a free download from the website, with or without graphics.

Massachusetts Advocates for Children (http://massadvocates.org/publications/): An independent agency working to reduce barriers to learning for all children and individual children. Free downloads of several related books are available on the website.

Professional Quality of Life Score (www.proqol.org/uploads/ProQOL_5_English_Self-Score_3-2012.pdf): Free self-test can be a great starting point for developing a self-care plan.

Road to Resilience Map (www.janeellenstevens.com/ACEsRoadmaptoResilience.html): All schools exist in communities, and this map presents simple steps to begin building community resilience. Jane Ellen Stevens began and is the editor of the ACEs Too High website.

Self-Care Starter Kit, School of Social Work, University of Buffalo (https://socialwork.buffalo.edu/resources/self-care-starter-kit.html): This site has it all! Definition, assessment, and developing a self-care plan.

Seven Types of Self-Care Activities for Dealing with Stress (www.psychology today.com/blog/shyness-is-nice/201403/seven-types-self-care-activities-coping-stress): Suggested activities in each of the following areas: sensory, pleasure, mental mastery, spiritual, emotional, physical, and social.

Trauma Center at the Justice Resource Institute (www.traumacenter.org/research/ascot.php): The mission of the Trauma Center is to help individuals, families, and communities affected by trauma and adversity using the ARC model.

Trauma Sensitive Schools (www.traumasensitiveschools.org): In addition to providing information on work in Massachusetts and academic articles, free downloads of several publications are available, including *Helping Traumatized Children Learn: Safe Supportive Learning Environments that Benefit All Children* (Book 1) and *Creating and Advocating for Trauma-Sensitive Schools* (Book 2).

Index